e-flux journal

The Internet Does Not Exist

Sternberg Press

Contents

Introduction

The internet does not exist. Maybe it did exist only a short time ago, but now it only remains as a blur, a cloud, a friend, a deadline, a redirect, or a 404. If it ever existed, we couldn't see it. Because it has no shape. It has no face, just this name that describes everything and nothing at the same time. Yet we are still trying to climb onboard, to get inside, to be part of the network, to get in on the language game, to show up on searches, to appear to exist. But we will never get inside of something that isn't there. All this time we've been bemoaning the death of any critical outside position, we should have taken a good look at information networks. Just try to get in. You can't. Networks are all edges, as Bruno Latour points out. We thought there were windows but actually they're mirrors. And in the meantime we are being faced with more and more—not just information, but the world itself. And a very particular world that has already become part of our consciousness. And it wants something. It doesn't only want to harvest our eyeballs, our attention, our responses, and our feelings. It also wants to condition our minds and bodies to absorb all the richness of the planet's knowledge.

There is something we used to call the internet that had an infrastructural base. And it worked a bit like its unconscious, storing all the things the glowing promises of free flow must repress in order to function. Looking under the hood, it turns out that its infrastructure was mostly based in the United States, mostly owned and operated by the United States. It was ARPANET that implemented the first successful packet switching network for the US Department of Defense in the late 1960s. From there the nodes slowly grew throughout the '70s and '80s until the network was decommissioned in the early '90s to make way for commercial internet service providers. Even though significant parts of the regulatory infrastructure over information exchange still falls under the oversight of the US government, whether directly or indirectly, the real shift in the 1990s came in realizing the commercial and economic potential of information exchange, placing it at the center of the era of globalization and acceleration in the financial sector.

Of course, the early 1990s also saw the dissolution of the Soviet Union, and it is no coincidence that information networks in the United States were transitioned from a military to an economic function at the same time. This was also the time of US right-wing philosopher Francis Fukuyama's famous declaration of the triumph of Western free market liberal democracy as the most just and emancipatory non-ideology to encompass an entire world finally free of communism. But when we look more closely, we start to see that information networks actually do have an ideological structure.

Here it becomes interesting to note how Soviet attempts under Khrushchev and Brezhnev to develop a nationwide computer network are largely considered to have failed due to Soviet bureaucracy's inability to fully internalize what Norbert Weiner and the American cyberneticists celebrated as the inherently liberal and libertarian values of networks. In the end, most attempts at a Soviet internet were never able to resolve the question of whether computers and cybernetic concepts were to be used as tools to manage a planned economy or to simply automate information processing tasks. And in the meantime, attempts to establish networks in many cases mirrored and even bloated existing managerial bodies with often secretive and isolated administration systems built specifically not to communicate with others for security reasons. All this in spite of the fact that one of the possible applications of a Soviet internet for a planned economy was the creation of a digital currency that would realize the Marxist dream of eliminating money, supposedly replacing it with a mechanism for registering and allocating resources—a strange reflection of contemporary forms of digital currency such as Bitcoin, or even financial instruments for that matter.

Still, as the story goes, the massive territorial and functional expansion of information networks in the 1990s came to be set up as not only an ideological triumph but also the technical application of liberal democratic concepts onto a planetary-scale economic system. For instance, networks produce, and are produced, by connectedness and free flow between nodes. They enjoy freedom from rigid structure, but only while inside the network and its exchange protocols—emancipation without end, but also without exit. Networks are often assumed to be democratic because they supposedly exist without central command, allowing non-hegemonic, noncoercive, individualistic freedom of movement, and encouraging some kind of distributed representation. All fine and well, but aren't we now a little suspicious of the all-encompassing inclusivity of these claims? Don't we know now that networks also produce stoppages, closures, dark spots, and their own particular forms of control and governance?

In order to understand how these forms of control materialize over networks, it might help to forget this thing we used to call the internet and look at just what it is that travels over the lines. Because what we once called the internet has unleashed something that we don't yet have a name for—possibly because it is made out of language itself. Language has increasingly become a primary currency for exchange—both as a way of explaining how money or financial assets function when they are no longer pegged to material assets that stabilize their value and float free, but also to explain the basic substance giving information its spin and its kick. From ones and zeroes moving between terminals to likes and pokes to manifestos and love letters to stock prices, the condition for anything to enter the network to become information is that it must first be abstracted into language.

But then how does language work? What is it pegged to? It is pegged to its own ability to create meaning, to its ability to refer to something. But language traveling over networks is not only about expression; it is also about addressing and location. As it was put elegantly in a 1981 DARPA Internet Program Protocol Specification: "A name indicates what we seek. An address indicates where it is. A route indicates how to get there." This might sound straightforward enough, but it's really not. Because when a location or address—which over a network is an ontological issue of whether something exists, or calls up a blank screen—doubles as a human expression, the ability to orient oneself in a meaningful way starts to melt. Furthermore, when words are put to auction and left to the highest bidder to determine where they point, what they will refer to, we face a scenario where just like with homes in the United States before the market crash, financial speculation will seek to squat a symbolic asset, whether a home or a name, regardless of its function or substance in physical or cognitive domains alike. With this, not only the names of countries start pointing to different laundry detergents, but linguistic meaning in general starts to liquidate and become noise.

It is strange to think how, in spite of so many young artists now playing with digital aesthetics, it was actually Warhol who saw it coming most clearly. The massive shift from depth to surface that Warhol explained with celebrity culture and advertising has now taken hold of language itself and spread across the planet. It's no wonder that since the 1990s the political, social, and economic aspects of artistic production have become increasingly interchangeable and hard to distinguish from one another. Planetary networks have become places of profound confusion and dislocation. We know from the start that we probably won't find what we're looking for, so we learn to search sporadically and asymmetrically just to see where we end up. This might look and feel like drifting, and traditional or conservative notions of substance will always try to dismiss its noise, its cat videos and porn, bad techno and bombastic contemporary art, but one should be careful not to underestimate the massive distances being crossed in the meantime.

These distances are themselves very quickly reformatting our consciousness and cognitive capacity to absorb entire worlds made of contradiction—not only in language but far beyond language as well. Some people might already be there: scammers and tricksters, the frazzled post-studio artist and the post-institutional independent militia, political dissidents and unruly journalists who know never to trust their maps. They know that contradictions don't resolve, rather you surf across them using empathy and solidarity, emotional blackmail, jokes, pranks, and vanguardism as norm. Our ability to traverse these contradictions may very well become the backbone of the global telecommunications network we used to think was an internet.

—Julieta Aranda, Brian Kuan Wood, Anton Vidokle

Hito Steyerl

Too Much World: Is the Internet Dead?

Is the internet dead?[1] This is not a metaphorical question. It does not suggest that the internet is dysfunctional, useless, or out of fashion. It asks what happened to the internet after it stopped being a possibility. The question is very literally whether it is dead, how it died, and whether anyone killed it. But how could anyone think it could be over? The internet is now more potent than ever. It has not only sparked but fully captured the imagination, attention, and productivity of more people than at any other point before. Never before have more people been dependent on, embedded into, surveilled by, and exploited by the web. It seems overwhelming, bedazzling, and without immediate alternative. The internet is probably not dead. It has rather gone all out. Or more precisely: it is all over!

This implies a spatial dimension, but not as one might think. The internet is not everywhere. Even nowadays when networks seem to multiply exponentially, many people have no access to the internet or don't use it at all. And yet, it is expanding in another direction. It has started moving offline. But how does this work?

Remember the Romanian uprising in 1989, when protesters invaded TV studios to make history? At that moment, images changed their function.[2] Broadcasts from occupied TV studios became active catalysts of events—not records or documents.[3] Since then it has become clear that images are not objective or subjective renditions of a preexisting condition, or merely treacherous appearances. They are rather nodes of energy and matter that migrate across different supports,[4] shaping and affecting people, landscapes, politics, and social systems. They acquired an uncanny ability to proliferate, transform, and activate. Around 1989, television images started walking through screens, right into reality.[5]

This development accelerated when web infrastructure started supplementing TV networks as circuits for image circulation.[6] Suddenly, the points of transfer multiplied. Screens were now ubiquitous, not to speak of images themselves, which could be copied and dispersed at the flick of a finger.

Data, sounds, and images are now routinely transitioning beyond screens into a different state of matter.[7] They surpass the boundaries of data channels and manifest materially. They incarnate as riots or products, as lens flares, high-rises, or pixelated tanks. Images become unplugged and unhinged and start crowding off-screen space. They invade cities, transforming spaces into sites, and reality into realty. They materialize as junkspace, military invasion, and botched plastic surgery. They spread through and beyond networks, they contract and expand, they stall and stumble, they vie, they vile, they wow and woo.

Just look around you: artificial islands mimic genetically manipulated plants. Dental offices parade as car commercial film sets. Cheekbones are airbrushed just as whole cities pretend to be YouTube CAD tutorials. Artworks are e-mailed to pop up in bank lobbies designed on fighter-jet software. Huge cloud storage drives rain down as skylines in desert locations. But by becoming real, most images are substantially altered. They get translated, twisted, bruised, and reconfigured. They change their outlook, entourage, and spin. A nail-paint clip turns into an Instagram riot. An upload comes down as a shitstorm. An animated GIF materializes as a pop-up airport transit gate. In some places, it seems as if entire NSA system architectures were built—but only after Google-translating them, creating car lofts where one-way mirror windows face inward. By

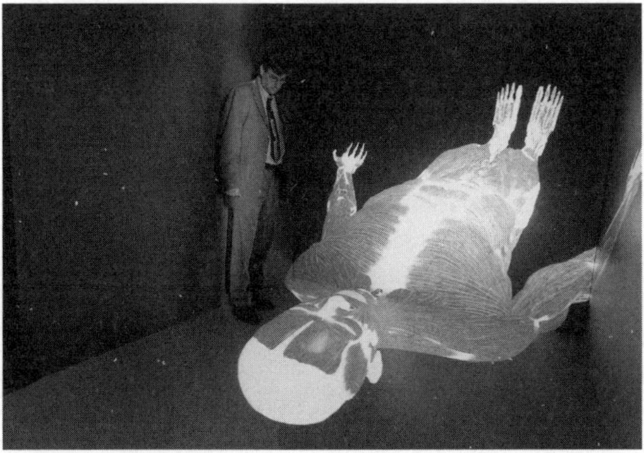

CAVEman is a 3-D virtual patient projected onto a holodeck, which allows doctors to visualize and diagnose ailments in high definition. Here scientist Christoph Sensen is pictured looking at his creation.

walking off-screen, images are twisted, dilapidated, incorporated, and reshuffled. They miss their targets, misunderstand their purpose, get shapes and colors wrong. They walk through, fall off, and fade back into screens.

Grace Jones's 2008 black-and-white video clip "Corporate Cannibal," described by Steven Shaviro as a pivotal example of post-cinematic affect, is a case in point.[8] By now, the nonchalant fluidity and modulation of Jones's posthuman figure has been implemented as a blueprint for austerity infrastructure. I could swear that Berlin bus schedules are consistently run on this model—endlessly stretching and straining space, time, and human patience. Cinema's debris rematerializes as investment ruins or secret "Information Dominance Centers."[9] But if cinema has exploded into the world to become partly real, one also has to accept that it actually did explode. And it probably didn't make it through this explosion either.

Post-Cinema

For a long time, many people have felt that cinema is rather lifeless. Cinema today is above all a stimulus package to buy new televisions, home projector systems, and retina display iPads. It long ago became a platform to sell franchising products—screening feature-length versions of future PlayStation games in sanitized multiplexes. It became a training tool for what Thomas Elsaesser calls the military-industrial-entertainment complex.

Everybody has his or her own version of when and how cinema died, but I personally believe it was hit by shrapnel when, in the course of the Bosnian War, a small cinema in Jajce was destroyed around 1993. This was where the Federal Republic of Yugoslavia was founded during World War II by the

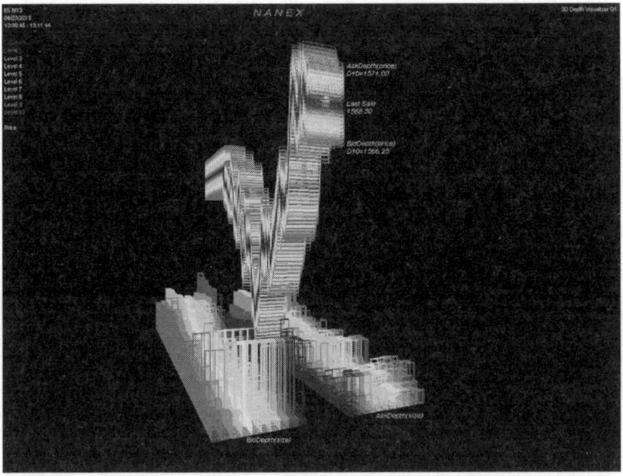

The market briefly lost $136 billion on April 23, 2013, when the Associated Press's Twitter feed was hacked and tweeted that the White House had been attacked and that President Obama had been injured.

Anti-Fascist Council for the National Liberation of Yugoslavia (AVNOJ). I am sure that cinema was hit in many other places and times as well. It was shot, executed, starved, and kidnapped in Lebanon and Algeria, in Chechnya and the Democratic Republic of the Congo, as well as in many other post–Cold War conflicts. It didn't just withdraw and become unavailable, as Jalal Toufic wrote of artworks after what he calls a surpassing disaster.[10] It was killed, or at least it fell into a permanent coma.

But let's come back to the question we began with. In the past few years many people—basically everybody—have noticed that the internet feels awkward, too. It is obviously completely surveilled, monopolized, and sanitized by common sense, copyright, control, and conformism. It feels as vibrant as a newly multiplexed cinema in the '90s showing endless reruns of *Star Wars: Episode 1*. Was the internet shot by a sniper in Syria, a drone in Pakistan, or a tear gas grenade in Turkey? Is it in a hospital in Port Said with a bullet in its head? Did it commit suicide by jumping out the window of an Information Dominance Center? But there are no windows in this kind of structure. And there are no walls. The internet is not dead. It is undead and it's everywhere.

I Am a Minecraft Redstone Computer

So what does it mean if the internet has moved offline? It crossed the screen, multiplied displays, transcended networks and cables to be at once inert and inevitable. One could imagine shutting down all online access or user activity. We might be unplugged, but this doesn't mean we're off the hook. The internet persists offline as a mode of life, surveillance, production, and organization—a form of intense voyeurism coupled with maximum nontransparency. Imagine an internet of things all senselessly "liking" each other, reinforcing the rule of a few quasi-monopolies. A world of privatized knowledge patrolled and defended by rating agencies. Of maximum control coupled with intense conformism, where intelligent cars do grocery shopping until a Hellfire missile comes crashing down. Police come knocking on your door for a download—to arrest you after "identifying" you on YouTube or CCTV. Do they threaten to jail you for spreading publicly funded knowledge? Or maybe beg you to knock down Twitter to stop an insurgency? Shake their hands and invite them in. They are today's internet in 4-D.

The all-out internet condition is not an interface but an environment. Older media as well as imaged people, imaged structures, and image objects are embedded into networked matter. Networked space is itself a medium, or whatever one might call a medium's promiscuous, posthumous state today. It is a form of life (and death) that contains, sublates, and archives all previous forms of media. In this fluid media space, images and sounds morph across different bodies and carriers, acquiring more and more glitches and bruises along the way. Moreover, it is not only form that migrates across screens, but also function.[11] Computation and connectivity permeate matter and render it as raw material for algorithmic prediction, or potentially also as building blocks for alternate networks. As Minecraft Redstone computers are able to use virtual minerals for calculating operations,[12] so is living and dead material increasingly integrated with cloud performance, slowly turning the world into a multilayered motherboard.[13]

But this space is also a sphere of liquidity, of looming rainstorms and unstable climates. It is the realm of complexity gone haywire, spinning strange feedback loops. A condition partly created by humans but also only partly controlled by them, indifferent to anything but movement, energy, rhythm, and complication. It is the space of the rōnin of old, the masterless samurai freelancers fittingly called wave men and women: floaters in a fleeting world of images, interns in dark net soap lands. We thought it was a plumbing system, so how did this tsunami creep up in my sink? How is this algorithm drying up this rice paddy? And how many workers are desperately clambering on the menacing cloud that hovers in the distance right now, trying to squeeze out a living, groping through a fog that may at any second transform both into an immersive art installation and a demonstration doused in cutting-edge tear gas?

Postproduction

But if images start pouring across screens and invading subject and object matter, the major and quite overlooked consequence is that reality now widely consists of images; or rather, of things, constellations, and processes formerly evident as images. This means one cannot understand reality without understanding cinema, photography, 3-D modeling, animation, or other forms of moving or still image. The world is imbued with the shrapnel of former images, as well as images edited, photoshopped, cobbled together from spam and scrap. Reality itself is postproduced and scripted, affect rendered as after-effect. Far from being opposites across an unbridgeable chasm, image and world are in many cases just versions of each other.[14] They are not equivalents, however, but deficient, excessive, and uneven in relation to each other. And the gap between them gives way to speculation and intense anxiety.

Under these conditions, production morphs into postproduction, meaning the world can be understood but also altered by its tools. The tools of postproduction: editing, color correction, filtering, cutting, and so on are not aimed at achieving representation. They have become means of creation, not only of images but also of the world in their wake. One possible reason: with digital proliferation of all sorts of imagery, suddenly too much world became available. The map, to use the well-known fable by Borges, has not only become equal to the world, but exceeds it by far.[15] A vast quantity of images covers the surface of the world—very much in the case of aerial imaging—in a confusing stack of layers. The map explodes on a material territory, which is increasingly fragmented and also gets entangled with it: in one instance, Google Maps cartography led to near military conflict.[16]

While Borges wagered that the map might wither away, Baudrillard speculated that on the contrary, reality was disintegrating.[17] In fact, *both* proliferate and confuse one another: on handheld devices, at checkpoints, and in between edits. Map and territory reach into one another to realize strokes on trackpads as theme parks or apartheid architecture. Image layers get stuck as geological strata while SWAT teams patrol Amazon shopping carts. The point is that no one can deal with this. This extensive and exhausting mess needs to be edited down in real time: filtered, scanned, sorted, and selected—into so many Wikipedia versions, into layered, libidinal, logistical, lopsided geographies.

This assigns a new role to image production, and in consequence also to people who deal with it. Image workers now deal directly in a world made of images, and can do so much faster than previously possible. But production has also become mixed up with circulation to the point of being indistinguishable. The factory/studio/tumblr blur with online shopping, oligarch collections, realty branding, and surveillance architecture. Today's workplace could turn out to be a rogue algorithm commandeering your hard drive, eyeballs, and dreams. And tomorrow you might have to disco all the way to insanity.

As the web spills over into a different dimension, image production moves way beyond the confines of specialized fields. It becomes mass postproduction in an age of crowd creativity. Today, almost everyone is an artist. We are pitching, phishing, spamming, chain-liking, or mansplaining. We are twitching, tweeting, and toasting as some form of solo relational art, high on dual processing and a smartphone flat rate. Image circulation today works by pimping pixels in orbit via strategic sharing of wacky, neo-tribal, and mostly US-American content. Improbable objects, celebrity cat GIFs, and a jumble of unseen anonymous images proliferate and waft through human bodies via Wi-Fi. One could perhaps think of the results as a new and vital form of folk art, that is if one is prepared to completely overhaul one's definition of folk as well as art. A new form of storytelling using emojis and tweeted rape threats is both creating and tearing apart communities loosely linked by shared attention deficit.

Circulationism

But these things are not as new as they seem. What the Soviet avant-garde of the twentieth century called productivism—the claim that art should enter production and the factory—could now be replaced by circulationism. Circulationism is not about the art of making an image, but of postproducing, launching, and accelerating it. It is about the public relations of images across social networks, about advertisement and alienation, and about being as suavely vacuous as possible.

But remember how productivists Mayakovsky and Rodchenko created billboards for NEP sweets? Communists eagerly engaging with commodity fetishism?[18] Crucially, circulationism, if reinvented, could also be about short-circuiting existing networks, circumventing and bypassing corporate friendship and hardware monopolies. It could become the art of recoding or rewiring the system by exposing state scopophilia, capital compliance, and wholesale surveillance. Of course, it might also just go as wrong as its predecessor, by aligning itself with a Stalinist cult of productivity, acceleration, and heroic exhaustion. Historic productivism was—let's face it—totally ineffective and defeated by an overwhelming bureaucratic apparatus of surveillance/workfare early on. And it is quite likely that circulationism—instead of restructuring circulation—will just end up as ornament to an internet that looks increasingly like a mall filled with nothing but Starbucks franchises personally managed by Joseph Stalin.

Will circulationism alter reality's hard- and software; its affects, drives, and processes? While productivism left few traces in a dictatorship sustained by the cult of labor, could circulationism change a condition in which eyeballs, sleeplessness, and exposure are an algorithmic factory? Are circulationism's Stakhanovites working in Bangladeshi like-farms,[19] or mining virtual gold in Chinese prison camps,[20] churning out corporate consent on digital conveyor belts?

Open Access

But here is the ultimate consequence of the internet moving offline.[21] If images can be shared and circulated, why can't everything else be too? If data moves across screens, so can its material incarnations move across shop windows and other enclosures. If copyright can be dodged and called into question, why can't private property? If one can share a restaurant dish JPEG on Facebook, why not the real meal? Why not apply fair use to space, parks, and swimming pools?[22] Why only claim open access to JSTOR and not MIT—or any school, hospital, or university for that matter? Why shouldn't data clouds discharge as storming supermarkets?[23] Why not open-source water, energy, and Dom Pérignon champagne?

If circulationism is to mean anything, it has to move into the world of offline distribution, of 3-D dissemination of resources, of music, land, and inspiration. Why not slowly withdraw from an undead internet to build a few others next to it?

This text comes from nearly two years of testing versions of it in front of hundreds of people. So thanks to all of you, but mostly to my students, who had to endure most of its live writing. Some parts of this argument were formed in a seminar organized by Janus Hom and Martin Reynolds, but also in events run by Andrea Phillips and Daniel Rourke, Michael Connor, Shumon Basar, Christopher Kulendran Thomas, Brad Troemel, and exchanges with Jesse Darling, Linda Stupart, Karen Archey, and many others. I am taking cues from texts by Redhack, James Bridle, Boris Groys, Jörg Heiser, David Joselit, Christina Kiaer, Metahaven, Trevor Paglen, Brian Kuan Wood, and many works by Laura Poitras. But the most important theoretical contribution to shape this text was my collaborator Leon Kahane's attempt to shoplift a bottle of wine for a brainstorming session.

1

This is what the term "post-internet," coined a few years ago by Marisa Olson and subsequently Gene McHugh, seemed to suggest while it had undeniable use value as opposed to being left with the increasingly privatized exchange value it has at this moment.

2

Cf. Peter Weibel, "Medien als Maske: Videokratie," in *Von der Bürokratie zur Telekratie: Rumänien im Fernsehen*, ed. Keiko Sei (Berlin: Merve, 1990), 124–49, 134f.

3

Cătălin Gheorghe, "The Juridical Rewriting of History," in *Trial/Proces*, ed. Cătălin Gheorghe (Iaşi: Universitatea de Arte "George Enescu" Iaşi, 2012), 2–4. See http://www.arteiasi.ro/ita/publ/Vector_CercetareCriticaIn Context-TRIAL.pdf.

4

Ceci Moss and Tim Steer in a stunning exhibition announcement: "The object that exists in motion spans different points, relations and existences but always remains the same thing. Like the digital file, the bootlegged copy, the icon, or Capital, it reproduces, travels and accelerates, constantly negotiating the different supports that enable its movement. As it occupies these different spaces and forms it is always reconstituting itself. It doesn't have an autonomous singular existence; it is only ever activated within the network of nodes and channels of transportation. Both a distributed process and an independent occurrence, it is like an expanded object ceaselessly circulating, assembling and dispersing. To stop it would mean to break the whole process, infrastructure or chain that propagates and reproduces it." See http://www.seventeengallery.com/exhibitions/motion-ceci-moss-tim-steer/.

5

One instance of a wider political phenomenon called "transition." Coined for political situations in Latin America and then applied to Eastern European contexts after 1989, this notion described a teleological process consisting of an impossible catch-up of countries "belatedly" trying to achieve democracy and free-market economies. Transition implies a continuous morphing process, which in theory would make any place ultimately look like the ego ideal of any default Western nation. As a result, whole regions were subjected to radical makeovers. In practice, transition usually meant rampant expropriation coupled with a radical decrease in life expectancy. In transition, a bright neoliberal future marched off the screen to be realized as a lack of health care coupled with personal bankruptcy, while Western banks and insurance companies not only privatized pensions, but also reinvested them in contemporary art collections. See http://transform.eipcp.net/correspondence/1145970626#redir.

6

Images migrating across different supports are of course nothing new. This process has been apparent in art-making since the Stone Age. But the ease with which many images morph into the third dimension is a far cry from ages when a sketch had to be carved into marble manually. In the age of postproduction, almost everything made has been created by means of one or more images, and any IKEA table is copied and pasted rather than mounted or built.

7
As the New Aesthetic tumblr has brilliantly demonstrated for things and landscapes (see http://new-aesthetic.tumblr.com/), and as the Women as Objects tumblr has done to illustrate the incarnation of image as female body (see http://womenasobjects.tumblr.com/). Equally relevant on this point is work by Jesse Darling and Jennifer Chan.

8
See Steven Shaviro's wonderful analysis in "Post-Cinematic Affect: On Grace Jones, *Boarding Gate* and *Southland Tales*," *Film-Philosophy* 14, no. 1 (2010): 1–102. See also his book *Post-Cinematic Affect* (London: Zero Books, 2010).

9
Greg Allen, "The Enterprise School," Greg.org, September 13, 2013, http://greg.org/archive/2013/09/13/the_enterprise_school.html.

10
Jalal Toufic, *The Withdrawal of Tradition Past a Surpassing Catastrophe* (2009). See http://www.jalaltoufic.com/downloads/Jalal_Toufic,_The_Withdrawal_of_Tradition_Past_a_Surpassing_Disaster.pdf.

11
"The Cloud, the State, and the Stack: Metahaven in Conversation with Benjamin Bratton," December 16, 2012, http://mthvn.tumblr.com/post/38098461078/thecloudthestateandthestack.

12
Thanks to Josh Crowe for drawing my attention to this.

13
"The Cloud, the State, and the Stack."

14
Oliver Laric, "Versions," 2012, http://oliverlaric.com/vvversions.htm.

15
Jorge Luis Borges, "On Exactitude in Science," in *Collected Fictions*, trans. Andrew Hurley (New York: Penguin, 1999), 75–82. "'In that Empire, the Art of Cartography attained such Perfection that the map of a single Province occupied the entirety of a City, and the map of the Empire, the entirety of a Province. In time, those Unconscionable Maps no longer satisfied, and the Cartographers Guilds struck a Map of the Empire whose size was that of the Empire, and which coincided point for point with it. The following Generations, who were not so fond of the Study of Cartography as their Forebears had been, saw that that vast Map was Useless, and not without some Pitilessness was it, that they delivered it up to the Inclemencies of Sun and Winters. In the Deserts of the West, still today, there are Tattered Ruins of that Map, inhabited by Animals and Beggars; in all the Land there is no other Relic of the Disciplines of Geography.' Suárez Miranda, Viajes de varones prudentes, Libro IV, Cap. XLV, Lérida, 1658."

16
L. Arlas, "Verbal Spat between Costa Rica, Nicaragua Continues," *Tico Times*, September 20, 2013, http://www.ticotimes.net/More-news/News-Briefs/Verbal-spat-between-Costa-Rica-Nicaragua-continues_Friday-September-20-2013. Thanks to Kevan Jenson for mentioning this to me.

17

Jean Baudrillard, "Simulacra and Simulations," in *Jean Baudrillard: Selected Writings*, ed. Mark Poster (Stanford, CA: Stanford University Press, 1988), 166–84.

18

Christina Kiaer, "'Into Production!': The Socialist Objects of Russian Constructivism," *Transversal* (September 2010). See http://eipcp.net/transversal/0910/kiaer/en. "Mayakovsky's advertising jingles address working-class Soviet consumers directly and without irony; for example, an ad for one of the products of Mossel'prom, the state agricultural trust, reads: 'Cooking oil. Attention working masses. Three times cheaper than butter! More nutritious than other oils! Nowhere else but Mossel'prom.' It is not surprising that Constructivist advertisements would speak in a pro-Bolshevik, anti-NEP-business language, yet the picture of the *Reklam-Konstruktor* advertising business is more complicated. Many of their commercial graphics move beyond this straightforward language of class difference and utilitarian need to offer a *theory* of the socialist object. In contrast to Brik's claim that in this kind of work they are merely 'biding their time,' I propose that their advertisements attempt to work out the relation between the material cultures of the prerevolutionary past, the NEP present and the socialist *novyi byt* of the future with theoretical rigor. They confront the question that arises out of the theory of Boris Arvatov: What happens to the individual fantasies and desires organized under capitalism by the commodity fetish and the market, after the revolution?"

19

Charles Arthur, "How Low-Paid Workers at 'Click Farms' Create Appearance of Online Popularity," *Guardian*, August 2, 2013, http://www.theguardian.com/technology/2013/aug/02/click-farms-appearance-online-popularity.

20

Harry Sanderson, "Human Resolution," *Mute*, April 4, 2013, http://www.metamute.org/editorial/articles/human-resolution.

21

And it is absolutely not getting stuck with data-derived sculptures exhibited in white cube galleries.

22

"Spanish workers occupy a Duke's estate and turn it into a farm," Libcom.org, Aug. 24, 2012, http://libcom.org/blog/spanish-workers-occupy-duke's-estate-turn-it-farm-24082012. "Earlier this week in Andalusia, hundreds of unemployed farmworkers broke through a fence that surrounded an estate owned by the Duke of Segorbe, and claimed it as their own. This is the latest in a series of farm occupations across the region within the last month. Their aim is to create a communal agricultural project, similar to other occupied farms, in order to breathe new life into a region that has an unemployment rate of over 40 percent. Addressing the occupiers, Diego Canamero, a member of the Andalusian Union of Workers, said that: 'We're here to denounce a social class who leave such a place to waste.' The lavish well-kept gardens, house, and pool are left empty, as the Duke lives in Seville, more than 60 miles away."

23
Thomas J. Michalak, "Mayor in Spain Leads Food Raids for the People," Workers.org, August 25, 2012, http://www.workers.org/2012/08/24/mayor-in-spain-leads-food-raids-for-the-people/. "In the small Spanish town of Marinaleda, located in the southern region of Andalusía, Mayor Juan Manuel Sánchez Gordillo has an answer for the country's economic crisis and the hunger that comes with it: He organized and led the town's residents to raid supermarkets to get the food necessary to survive." See also http://theextinctionprotocol.wordpress.com/2012/08/25/economic-crisis-riots-food-raids-and-the-collapse-of-spain/.

Keller Easterling

An Internet of Things

I.

An "internet of things" describes a world embedded with so many digital devices that the space between them consists not of dark circuitry but rather the space of the city itself. The computer has escaped the box, and ordinary objects in space are carriers of digital signals. This capacity seems to finally fulfill the dream of artists and architects of the mid- to late twentieth century, among them Jack Burnham, Cedric Price, Archigram, and Christopher Alexander, who experimented with a cybernetic apparatus for modeling space. It might also be the practical answer to quests by Nicholas Negroponte's *Architecture Machine Group* and architects exploring Artificial Intelligence, who rehearse interplay between digital machines and the space of the city and the body—reciprocal modeling that enhances the capacities of each. On the contemporary scene, manifestos like Carlo Ratti's "Open Source Architecture" imagine that in digitized space—this web of things—architecture can be constructed in much the same way that a wiki is assembled.

As art and architecture adopt technologies to embrace a new imaginary or model a new relationship, digital technologies often become an essential prosthetic for an idea about form-making. Yet these nourishing and exciting projects also perhaps prematurely stop short of, or even foreclose on, a much more expansive investigation. Even when resisting the vampiric modernist impulse to declare a new regime, these projects may be drawn into a cul-du-sac; their production of artifacts risks being yet another anecdotal, even marginal, expression in a succession of ideas.

A non-modern question—the artifacts of which have always been with us, the boundaries of which include but exceed all of the above experiments, and the answer to which we already know—is how space, without digital or media enhancement, is itself information.[1]

We are not accustomed to the idea that non-human, inanimate objects possess agency and activity, just as we are not accustomed to the idea that they can carry information unless they are endowed with code/text-based information technologies. While accepting that a technology like mobile telephony has become the world's largest shared platform for information exchange, we are perhaps less accustomed to the idea of space as a technology or medium of information—undeclared information that is not parsed as text or code. Indeed, the more ubiquitous code/text-based information devices become, the harder it is to see spatial technologies and networks that are independent of the digital. Few would look at a concrete highway system or an electrical grid and perceive agency in their static arrangement. Agency might only be ascribed to the moving cars or the electrical current. Spaces and urban arrangements are usually treated as collections of objects or volumes, not as actors. Yet the organization itself is active. It is *doing* something, and changes in the organization constitute information. Even so, the idea that information is carried in *activity*, or what we might call active form, must still struggle against many powerful habits of mind.

II.

The projects of Cedric Price and Christopher Alexander are on the threshold of designing an architecture that has become information. It is instructive then to examine why their practices are sometimes relegated to historical oddities or novelties. Price, a London architect active from the 1960s to the early years of the twenty-first century, artfully prefigures the discussion of active form and spatial software or protocol. Fascinated by networks, infrastructure, and the movement of populations, Price puzzled over variable cocktails of skeletal authorship and improvisation. He designed spatial repertoires, building details, infrastructural networks, games, and toys. His constructions were essentially choreographies of human and nonhuman actors unfolding over time. Price steered his work away from objects, signature buildings, and monuments toward encounter and performance. He found "delight in the unknown." He was interested in "doing less" and wrote that "calculated indolence on the part of the architect [...] produces great work by others."[2] Price chose to practice like a performer, noting that the architect was usually a "poor performer," "consistently bad."[3] Like a good performer, he focused on interplay. He was relaxed within the power of object form and active form and enjoyed how they worked together to create their own epidemics in the environment. He wrote:

> I consider it unlikely that architecture and planning will match the contribution HushPuppies have made to society today, let alone approach that of the transistor or loop, until a total reappraisal of its particular expertise is self-imposed, or inflicted from outside.
>
> Designers and architects would be better employed in devising new languages of comparison from computers, than in using them to confirm the obvious. I would like to suggest that the socio-environmental factors that would stop lonely old people from going mad could be utilized in determining the economic

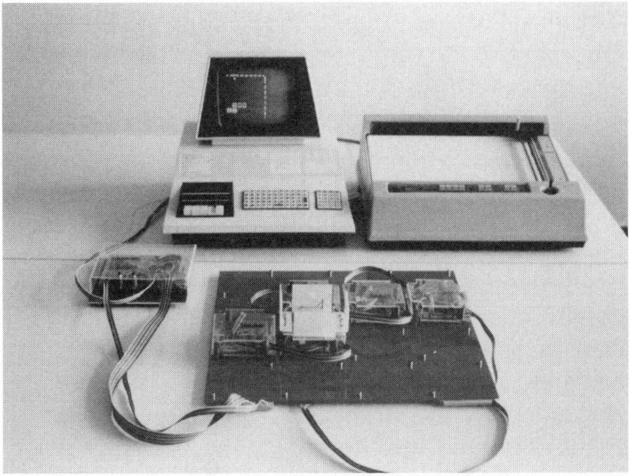

Cedric Price, *View of working electronic model of the Generator project*, c. 1976–79. Chromogenic color print adhered to cardboard.

viability of particular intervals of rental vacancy within a newly completed office block—just a suggestion.[4]

At their best, Price's schemes were time-released, located beyond a single site or stage, and poised to upset holistic cybernetic dreams. However, some of Price's projects also aspired to the predictability and predetermination of the holistic scripts of cybernetics, with its quest for homeostasis. For instance, *Potteries Thinkbelt* and *Fun Palace*, collaborations with theater director Joan Littlewood and cybernetician Gordon Pask, were theatrical and educational spaces proposed for London but never built. Price, interested in transportation landscapes, incorporated equipment used in container shipping to choreograph the programmatic components to be kinetic, interactive, and responsive to the user. His *Generator* project, a landscape with minimal construction planned for a wooded area in Florida, was the spatial reflection of a computer game that assigned a repertoire of moves to various players and objects in the landscape. The degree to which these projects were choreographed as tightly integrated, even prescriptive, cybernetic science perhaps foreclosed on their experimentation.

Christopher Alexander's direct application of set theory and network topology to urban morphology similarly illustrates the perils of codification and predetermination. Trained in physics, mathematics, computer science, information science, and architecture, Alexander's work engages both object form and active form, as well as human and nonhuman actors. But using these techniques he constructs a science that forecloses on the very territory about which he speculates. In his 1965 article "The City Is Not a Tree," he critiqued what he deemed to be the infrastructural or organizational template of many settlements and cities. A "tree," in Alexander's parlance, is a branching structure in which sets are either completely disconnected from one another or entirely contained within one set without overlapping sets. The branches do not grow together but emanate separately from a single trunk. Alexander demonstrates that Greenbelt, Maryland; Levittown, New York; the Greater London Plan, Brasília, Kenzo Tange's Tokyo Plan; Chandigarh, India; Hilberseimer's settlement patterns, and other well-known plans are "trees." He asserts that settlements in "traditional society" developed interconnections and overlaps that did not resemble an arborescent structure, primarily due to the activities of inhabitants rather than the authority and administration of planners. Authority always generates a tree and therefore, in his terms, an "artificial" city.[5]

Alexander observed activity in urban space as information. In "The City Is Not a Tree" he gave a now famous example:

> For example, in Berkeley at the corner of Hearst and Euclid, there is a drugstore, and outside the drugstore a traffic light. In the entrance to the drugstore there is a newsrack where the day's papers are displayed. When the light is red, people who are waiting to cross the street stand idly by the light; and since they have nothing to do, they look at the papers displayed on the newsrack which they can see from where they stand. Some of them just read the headlines, others actually buy a paper while they wait.
>
> This effect makes the newsrack and the traffic light interactive; the newsrack, the newspapers on it, the money going from people's pockets to the dime slot, the people who stop at the light

> and read papers, the traffic light, the electric impulses which make the lights change, and the sidewalk which the people stand on form a system—they all work together.[6]

For Alexander, this urban system is like a semi-lattice in set theory. Two sets of objects and activities overlap at the newsrack. If diagrammed like a branching structure, the branches overlap and connect. The semi-lattice diagrams "natural" cities like Siena, Liverpool, Kyoto, or Manhattan. The tree segregates urban functions in an organization, while the semi-lattice offers "ambiguity" and "multiplicity" in a structure that is "thick, tougher, more subtle, and more complex." On the one hand, Alexander expands the repertoire of design to include activity. But on the other, he quickly codifies and taxonomizes that activity. He mimics the object of his own critique by reforming the artificial with a "natural" corrective—instead of the tree, the semi-lattice becomes the placeholder. Despite his attempt to incorporate active form and information, Alexander only creates another immobilized form.[7]

III.

Far from what may be considered the more obscure experiments of architects, the most consequential architecture in the world has already become information. Still somewhat obscure only because of its overwhelming ubiquity, space is itself an infrastructural technology that is mobile and monetized, traveling around the world as a repeatable phenomenon. Compared to the relative trickle of space made by special practitioners, these technologies produce a fire-hose blast. The most radical changes to the globalizing world are being written in the protocols or softwares of infrastructural space.

Avoiding some modern habits that shape the projects of Price and Alexander, another kind of artistic endeavor, not reliant on either the digital prosthetic or the predictable cybernetic system, can address this new global infrastructure space. This is not a new but an extra art and mode of making in which *the action is the form*. Action is not necessarily movement but is rather embodied in relationship, relative position, and potential in organizations. Action is immanent in the *disposition* of an organization. There is no prescription for architecture, only a technique for performing it. Active forms design a disposition—a set of capacities for shaping space over time. Active forms are forms for handling forms.

The shift from nominative to active that requires so much ideation and analysis in some schools of thought, such as design, is completely ordinary and natural in other disciplines, such as theater. As Price recognized, an aesthetic training in this extra art might resemble that of theater. It requires no special technological apparatus. The construction of action is the theater performer's stock in trade. An actor adheres to a script but the scripted words are regarded only as traces or artifacts that hint at underlying action. A scene is a string of actions that carry meaning. Actors rarely deal with nominative or descriptive expressions—states of being or mood. One cannot, for instance, play "being a mother." Attempting to do so leads to what is known in the theater as "indicating." As Deleuze has written, "mediocre actresses must weep in order to signify grief."[8] In the theater, infinitive expressions, not representations, are the currency. The director asks the actor, "What are you doing?" It is generally agreed that leading with action or letting a vivid action carry the words rather than the other way around is a durable technique. Again, the action that leads the performance is not necessarily a movement or a gesture. It is rather the driving intent expressed as an active verb. An actor would not play "being a mother," but rather "smothering a child." Uncertainty, or the inability to fix meaning, does not paralyze the actor but rather allows more agility and interaction with other actors. Action is the bearer of information, consequence, change, or event. Action is the material used to make things and create meaning. The actor crafts variables and intentions to shape the information of the play.

While the model of a software as computer code is vivid, one can back out of that model and into a software made of active forms, deltas, and variables in *space itself*. For instance, Bruno Latour critiqued those architectural manipulations in computing or CAD environments "where objects move without being transformed" and are "geometrically manipulated or projected." Stepping back from these practices, Latour writes that "with this kind of project, you do not move an inch out of the modernism framework. You are still focused on the *object* rather than the *thing*." He has mused about an active software that would not simply reify form as geometry but would instead be intelligent enough to instantly pull up a web of cultural, political, and economic information, thus demonstrating the expanded reach of object form partnered with active form. But stepping back even further, one can only see this imagined software as an enhancement to Latour's larger model of interplay in his actor-network theory, a theory that does not need software or special equipment to exist. The activity in a spatial environment is not reliant on the digital environment. It may be enhanced by a code/

text-based software, but a spatial software or protocol can be any platform that establishes variables for space as information.[9]

Dispositional expressions and active forms can be spatial softwares, protocols, or diagrams. A diagram, as Deleuze and Guattari render the idea, is not a representational sketch of an single arrangement but rather an "abstract machine" that is generative of a "real that is yet to come."[10] Similarly, Deleuze discusses Foucault's notions of "dispositif" and "social apparatus" as "lines of force," trajectories or "names given to variables."[11] Gregory Bateson wrote that "the switch is the thing that is not except at the moments of its change of setting, and the concept 'switch' has thus a special relation to time. It is related to the notion 'change' rather than to the notion 'object.'"[12] Active forms in urban space can serve as expressions of variability and interdependence, like a calculus function or cosx—a software that facilitates relationships while not controlling every outcome. Cosx is an explicit expression and yet only manages a multiple set of values. Knowing all of those values is less important than understanding the disposition to form, when graphed, a particular curve.

This extra art is non-modern because active form does not need to kill object form to exist. There is no need for succession, segregation, and competition between these ideas, which already often coexist on a continuum. Object form can be resolutely disengaged from or, alternatively, positioned to become, active form, like a stone in the water. There is no necessity to create active form and no necessity to corral a fixed set of meanings under a new term.[13] There is only the observation that there are modes of form-making that exceed object form in substantial ways—only the need to point to a project that offers additional artistic pleasures and political powers.

The extra art of active form and disposition rehearse an internet of things without the internet.

This article is an adaptation of material from the book *Extrastatecraft: Global Infrastructure and Political Arts* (London: Verso, 2014).

1
I borrow the expression "non-modern" from Bruno Latour. Bruno Latour, *We Have Never Been Modern* (Cambridge, MA: Harvard University Press,1993), 48.

2
Cedric Price, *Works II* (London: Architectural Association, 1984), 18.

3
Cedric Price and Hans Ulrich Obrist, *Re:CP* (Basel: Birkhäuser, 1999), 64.

4
"Cedric Price Talks at the AA," *AA Files* 19 (Spring 1990): 33.

5
Christopher Alexander, "The City Is Not a Tree," *Architectural Forum* 122, no. 1 (April 1965): 58–62 (part I); and 122, no. 2 (May 1965): 58–62 (part II).

6
Ibid.

7
Ibid.

8
Gilles Deleuze, *Proust and Signs: The Complete Text*, trans. Richard Howard (Minneapolis: University of Minnesota Press, 2000), 39.

9
"Interview with Bruno Latour: Decoding the Collective Experiment," by María J. Prieto and Elise S. Youn, Agglutinations.com, July 5, 2004. (No longer available online.)

10
Gilles Deleuze, *Foucault*, trans. S. Hand (Minneapolis: University of Minnesota Press, 1988), 37; and Gilles Deleuze and Félix Guattari, "On Several Regimes of Signs," *A Thousand Plateaus*, trans. Brian Massumi (Minneapolis: University of Minnesota Press, 1987), 141–42.

11
Gilles Deleuze, "What Is Dispositif?," in *Michel Foucault: Philosopher* (New York: Routledge, 1991), 160, 166.

12
Gregory Bateson, "Criteria of Mental Process 1-4," *Mind and Nature: A Necessary Unity* (New York: Dutton, 1979), 109.

13
This argument is very careful to avoid modern pronoucements, preferring an inclusive position. For instance, Nicolas Bourriaud's notion of "relational form" is sympathetic, as is his "altermodern" position. Still, this argument hopes to broaden the field in which it and similar notions can be applied. Nicolas Bourriaud, *Relational Aesthetics*, trans. Simon Pleasance and Fronza Woods (Paris: Les presses du réel, 2002).

Bruno Latour

Some Experiments in Art and Politics

The word "network" has become a ubiquitous designation for technical infrastructures, social relations, geopolitics, mafias, and, of course, our new life online.[1] But networks, in the way they are usually drawn, have the great visual defect of being "anemic" and "anorexic," in the words of philosopher Peter Sloterdijk, who has devised a philosophy of *spheres* and *envelopes*.[2] Unlike networks, spheres are not anemic, not just points and links, but complex ecosystems in which forms of life define their "immunity" by devising protective walls and inventing elaborate systems of air conditioning. Inside those artificial spheres of existence, through a process Sloterdijk calls "anthropotechnics," humans are born and raised. The two concepts of networks and spheres are clearly in contradistinction to one another: while networks are good at describing long-distance and unexpected connections starting from local points, spheres are useful for describing local, fragile, and complex "atmospheric conditions"—another of Sloterdijk's terms. Networks are good at stressing edges and movements; spheres at highlighting envelopes and wombs.

Of course, both notions are indispensable for registering the originality of what is called "globalization," an empty term that is unable to define from which localities, and through which connections, the "global" is assumed to act. Most people who enjoy speaking of the "global world" live in narrow, provincial confines with few connections to other equally provincial abodes in far away places. Academia is one case. So is Wall Street. One thing is certain: the globalized world has no "globe" inside which it could reside. As for Gaia, the goddess of the earth, we seem to have great difficulty housing her inside our global view, and even more difficulty housing ourselves inside her complex cybernetic feedbacks. It is the globe that is most absent in the era of globalization. Bad luck: when we had a globe during the classical age of discoveries and empire, there was no globalization; and now that we have to absorb truly global problems ...

1. Saraceno's *Galaxies Forming along Filaments*

So how can we have both networks and spheres? How do we avoid the pitfalls of a globalization that has no real globe in which to place everything? In a work presented at the Venice Biennale in 2009, Tomás Saraceno provided a great, and no doubt unintended, metaphor for social theory. In an entire room inside the Biennale's main pavilion, *Galaxies Forming along Filaments, Like Droplets along the Strands of a Spider's Web* (2009) consisted of carefully mounted elastic connectors that produced the shape of networks *and* spheres. If you were to avoid the guards' attentive gaze and slightly shake the elastic connectors—strictly forbidden—your action would reverberate quickly through the links and points of the network paths, but much more slowly through the spheres. This is not to say that spheres are made from different stuff, as if we must choose between habitation and connection, between local and global, or indeed between Sloterdijk and, let's say, actor-network theory. What Saraceno's work of art and engineering reveals is that multiplying the connections and assembling them closely enough will shift slowly from a network (which you can see through) to a sphere (difficult to see through). Beautifully simple and terribly efficient.

We should have known this all along: a cloth is nothing but a finely woven network, with a clear transition between one thread and the

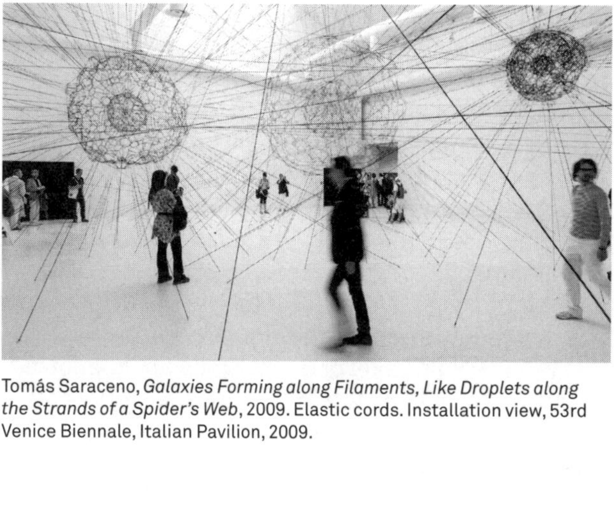

Tomás Saraceno, *Galaxies Forming along Filaments, Like Droplets along the Strands of a Spider's Web*, 2009. Elastic cords. Installation view, 53rd Venice Biennale, Italian Pavilion, 2009.

next, depending on the density of the stitching. By deploying this "obvious" truth within the main exhibition space of the Italian Pavilion, Saraceno performed precisely the task of philosophy according to Sloterdijk, namely of *explicating* the material and artificial conditions for existence. The task is not to overthrow but to make explicit. As Deleuze and Guattari have shown, a *concept* is always closely related to a *percept*.[3] By modifying our percept, *Galaxies Forming along Filaments* allows those who try to redescribe the loose expression of globalization to explore new concepts. Instead of having to choose between networks and spheres, we can have our cake and eat it too. There is a principle of connection—a kind of movement overlooked by the concepts of networks and spheres alike—that is able to generate, in the hands of a clever artist, both networks and spheres; a certain topology of knots that may thread the two types of connectors in a seamless web.

More interesting still is the theory of envelopes—the concept implied by this percept. In this proposition, walls or quasi-walls are supported by both external and lateral linkages. Again, we all know, or should know, that identities—the walls—are made possible only through the double movement of connecting distant anchors and stitching together local nodes. If you believe that there are independent bubbles and spheres that can sustain themselves, you are clearly forgetting the whole technology of envelopes. But it is one thing to say it, for instance in political philosophy—that no identity exists without relations with the rest of the world—and it is quite another to be reminded *visually* and *experientially* of the way this could be done.

Standing in the middle of Saraceno's work, the experience is inescapable: the very possibility of having an envelope around a local habitat is given by the length, number, and solidity of the connectors that radiate out in all directions.

I would have loved to see, when the exhibition was dismantled, how quickly the spherical patterns would have collapsed once a few of their outside links had been severed. A powerful lesson for ecology as well as for politics: the search for identity "inside" is directly linked to the quality of the "outside" connection—a useful reminder at a time when so many groups clamor for a solid identity that would "resist globalization," as they say. As if being local and having an identity could possibly be severed from alterity and connection.

Another remarkable feature of Saraceno's work is that such a visual experience is not situated in any fixed ontological domain, nor at any given scale: you can take it, as I do, as a model for social theory, but you could just as well see it as a biological interpretation of the threads that hold the walls and components of a cell, or, more literally, as the weaving of some monstrously big spider, or the utopian projection of galactic cities in 3-D virtual space. This is very important if you consider that all sorts of disciplines are now trying to cross the old boundary that has, until now, distinguished the common destiny of increasing numbers of humans and nonhumans. No visual representation of humans as such, separated from the rest of their support systems, makes any sense today. This was the primary motive for Sloterdijk's notion of spheres, as well as for the development of actor-network theory; in both cases the idea was to simultaneously modify the scale and the range of phenomena to be represented so as to renew what was so badly packaged in the old nature/society divide. If we have to be connected with climate, bacteria, atoms, and

DNA, it would be great to learn about how those connections could be represented.

The other remarkable feature of the work is that although there are many local orderings—including spheres within spheres—there is no attempt at nesting all relations within one hierarchical order. There are many local hierarchies, but they are linked into what appears visually as a heterarchy. Local nesting, yes; global hierarchy, no. For me, this is a potent attempt at shaping today's political ecology—by extending former natural forces to address the human political problem of forming livable communities. Too often, when ecologists—whether scientists or activists—appeal to nature, they speak as if it were the big global container *inside which* all other entities are arrayed in order of importance, from, let's say, the climate system to the earthworms and the bacteria, while humans meanwhile are situated somewhere in between. This gives a youthful image to the old image of the *scala naturae*, the great chain of being from the Renaissance.

But this is not the representation that Saraceno explores, as there is no overall container to his work. (Well, there is one, obviously, but it is only the physical quadrilateral of the Italian Pavilion's great hall. If you speak metaphorically, and to borrow another metaphor from Sloterdijk, this container must necessarily be the Crystal Palace of the international art market in which the artist's creation is "embedded.") In his work, every container or sphere is either inside another local one or "inside" the network of outside connections. But that's the point: networks have no inside, only radiating connectors. They are all edges. They provide connections but no structure. One does not reside in a network, but rather moves to other points through the edges.

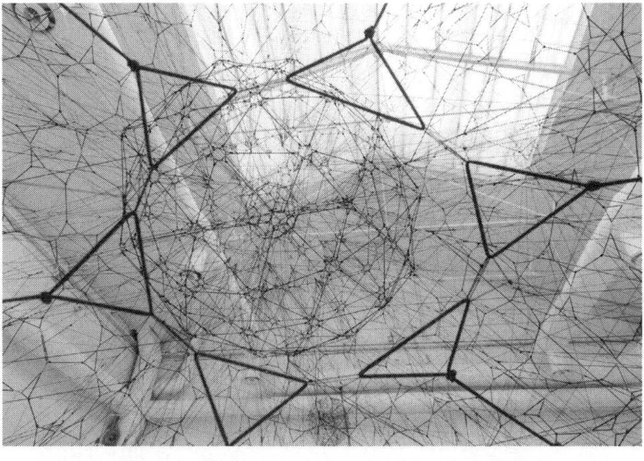

Tomás Saraceno, *Galaxies Forming along Filaments, Like Droplets along the Strands of a Spider's Web*, 2009. Elastic cords. Installation view, 53rd Venice Biennale, Italian Pavilion, 2009.

To think in these terms is to find a way to avoid modernism—in which case the hierarchy moves from bigger to smaller elements from a central point—but to also avoid, if I dare say, post-modernism—in which case there would be no local hierarchies and no *homogeneous* principle by which to establish the connections (in this case the elastic tensors that provide the language for the whole piece). For me, that is the beauty of Saraceno's work: it gives a sense of order, legibility, precision, and elegant engineering, and yet has no hierarchical structure. It is as if there were a vague possibility of retaining modernism's feeling of clarity and order, but freed from its ancient connection with hierarchy and verticality.

2. Who Owns Space and Time?

To explore the artistic, philosophical, and political questions raised by Saraceno's work, it might be useful to turn to another *locus classicus*—not the sphere versus network debate, but the debate over who owns the space in which we live collectively. There is no better way to frame this question than the bungled dialogue (well, not really a "dialogue," but that's the point) between Henri Bergson and Albert Einstein in Paris in 1922. Bergson had carefully studied Einstein's theory of relativity and wrote a thick book about it, but Einstein had only a few dismissive comments about Bergson's argument.[4] After Bergson spoke for thirty minutes, Einstein made a terse two-minute remark, ending with this damning sentence: "Hence there is no philosopher's time; there is only a psychological time different from the time of the physicist." While Bergson had argued that his notion of space and time had a *cosmological* import that was to be carefully meshed within Einstein's remarkable discoveries, Einstein argued that there was only one time and space—that of physics—and that what Bergson was after was nothing more than *subjective* time—that of psychology. We recognize here the classical way for scientists to deal with philosophy, politics, and art: "What you say might be nice and interesting but it has no cosmological relevance because it only deals with the subjective elements, the lived world, not the real world." The funny thing is that everyone—including, in a way, Bergson—was convinced that he had lost, and that indeed the whole question was another episode in the gigantomachy of objective reality versus subjective illusion. To the scientists, the cosmos, and to the rest of us, the phenomenology of human intentionality. So the answer to the question "Which space do we live in?" is clearly: we live in a subjective world with no reality for physics. Einstein: winner.

But this was the beginning of the twentieth century. Can we do better at the beginning of the twenty-first century? In other words, is it possible to give Bergson another chance to make his case that, no, he is not talking about subjective time and space, but is rather proposing an alternative to Einstein's cosmology? To explore such a possibility, I decided to rely on the fascinating genre of the reenactment. As many artists have shown, especially Rod Dickinson in the amazing staging of Milgram's experiment, reenactment is not a mere facsimile of the original but a second version, or a *second print* of the first instance, allowing for the exploration of its originality.[5] This is why, in a series of lectures at the Pompidou Center in June 2010, I invited, among many others, the artist Olafur Eliasson and two scholars, a historian of science, Jimena Canales, and a philosopher, Elie During, to reenact the famous debate by allowing the conclusion to shift somewhat, thus reopening a possibility that had been closed in the twentieth century.[6]

Who *owns* the concepts of space and time? Artists? Philosophers? Scientists? Do we live in the space-time of Einstein without realizing it, or, as Bergson vainly argued, does Einstein, the physicist, live in the time of what Bergson called *duration*? Those questions, it seemed to me, were just as important for physicists, historians, and philosophers as they are for an artist like Eliasson, who has populated museums and cities around the world by publicly demonstrating, through many artful connections between science, technology, and ecology, that there are many alternatives to the visual experience of common sense. The art form—or forum—that I chose consisted of asking the three of them to conjoin their forces in presenting films and photographs to set the stage for this famous debate, with Eliasson "refereeing" the debate through his own work.[7]

It may seem silly to ask an artist to adjudicate a debate between a philosopher and a physicist—especially a debate whose pecking order had been historically settled once and for all: the physicist speaks of the real world, and the philosopher "does not understand physics"; the artist is irrelevant here. But that was precisely the point, a point shared by Saraceno's heterarchy: that it is now possible to complicate the hierarchy of voices and make the conversation between disciplines move ahead in a way that is more representative of the twenty-first century than of the twentieth. No discipline is the final arbiter of any other.

That is exactly what Elie During did in a brilliant piece of philosophical fiction in which he entirely rewrote the 1922 dialogue as if Einstein had actually paid attention to what Bergson had told him. In the end, Zweistein—that is, the Einstein of 2010—was not, of course, convinced (that would have been a falsification, and no longer a fiction), but he had to admit that there might be more philosophy in his physics than he had claimed in 1922. Where Einstein had won, Zweistein had to settle for a draw.[8] So now we have a more balanced situation: the space and time in which we live—experientially, phenomenologically—might not be a mere mistake of our subjective self, but might have some relevance for what the world is really like. Instead of accepting the divide between physics and philosophy, this reenactment was a means of answering Alfred North Whitehead's famous question: "When red is found in nature, what else is found there also?"[9] Likewise, is it possible to imagine a world where scientific knowledge is able to *add* to the world instead of *dismissing* the experience of being in the world?

3. Composition?

One could object that such a reenactment, no matter how intriguing in its own right, does not have much to do with politics. The question has been asked many times by the public, especially when, during one of the keynote lectures I had organized to launch a new master's program in arts and politics, I invited Donna Haraway and Isabelle Stengers to present their understanding of "the political arts."[10] To the total dismay of many politically minded French citizens, Haraway spoke mainly about learning how to behave politically anew from her dog.[11] "From her dog! What does this have to do with politics? Tell us more about domination, inequalities, power struggles, elections, and revolutions." And yet, as Isabelle Stengers quietly but forcefully explained, the new vocabulary of politics—what, for this reason, she calls "cosmopolitics"—will come precisely from a new attention to other species and other types of agencies.[12] Here again, art, philosophy, ecology, activism, and politics exchanged their repertoire in order to redefine the actors, the aims, the forums, and the emotions of political involvement.

I have come to use the word "composition" to regroup in one term those many bubbles, spheres, networks, and snippets of arts and science.[13] This concept plays the same role as Saraceno's percept of elastic tensors. It allows us to move from spheres to networks with enough of a common vocabulary, but without a settled hierarchy. It is my solution to the modern/postmodern divide. Composition may become a plausible alternative to modernization. What can no longer be modernized, what has been postmodernized to bits and pieces, can still be composed.

1
Bruno Latour, *Reassembling the Social: An Introduction to Actor-Network Theory* (Oxford: Oxford University Press, 2005).

2
Peter Sloterdijk, *Sphären III – Schäume* (Frankfurt: Suhrkamp, 2004) [partial translation: Peter Sloterdijk, *Terror from the Air*, trans. Amy Patton and Steve Corcoran (Los Angeles: Semiotext(e), 2009)]; see also Peter Sloterdijk, "Foreword to the Theory of Spheres," in *Cosmograms*, ed. Melik Ohanian and Jean-Christophe Royoux (New York and Berlin: Lukas and Sternberg, 2005), 223–41. See http://www.sed.manchester.ac.uk/research/marc/news/seminars/latour/COSMOGRAM-INTER-GB_Spheres.pdf.

3
Gilles Deleuze and Félix Guattari, *What Is Philosophy?*, trans. Janis Tomlinson and Graham Burchell III (New York: Columbia University Press, 1996).

4
Henri Bergson, *Durée et simultanéité: À propos de la théorie d'Einstein* (Paris: PUF, 2009).

5
See http://www.roddickinson.net/pages/index.php.

6
Jimena Canales, *A Tenth of a Second: A History* (Chicago: University of Chicago Press, 2009).

7
This reenactment was pursued in February 2011 at Eliasson's Institut für Raumexperimente in Berlin and is still in progress.

8
Elie During, *Bergson et Einstein: La querelle du temps* (Paris: Presses Universitaires de France, 2011).

9
Alfred North Whitehead, *Concept of Nature* (Cambridge: Cambridge University Press, 1920).

10
See http://speap.sciences-po.fr/fr.php?item.1; and http://www.centrepompidou.fr/videos/2010/20100630-latour/index.html.

11
See Donna J. Haraway, *When Species Meet* (Minneapolis: University of Minnesota Press, 2007).

12
Isabelle Stengers, *Cosmopolitics I*, trans. Robert Bononno (Minneapolis: University of Minnesota Press, 2010).

13
Bruno Latour, "Steps toward the Writing of a Compositionist Manifesto," *New Literary History* 41 (2010): 471–90.

Ursula K. Heise

From the Blue Planet to Google Earth

1. Vaster Than Empires

In her short story "Vaster Than Empires and More Slow," science-fiction novelist Ursula K. Le Guin describes the encounter of a group of humans with an ecosystem that cannot be understood as encompassing anything less than an entire planet. When a team of scientific explorers arrives on the planet called only World 4470, after a journey that has taken just a few hours in their personal time but 250 years in Earth time, they find all its continents inhabited exclusively by plants, from grasslike to treelike species. Their scientific study of this world is from the beginning impaired by the peculiarities of their life as a group: since only psychologically or socially alienated individuals volunteer for a mission that will take them 500 years into the future (returning to Earth will take another 250), conflicts continuously erupt between the team members. One of the scientists, Osden, proves particularly problematic, as his "wide-range bioempathic receptivity," a psychological condition that enables him to "share lust with a white rat, pain with a squashed cockroach, phototropy with a moth," also leads him blindly to reflect back any human emotions he senses in his surroundings.[1] Since most of his colleagues approach him with suspicion or latent hostility, he cannot help but respond with scorn and hatred, which ends up estranging even the most patient and compassionate among them. To minimize the disruptive effects of this condition, he moves away from the team to take on the biological exploration of a nearby forest.

But the tension that Osden's presence had caused is soon replaced by a vague feeling of unease that most members of the group experience in and around this forest. Lingering apprehension erupts into crisis when Osden misses his radio transmissions, and is found bleeding and unconscious on the forest soil by two scientists who go out to search for him. As they pick him up, they are seized by an overwhelming and irrational fear that they hardly know how to control. When they discuss their experiences as Osden regains consciousness, it becomes clear that the plant life in the forest has some kind of sentience that he was able to identify mostly by its fear: "I suppose I could feel the roots. Below me in the ground, down under the ground ... I felt the fear. It kept growing. As if they'd finally *known* I was there, lying on them there, under them, among them, the thing they feared, and yet part of their fear itself. I couldn't stop sending the fear back, and it kept growing, and I couldn't move, I couldn't get away."[2] Several of the scientists contradict him by pointing out that the treelike plants have no nervous system that would enable them to react to their surroundings in such a way. But others observe that all the plants are linked by an intricate root system and a network of epiphytes so as to create what might be a far-reaching web of connections. One of them argues, "sentience or intelligence isn't a thing, you can't find it in, or analyze it out from, the cells of a brain. It's a function of the connected cells. It is, in a sense, the connection: the connectedness." Osden sums up his experience of this utterly alien form of intelligence by characterizing it as "sentience without senses. Blind, deaf, nerveless, moveless. Some irritability, response to touch. Response to sun, to light, to water, and chemicals in the earth around the roots. Nothing comprehensible to an animal mind. Presence without mind. Awareness of being, without object or subject. Nirvana."[3]

In such an ecosystem, the only agent that could have attacked Osden is another human, and one of the scientists finally admits that he mistook the psychological effect of the forest for Osden's influence and wanted to rid the mission of his interference. To break the impact of the alien forest, the crew decides to relocate their camp to another continent. But the same unease as before revisits them on a vast prairie covered with grasslike plants, forcing them to realize, as the team's biologist points out, that the entire planet's vegetation constitutes one large "network of processes. [...] There are no individual plants, then, properly speaking. Even the pollen is part of the linkage, no doubt, a sort of windborne sentience, connecting overseas. But it is not conceivable. That all the biosphere of a planet should be one network of communications, sensitive, irrational, immortal, isolated."[4] Le Guin's title allusion to Andrew Marvell's well-known poem "To His Coy Mistress," with its reference to "vegetable love," is translated into "vegetable fear" as Osden infers that the planet's apprehension must have been triggered by its dawning awareness of other beings where there had never been anything but itself. As Osden and the other humans perceive and retransmit this fear to the alien intelligence, they are locked into a self-reinforcing feedback loop with their environment.

Humans' interaction with a global environment is here articulated through a series of conceptual tensions: the forest's contemplative immobility versus the humans' movements; its indifference to them as against their investigation of it; its unconcern over space and time, which contrasts both with the humans' separation from their own world and history, and their longing to overcome the limitations of their biological form; its silence as against their language; its total unity (signaled here by the pollen, which connects the plants even across oceans) versus their plurality and individuality. At the same time, the lyrical quality of the passage, which culminates in the quotation from Marvell's poem and echoes the story's title, also conveys the sense that the forest possesses a kind of being that humans have always aspired to: a collective experience of "world enough and time," where temporality and space are no longer issues of existential concern. Even as the scientists, like Marvell's lovers, cannot share this experience, they seem to participate in it temporarily by "walk[ing] under the trees":[5] rootedness in its original, botanical sense and indifference to space coexist in the same experience.

Published in 1971, this short story articulates a vision of global ecology that had gained great popularity at the time. The idea that all the planet's life forms are linked in such a way that they come to form one world-encompassing, sentient superorganism echoes James Lovelock's well-known Gaia hypothesis, according to which Planet Earth constitutes a single overarching feedback system that sustains itself.[6] At the same time, the scientists' taxonomic approach to World 4470's biology—surveying the land, counting and identifying species, analyzing chemical processes—is complemented and in the end superseded by what the narrator calls Osden's "love," his willingness to merge physically and psychologically with the environment so as to communicate with it, in a transparent allusion to the holistic, synthetic modes of thought that were being advocated as superior to conventional, analytic science in the 1960s and 1970s. "Vaster than empires," this biosphere cannot be grasped in any of its parts unless their underlying planetary connectedness is understood first.

In asking how humans might be able to relate to such a planetwide organic "network of

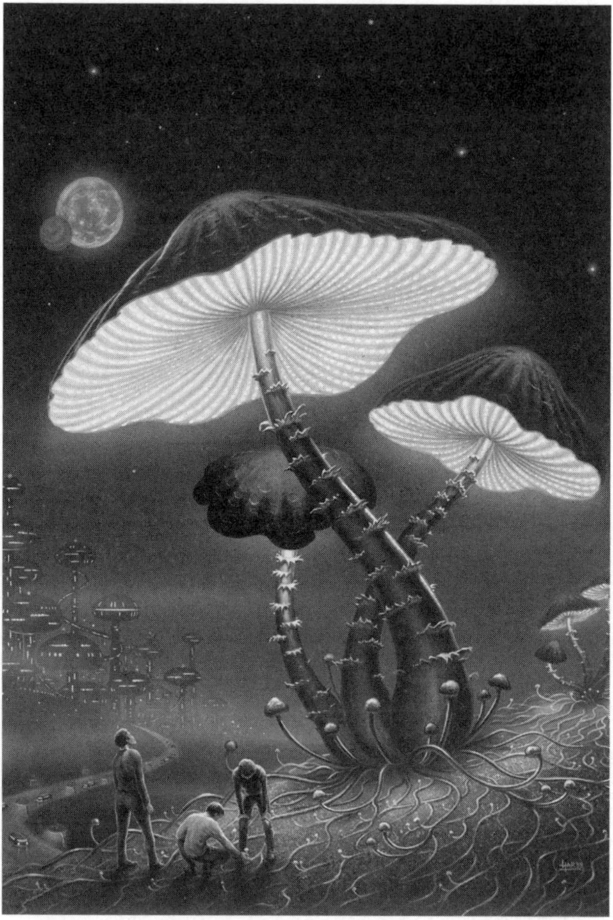

David A. Hardy, *Fairyland of Fungi*, from the illustration series “Galactic Tours,” 1981. Gouache on illustration board. This illustration originally prompted a short story by science-fiction writer Bob Shaw.

communications," Le Guin responds to powerful allegorizations of the global in the 1960s, from the "global village" to "Spaceship Earth," and to some extent participates in their romanticizations of global connectedness as mergers with a techno-logical or ecological sublime. Yet it is impossible to overlook that her short story also complicates such romanticizations, in that the global organism presents itself to the human observers as thoroughly alien, a world far from their own in both space and time. Osden's merger with it—enabled, it is worth noting, by psychopathology—comes at the price of his individual identity, while the other explorers remain just visitors who return to their own planets after a few months. Far from idyllic or utopian, the biosphere's total connectedness is what makes it even more strange than its remoteness or its unfamiliar species. Humans have no "natural" way of relating to such sentient connectivity, in whose context they themselves appear as alien Others. All the terms—cognitive, affective, and linguistic—by means of which they approach the planet have to be questioned as to whether they do not unduly project the terms of a quite different biological frame of reference, as one of the scientists implies when he refers to the treelike plants of this "totally alien environment, for which the archetypical connotations of the word 'forest' provide an inevitable metaphor."[7] Rather than describing awareness of the global biosphere as a reassuring (re)turn to Mother Earth, Le Guin's story portrays it as a difficult and thoroughly mediated step for the human imagination.

2. Sense of Planet

In spite of their conceptual differences, what all of these ecological allegories have in common is a sense that the earth's inhabitants, regardless of their national and cultural differences, are bound together by a global ecosystem whose functioning transcends human-made borders. It is easy to see how such a conception of ecology, derived from an attempt to practice science in a more synthetic and holistic fashion, lent itself to extrapolation into the political and social sphere. Countercultural aspirations toward global peace and the "brotherhood of man" could effortlessly be associated with the image of the Blue Planet and indeed be understood to derive directly from the planet's ecological functioning. Ecological systems, in this understanding, are naturally balanced, harmonious, and self-regenerating, and much of the utopian energy of the 1960s derived implicitly or explicitly from the inference that sociocultural systems might also return to such a state if they were freed from artificial constraints and distortions. Whatever the critiques one might want to formulate vis-à-vis this understanding of ecology and its sociocultural ramifications from the perspective of current cultural theory—justifiably much more suspicious of such notions of the natural—one cannot underestimate the galvanizing influence such thinking exerted on the burgeoning environmentalist movement, as well as on other new social movements in the 1960s.

But as Garrett Hardin's 1963 warning about the possible "tragedy" of the global commons already indicates, visions of global connectedness did not always entail utopian sociocultural projects. Paul R. Ehrlich's *Population Bomb*, Donella and Dennis Meadows's *Limits to Growth*, and Lester Brown's *Twenty-Ninth Day*, on the contrary, emphasized the possibility of catastrophic collapse on a planetary scale if contemporary trends in demographic growth, resource use, and pollution continued. The widespread use of apocalyptic narrative in environmentalist rhetoric of the 1960s and 1970s is well documented,[8] as is the transfer of Cold War language to environmentalist scenarios in Ehrlich's metaphorization of population growth as a "bomb" or Rachel Carson's description of chemical pollution as a "grim specter stalk[ing] the land."[9] Environmentally oriented science-fiction stories, by both scientists like Paul Ehrlich and literary authors, similarly portrayed global agricultural landscapes gone so toxic they could only be worked by robots (as in Brian Aldiss's 1967 *Earthworks*), nightmarish urban crowding, food riots, and famine (in a multitude of texts and films), or the entire planet laid to waste in misery, pollution, and disease (as in John Brunner's 1972 novel *The Sheep Look Up*). As Killingsworth and Palmer have pointed out, the horror of such millennial scenarios was in many cases intended less as a probable assessment of things to come than as a means of driving home the urgency of the environmentalist call for social change;[10] the presentation of collapse as global rather than local or national functioned as one important way of conveying the deadly seriousness of the crisis.

If nuclear fear and environmental concern shared such narrative patterns, derived in the last instance from biblical apocalypse, a more subtle but no less terrifying vision of global connectedness emerged from fears of corporate conspiracy that had circulated since the 1950s and made themselves explicit in the countercultural resistance to "the Man" or "the System." While social critics in earlier decades had emphasized the dangers of totalitarian states that might expand to worldwide rule, from the 1950s on, transnational corporations became the prime suspects of aspirations to global hegemony. Anticipated in novels such as Cyril Kornbluth and Frederik Pohl's *Space Merchants* (1953), this fear found its most influential cultural expression in the indictments of the corporate "moloch" and characters' persistently paranoid states of mind in the poetry and fiction of Allen Ginsberg, William Burroughs, and above all, Thomas Pynchon. As a form of resistance to capitalism and specifically to the mass consumerism that escalated in scale and scope after 1945, this paranoid vision of a global corporate conspiracy aiming to control the lives of individuals, communities, and nations, up to and including the triggering of world wars, was not in its original formulations specifically environmentalist. But it made its way into environmental rhetoric in the 1970s, when it surfaced in, for example, Edward Abbey's ecoclassic *The Monkey Wrench Gang* (1975), whose protagonists struggle against what they perceive as a "megalomaniacal megamachine":

> U.S. Steel intertwined in incestuous embrace with the Pentagon, TVA, Standard Oil, General Dynamics, Dutch Shell, I.G. Farben-industrie [sic]; the whole conglomerated cartel spread out upon half the planet Earth like a global kraken, pan-tentacled, wall-eyed and parrot-beaked, its brain a bank of computer data centers, its blood the flow of money, its heart a radioactive dynamo.[11]

Part of today's antiglobalization rhetoric, with its allegorization of villainous transnational corporations, descends directly from this corporate conspiracy discourse of the 1960s and 1970s. This intensely ambivalent legacy of global visions may help explain why the environmentalist movement today is uneasily extended from organizations that operate internationally and regularly make their voices heard in global political affairs using the diplomatic, economic, legal, and social languages of international institutions, all the way to a fervently antiglobalist wing of activists who demonstrate in the streets against the actions of precisely such institutions. The current political influence of international environmental nongovernmental organizations depends on their willingness to engage in and shape global processes in view of environmentalist goals, while the running battles of activists against the police at the Seattle World Summit in 1999 and the G8 Summit in Genoa in 2001 reflect a different assessment of globalization as dominated by corporate interests and therefore in need of being vigorously resisted. While the term "antiglobalization movement" has become popular in the media, many activists prefer the terms "anti-global capitalism movement" or "global justice movement," as they seek to foreground their opposition to the way politics has been dominated by transnational corporations.

But while this ambivalence of engagement in and resistance to the global, as I have shown, has a history that is several decades old, both the apocalyptic and the utopian dimensions of environmentalist visions of the planet have substantially weakened. Frederick Buell has persuasively demonstrated how the expectation of future collapse, prevalent in the 1960s, has transmuted into an awareness of ongoing crisis in the present.[12] Instead of anticipating disaster, he argues, most populations have learned to live with, and sometimes to accommodate, a multitude of daily ecological risk scenarios. Utopian hopes have diminished along with all-encompassing millennial visions. Attempts to project a future course for the planet under the label "sustainable development," widely discussed since the 1987 Brundtland Report, and more recent revisions of the development philosophy that undergirded this notion in the context of "environmental justice," are themselves contested and have not to date generated the kind of powerful images that dominated the debates of the 1960s and 1970s.[13] To the extent that most environmentalists see the world as unified today, it is either as a world dominated by corporate capitalism or as a world at risk.

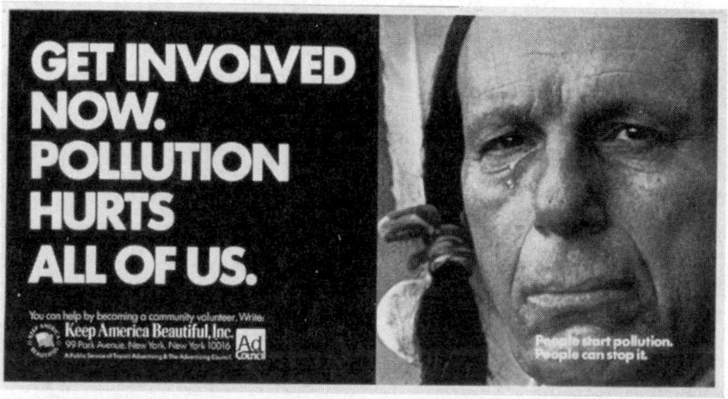

Ad campaign against pollution evoking American Indians as environmentally conscious. This 1971 campaign was notorious for featuring "Iron Eyes" Cody, a Hollywood actor of Italian origin who was frequently cast as an American Indian.

3. Localism and Modernity: The Ethic of Proximity

Environmental justice activists have often taken issue with the underlying assumptions of race, class, and gender that tend to be taken for granted in the environmental ethics of white, male, middle-class writers, including Wendell Berry and Scott Russell Sanders. They have rightly emphasized not only that the privileges of encounters with nature as well as the risks associated with some branches of agribusiness and industry are unevenly distributed but that in fact this uneven distribution has in some instances helped to perpetuate environmentally unsound practices whose consequences have often not been suffered or even noticed by the middle class.[14] Given the environmental justice movement's leftist, antihegemonic, and radical political rhetoric, it comes as somewhat of a surprise to find one environmental justice ecocritic deploring how "globalization [...] alters traditional values of place, life, and meaning" and "trigger[s] [...] chaos,"[15] as if tradition and order were self-evidently worth perpetuating, and to see others relying on conceptions of place-based identity that do not differ from those of the white, male, middle-class environmentalists they criticize as much as one might expect. [...]

I would argue, then, that in spite of significant differences in social outlook, certain features recur across a wide variety of environmentalist perspectives that emphasize a sense of place as a basic prerequisite for environmental awareness and activism. Many of them, as I have attempted to show, associate spatial closeness, cognitive understanding, emotional attachment, and an ethic of responsibility and "care." Put somewhat more abstractly, they share what philosophers Hans

Jonas and Zygmunt Bauman, as well as the sociologist John Tomlinson, have in a broader context called an "ethic of proximity." As Bauman puts it:

> The morality which we have inherited from premodern times—the only morality we have—is a morality of proximity, and as such is woefully inadequate in a society in which all important action is an action on distance. [...] Moral responsibility prompts us to care that our children are fed, clad and shod; it cannot offer us much practical advice, however, when faced with numbing images of a depleted, desiccated and overheated planet which our children, and the children of our children will inherit and have to inhabit in the direct or oblique result of our collective unconcern.[16]

Bauman sums up the dilemma that this approach to ethics raises in an increasingly global context by claiming:

> The cancelling of spatial distance as measured by the reach of human action—that sometimes applauded, but ever more often bewailed feat of modern technology—has not been matched by the cancellation of moral distance, measured by the reach of moral responsibility; but it should be so matched. The question is, how this can be done, if at all.[17]

This skepticism as to whether an ethical code based on what is geographically or socially nearby will be able to cope with larger contexts such as the nation or the transnational realm is echoed by many environmentalist thinkers. The Norwegian philosopher Arne Naess, for example, a highly influential figure for American environmentalism, declares categorically that "the nearer has priority over the more remote—in space, time, culture, species."[18] His call for "a coherent, local, logical, and natural community" assumes, as do many other celebrations of the sense of place, that sociocultural, ethical, and affective allegiances arise spontaneously and "naturally" at the local level, whereas any attachments to larger entities such as the nation or beyond require complex processes of mediation.[19]

Frequently, the assumption that there can be no compelling ethical interpellation other than that of proximity becomes the foundation for a more general critique of modern sociopolitical structures in environmentalist thought, a deep-seated skepticism vis-à-vis the long-distance, mediated, and abstract structures and institutions that shape modern societies. Naess himself is quite explicit about his rejection of social modernity: "Locality and togetherness in the sense of community are central key terms in the deep ecological movement. There is, so to say, an 'instinctive' reaction against being absorbed in something that is big but not great—something like our modern society."[20] For this reason, the bioregionalist movement, which is heavily indebted to Naess, has consistently advocated a geographical, political, and economic reorganization of nations into bioregions whose boundaries would follow ecological dividing lines like climate zones, species distribution, watersheds, or mountain ranges. Such a reorganization, according to prominent bioregionalist Kirkpatrick Sale, would liberate people from the large-scale social structures that interpose themselves between people's actions and the visibility of their consequences:

> The only way people will apply "right behavior" and behave in responsible ways is if they have been persuaded to see the problem concretely and to understand their own connections to it directly—and this can be done only at a limited scale. [...] People will do the environmentally "correct" thing not because it is thought to be the *moral*, but rather the *practical*, thing to do. That cannot be done on a global scale, nor a continental, nor even a national one, because the human animal, being small and limited, has only a small view of the world and a limited comprehension of how to act within it.[21]

Sale's central idea, that the ecologically right course of action will impose itself as the obvious one at the local but not at larger levels of scale, may seem something short of compelling to anyone who has ever engaged in local politics (a point I will return to later). What persuasive power it has surely derives from its widely shared mistrust of the large-scale, abstract, and often invisible networks of authority, expertise, and exchange that structure modern societies.[22]

4. Sense of Place

The idea of the "cultural construction" of place similarly revolves around the assumption that places are not simply given in advance of human understanding, but its emphasis lies more on the cultural practices of particular communities in creating them than on the mechanisms of capitalist economies. Both the characters of particular places and the modes of belonging to them are defined by human intervention and cultural history more than by natural processes, cultural constructionists argue; local citizenship, far from coming naturally, is painstakingly established and safeguarded through a multiplicity of political, social, and cultural practices and procedures. As anthropologist Arjun Appadurai has argued, this is even and especially the case in premodern tribal communities: against a view of such communities as more spontaneously and directly bonded to place than modern societies, Appadurai insists that, on the contrary, elaborate rituals of home building, gardening, or initiation can all be read as strategies to define an always uncertain and embattled local citizenship rather than as signs of its self-evidence and stability.[23] More broadly, the basic goal of work in cultural studies for the last twenty years has been to analyze and, in most cases, to dismantle appeals to "the natural" or "the biological" by showing their groundedness in cultural practices rather than facts of nature. The thrust of this work, therefore, invariably leads to skepticism about the possibility of returning to nature as such, or of the possibility of places defined in terms of their natural characteristics that humans should relate to.

A somewhat different, but related, set of criticisms has emphasized not so much the difficulties of defining the local as the ambivalent ethical and political consequences that might follow from encouraging attachments to place. In the passage quoted earlier, for example, Kirkpatrick Sale assumes that at the local and regional level, environmentalist considerations will simply impose themselves as the most "practical" course of action because people will be directly aware of and affected by the consequences of their decisions. But it remains unclear why this would be the case. Surely in a local or regional context, decision-makers have to weigh different kinds of "practicalities" against each other just as those in national or transnational contexts do: the interests of different social groups, short-term versus long-term practicalities, the interests of present versus future generations, diverging predictions of what consequences a particular course of action might entail, competition between different interests the community holds in common (e.g., the need for access to transportation vs. the interest in preserving natural areas), and so on. Since many such decisions depend on value judgments about the kind of community and environment that are considered most desirable, and on courses of action whose outcome cannot be predicted with complete certainty, "practical" reason of the kind Sale postulates cannot function as an unambiguous guide for how communities should reconnect to nature. A change in scale from large to small entities, therefore, does not in and of itself guarantee anything in the way of more ecologically sustainable modes of living. The history of environmental politics includes many examples of local communities voting in favor of their own economic interest and against environmental preservation, decisions that have sometimes been overruled by a national community with fewer direct gains to hope for from development or exploitation of local resources. Similarly, supranational entities such as the European Union have in some cases passed environmental laws whose stringency exceeds national and local ones.

As quite a few critics of deep ecology have pointed out, in addition, one of the risks in attempting to derive political and ethical norms and imperatives directly from nature is that of underestimating the diversity of political projects at whose service such derivations can be put. The most extreme and frequently quoted example is no doubt the National Socialist rhetoric of Germans' natural connectedness to "blood and soil" (*Blut und Boden*), which helped legitimate fascist political structures, military expansion of the "life space" (*Lebensraum*), and unprecedented violence both within and outside what was claimed to be Germans' legitimate space of domination in the 1930s and 1940s.[24] But there is no need to rely only on this in many ways extraordinary case to argue that a sense of place can lend equal support to both conservative and progressive politics. [...] The political consequences of encouraging people to develop a sense of place, therefore, are far from straightforward and predictable, and environmentalists need to be aware that place awareness can be deployed in the service of political ideals they may not judge desirable. There is nothing in the idea of localism itself that guarantees its connection with the grassroots-democratic and egalitarian politics that many environmentalists envision when they advocate place-based communities.

5. Deterritorialization and Eco-Cosmopolitanism

In the later 1990s, as discussions of globalization spread from the social sciences to the humanities, studies of the relationship of identity to various kinds of space also shifted in emphasis to concepts such as "transnationalism" or "critical internationalism." Theorists from a variety of fields, at the same time, began to recuperate the term "cosmopolitanism" as a way of imagining forms of belonging beyond the local and the national. Philosophers Anthony Appiah and Martha Nussbaum, anthropologists James Clifford and Aihwa Ong, sociologists Ulrich Beck, Anthony Giddens, Ulf Hannerz, and John Tomlinson, political scientists Patrick Hayden, David Held, and Anthony McGrew, as well as literary critics such as Homi Bhabha, Pheng Cheah, Walter Mignolo, and Bruce Robbins, among others, have all engaged with this notion in the attempt to free it from the connotations of social privilege and leisure travel that accompanied it in earlier periods. While there are considerable differences in the way these theorists rethink cosmopolitanism, they share with earlier theorists of hybridity and diaspora the assumption that there is nothing natural or self-evident about attachments to the nation, which are on the contrary established, legitimized, and maintained by complex cultural practices and institutions. But rather than seeking the grounds of resistance to nationalisms and nation-based identities in local communities or groups whose mobility places them at the borders of national identity, these theorists strive to model forms of cultural imagination and understanding that reach beyond the nation and around the globe. In one way or another, all of them are concerned with the question of how we might be able to develop cultural forms of identity and belonging that are commensurate with the rapid growth in political, economic, and social interconnectedness that has characterized the last few decades.

Cogent as this reasoning is in its search for new forms of transnational cultural identity, it has not gone unchallenged. Historian Arif Dirlik, literary critic Timothy Brennan, and other theorists have recently reemphasized the value of local and national identities as forms of resistance to some dimensions of globalization. Critiques of the "essentialism" of local identities and of national belonging, Dirlik and Brennan argue, omit consideration of the ways localism and nationalism can serve progressive political objectives and legitimate emancipatory projects, especially in the developing world and in a context of rapid economic globalization.[25] Several recent anthologies—Prazniak and Dirlik's *Places and Politics in the Age of Globalization*, Mirsepassi, Basu, and Weaver's *Localizing Knowledge in a Globalizing World*, or Jasanoff and Martello's *Earthly Politics*, for example—all seek to revalidate local and national foundations of identity as a means of resisting the imperialist dimensions of globalization.

With this wave of counter-critiques, the theoretical debate has arrived at a conceptual impasse: while some theorists criticize nationally based forms of identity and hold out cosmopolitan identifications as a plausible and politically preferable alternative, other scholars emphasize the importance of holding on to national and local modes of belonging as a way of resisting the imperialism of some forms of globalization. Fredric Jameson sums up this quandary when he highlights how local and regional identities used to be pitched against the homogenizing force of the nation, only to point out:

> When one positions the threats of Identity at a higher level globally, then everything changes: at this upper range, it is not national state power that is the enemy of difference, but rather the transnational system itself, Americanization and the standardized products of a henceforth uniform and standardized ideology and practice of consumption. At this point, nation-states and their national cultures are suddenly called upon to play the positive role hitherto assigned—against them—to regions and local practices. [...] And as opposed to the multiplicity of local and regional markets, minority arts and languages, whose vitality can certainly be acknowledged all over the world uneasily coexisting with the vision

[...] of their universal extinction, it is striking to witness the resurgence—in an atmosphere in which the nation-state as such, let alone "nationalism," is a much maligned entity and value—of defenses of national culture on the part of those who affirm the powers of resistance of a national literature and a national art.[26]

This conflict between a conceptualization of national identity as either an oppressive hegemonic discourse or a tool for resistance to global imperialism, and of local identity as either an essentialist myth or a promising site of struggle against both national and global domination, leads Arif Dirlik even more pointedly to declare a theoretical stalemate. He acknowledges the

intractability of the problem [...] with existing discussions of place/space in which the defense and the repudiation of place both carry considerable theoretical plausibility and for that same reason seem in their opposition to be confined within a theoretical world of their own out of which there is no exit that is to be revealed by theory.[27]

If Dirlik falls prey to a rather comical non sequitur by following up this categorical rejection of a theoretical solution with a sustained theoretical defense of place—against his own suggestion that the entire discussion should be shifted to the level of specific case studies—he and Jameson nevertheless accurately pinpoint the conceptual contradictions in many current discourses about place. It might be more useful to think of such contradictions as a starting point for reflecting on the kinds of categories and abstractions that are commonly used in cultural theory than to reject them wholesale, since such rejection would presumably lead back to the theory resistance and hyper-specific analyses of detail that were already rehearsed (and later abandoned) in cultural studies in the early 1990s. But Dirlik is surely right that no obvious theoretical solution presents itself to the conceptual dilemmas in current theories regarding the relationship of identity and place.

Such problems in rethinking the relation of local inhabitation to global citizenship are by no means limited to environmentalist rhetoric but have surfaced in a variety of fields from identity politics to globalization theories. Several waves of debate about notions involving rootedness in the local or the nation on the one hand and concepts such as diaspora, nomadism, hybridity, *mestizaje*, borderlands, and exile on the other have led to an impasse, where advocacies of local and of global consciousness have achieved equal plausibility when they are formulated at an abstract theoretical level. It no longer makes sense to rely mechanically on a particular set of terms with the assumption that it always describes the ideologically preferable perspective: for example, the frequent assumption that hybridity is inherently preferable to claims to cultural authenticity, that an emphasis on migration and diaspora is superior to one on rootedness or, conversely, that nomadism is destructive while place attachments are not. But acknowledging this impasse does not imply that such arguments no longer make sense or that they have become superfluous in specific political and discursive contexts.

In Le Guin's "Vaster Than Empires and More Slow," Osden, after becoming enveloped by World 4470's "vegetable fear," realizes the only way to break the humans' self-sustaining feedback loop with their new environment is either to leave the planet and thereby abort the mission or self-sacrifice. He chooses the latter, venturing into the forest on his own with a conscious effort to absorb rather than reflect back its fear, and to transmit the humans' absence of hostility. Doing so implies that he has to disrupt the psychic mechanisms that have allowed him to survive in human company, and he therefore remains in the forest when the rest of the expedition returns to Earth, merging with an intelligence that, in his perception, "know[s] the whole daylight [...] and the whole night. All the winds and lulls together. The winter stars and the summer stars at the same time. To have roots, and no enemies. To be entire. [...] No invasion. No others. To be whole."[28] The team members, for the rest of their stay, live immersed in this sentient environment whose planet-encompassing existence is unimaginably alien to their own:

> The people of the Survey team walked under the trees, through the vast colonies of life, surrounded by a dreaming silence, a brooding calm that was half aware of them and wholly indifferent to them. There were no hours. Distance was no matter. Had we but world enough and time. [...] The planet turned between the sunlight and the great dark; winds of winter and summer blew fine, pale pollen across the quiet seas.[29]

This text is an edited excerpt from the chapter "From the Blue Planet to Google Earth: Environmentalism, Ecocriticism, and the Imagination of the Global," in Ursula K. Heise, *Sense of Place and Sense of Planet: The Environmental Imagination of the Global* (New York: Oxford University Press, 2008).

1
Ursula K. Le Guin, "Vaster Than Empires and More Slow," in *Buffalo Gals and Other Animal Presences* (New York: Plume, 1987), 97.

2
Ibid., 113.

3
Ibid., 118.

4
Ibid., 122.

5
Ibid., 127.

6
In the 1987 introduction to the story, Le Guin does not mention Lovelock's Gaia hypothesis explicitly but does refer to "Deo, Demeter, the grain-mother, and her daughter/self Kore the Maiden called Persephone" as ancient mythological paradigms for envisioning humans' relationship to the plant world. See ibid, 83.

7
Ibid., 115.

8
For detailed analyses of this rhetoric, see Greg Garrard, *Ecocriticism* (London: Routledge, 2004), 85–107; Lawrence Buell, *The Environmental Imagination: Thoreau, Nature Writing, and the Formation of American Culture* (Cambridge, MA: Harvard University Press, 1995), 280–308; Jimmie M. Killingsworth and Jacqueline S. Palmer, "Millennial Ecology: The Apocalyptic Narrative from *Silent Spring* to *Global Warming*," in *Green Culture: Environmental Rhetoric in Contemporary America*, ed. Carl G. Herndl and Stuart C. Brown (Madison: University of Wisconsin Press, 1996); and Frederick Buell, *From Apocalypse to Way of Life: Environmental Crisis in the American Century* (New York: Routledge, 2003), 177–208.

9
Rachel Carson, *Silent Spring* (Boston: Houghton Mifflin, 1962), 3.

10
Killingsworth and Palmer, "Millennial Ecology," 41.

11
Edward Abbey, *The Monkey Wrench Gang* (New York: Perennial, 2000), 167, 172. Shell and IG Farben also figured prominently in Pynchon's vision of corporate conspiracy in *Gravity's Rainbow*, published only two years before *The Monkey Wrench Gang*.

12
Buell, *From Apocalypse to Way of Life*, 177–208.

13
For a more detailed summary of the debates about the notion of human and/or economic development that surround these terms, see Patrick Hayden, *Cosmopolitan Global Politics* (Aldershot: Ashgate, 2005), 121–51.

14
See T. V. Reed, "Toward an Environmental Justice Ecocriticism," in *The Environmental Justice Reader: Politics, Poetics, and Pedagogy*, ed. Joni Adamson, Mei Mei Evans, and Rachel Stein (Tucson: University of Arizona Press, 2002), 151.

15
Julie Sze, "From Environmental Justice Literature to the Literature of Environmental Justice," in ibid., 168.

16
Zygmunt Bauman, *Postmodern Ethics* (Oxford: Blackwell, 1993), 217–18.

17
Ibid., 219.

18
Arne Naess, "Identification as a Source of Deep Ecological Attitudes," in *Deep Ecology*, ed. Michael Tobias (San Diego, CA: Avant Books, 1985), 268.

19
Arne Naess, *Ecology, Community and Lifestyle*, trans. David Rothenberg (Cambridge: Cambridge University Press, 1989), 144.

20
Ibid.

21
Kirkpatrick Sale, *Dwellers in the Land*, 2nd ed. (Athens: University of Georgia Press, 2000), 53.

22
This opposition to modernity as a general sociopolitical structure is also clearly articulated by some environmentalist thinkers who draw on more leftist traditions of thought. British philosopher Mick Smith argues that "radical environmentalism is engaged in a fundamental critique of modernism; its alternative culture challenges modern life to its very core." (Mick Smith, *An Ethics of Place: Radical Ecology, Postmodernity, and Social Theory* [Albany: State University of New York Press, 2001], 164–65.) Yet in Smith's thought, "place" is quite deliberately used as an ambiguous concept that sometimes refers to actual localities (as in his discussion of the British anti-roads movement) and sometimes to a more general reliance on the concrete rather than on abstract categories.

23
Arjun Appadurai, *Modernity at Large: Cultural Dimensions of Globalization* (Minneapolis: University of Minnesota Press, 1996), 183–86.

24
Janet Biehl, "'Ecology' and the Modernization of Fascism in the German UltraRight," *Society and Nature* 1 (1993): 131–33; Janet Biehl and Peter Staudenmaier, *Ecofascism: Lessons from the German Experience* (Edinburgh: AK Press, 1995); Anna Bramwell, *Blood and Soil: Richard Walther Darré and Hitler's "Green Party"* (Abbotsbrook: Kensal Press, 1985).

25
Arif Dirlik, "Place-Based Imagination: Globalism and the Politics of Place," in *Places and Politics in an Age of Globalization*, ed. Roxann Prazniak and Arif Dirlik (Lanham: Rowman and Littlefield, 2001), 35–42; Timothy Brennan, *At Home in the World: Cosmopolitanism Now* (Cambridge, MA: Harvard University Press, 1997), 44–65.

26
Fredric Jameson, "Notes on Globalization as a Philosophical Issue," in *The Cultures of Globalization*, ed. Fredric Jameson and Masao Miyoshi (Durham, NC: Duke University Press, 1998), 74–75.

27
Dirlik, "Place-Based Imagination," 23–24.

28
Le Guin, "Vaster Than Empires and More Slow," 123.

29
Ibid., 127.

Gean Moreno

Notes on the Inorganic, Part I: Accelerations

For capitalism to sustain itself, to reproduce indefinitely, it needs to incrementally gobble up more and more. It must continually overturn any balanced cycles, as they can lead to stagnation and lost opportunities for growth. Extinctions are drawn to it like filaments to a magnet. The imperative to grow and the need for unrestricted license to devastate are two sides of the same coin—not only mutually dependent but structurally essential. Yet, however deplorable, growth and devastation can be aesthetically generative: they set us on a course toward imagining what the world will look like as it slides toward the inorganic.

By constantly invading and liquidating resource-rich contexts, capitalism encourages images that project what will inevitably be left in its wake: a dead world. And just as one can imagine (or see) patches of devastated and desolate land, a kind of localized post-extraction desertification, one can just as easily imagine this becoming a planetary condition: the globe as a rotating, dead lithosphere, coated in a fine dust of decomposing once-organic particles. Individual patches of dead world synthesized into a continuous crust.

1. Gray Goo

In 1986, Dr. K. Eric Drexler, at the time a research affiliate at MIT's Artificial Intelligence Laboratory, published *Engines of Creation*, a book celebrating the growing productive capabilities of nanotechnology and the coming age of mechanochemical manufacturing. He was preparing us for the "assembler breakthrough"—the moment when self-replicating machines as small as molecules would become the driving engines of contemporary technology. Like science fiction, it was a testament of—or from—the future. It came in a warm language of affirmation and delight: a less arduous life was guaranteed by the inevitable emergence of molecular technology. We were moving up, pushing forward, relieving ourselves of unseemly burdens such as those of aging and dying or having to work for a living. But in one chapter in the book—chapter 11, "Engines of Destruction"—Drexler slips out of character and offers a simple and formal warning, one with enough seductive charge and narrative potential to take on a life of its own:

> The early transistorized computers soon beat the most advanced vacuum-tube computers because they were based on superior devices. For the same reason, early assembler-based replicators could beat the most advanced modern organisms. "Plants" with "leaves" no more efficient than today's solar cells could out-compete real plants, crowding the biosphere with an inedible foliage. Tough omnivorous "bacteria" could out-compete real bacteria: they could spread like blowing pollen, replicate swiftly, and reduce the biosphere to dust in a matter of days. Dangerous replicators could easily be too tough, small, and rapidly spreading to stop—at least if we make no preparation. We have trouble enough controlling viruses and fruit flies.[1]

In the wake of Drexler's book, the threat related in this paragraph became popularized as the "gray goo problem." It was abhorred in nanotechnology circles, but among science-fiction writers and aficionados, it was fashionable and much loved. The tale, in a more developed stage, involves a swarm of self-replicating, biovorous nano-assemblers run amok. If what it relates was to actually occur, it would be the first and only environmental disaster caused by the field of molecular mechanochemical manufacturing, with a total consumption of the planet taking place in as little as ~10^4 seconds after the chain of reproduction was first triggered.[2] Either by mimicking biological replicators like bacteria but aborting or overstepping the boundaries of their intended use (in the sci-fi version), or by being produced in a lab with the capacity to function autonomously (in the scientist's hypothetical version), these molecule-sized machines multiply exponentially by transferring "genetic" algorithms to new units and using our biosphere as fuel. They reproduce until they ingest all life on the planet and leave behind a desolate landscape of gray slime. "Ecophagic nanorobots would regard living things as environmental carbon accumulators and biomass as a valuable ore to be mined for carbon and energy," writes Robert A. Freitas Jr. "Of course, biosystems from which all carbon has been extracted can no longer be alive but would instead become lifeless chemical sludge."[3]

The world ends, then, as a dead, undifferentiated, slimy surface—a massive lithosphere covered in lifeless sludge and nanomass wreckage. The scenario is one of mass, if unintentional, "species" suicide (the replibots) and full biological elimination, fated by the meeting of machines programmed for infinite non-mutational reproduction and an environment with finite energy-producing resources. One ecology doesn't emerge by eating and metabolizing another—an affirmationist escape hatch available to certain flinching strands of apocalyptic sci-fi. This isn't a machines-take-over story. These replibots eat the environment for no reason but to proliferate more replibots, unaffected by the useless gray goo they generate and the acceleration of their own demise. This isn't the production of a new world, but a sped-up, unintentional dissolution of the existing one. One world isn't being transfigured into another; rather, a world is being transfigured into a non-world, dissolved into inorganic slime. Articles challenging this gray goo scenario quickly appeared, multiplying exponentially like the replibots they targeted. This was hardly surprising. Dependent on large public research grants and seeking application in the private manufacturing sector, the field of nanotechnology quickly deployed its reactive forces. The last thing it needed to contend with was an unsubstantiated speculative doomsday scenario. Drexler himself was at the forefront of efforts to argue that his scenario is highly unlikely and that advances in safety since he wrote his book render it all but impossible.

In the end, the mythological space opened by his gleeful slip into the apocalyptic needed to be fenced off and eradicated. As Drexler explicitly stated in his book—giving us a furtive glance at the economic imperative that guides the project of molecular technology—the market is the "ultimate test." And we all know that a capricious market may suddenly recoil from this sort of risk (even if not from others, as we've come to learn lately), particularly where long-term and high-investment projects that involve untested technologies are concerned. But what is interesting, beyond considering just how irreversibly bound science and the market are, is attempting to explain why this gray goo scenario found such a warm reception beyond cloistered nanotechnology circles, in the culture it was thought to abolish. Why does the scenario still have currency as narrative, while having been completely debunked as hard science? For what amorphous, slippery collective feeling does this scenario serve as an outlet or allegory?

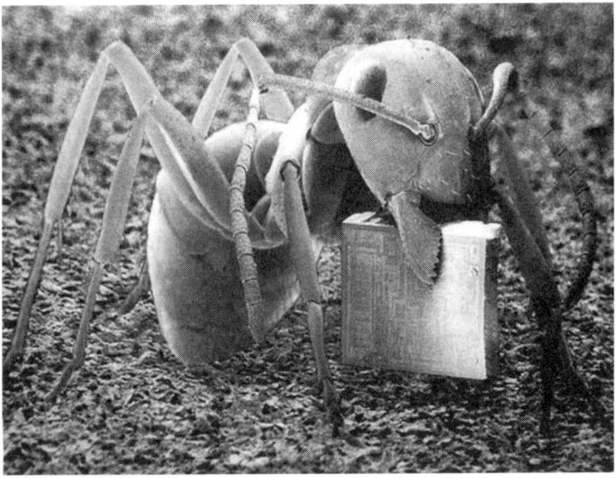

Image of an ant captioned "Nanotechnology makes possible devices thousands of times smaller than this ant's microchip."

2. The Deeper Cut

The pages that precede the introduction of the gray goo problem in Drexler's book are concerned with the eliminations that will accompany the proliferation of assembler-based replicators and thinking machines. He mentions specifically the elimination of global trade (automated engineering can be localized and shrunk), the elimination of the current parameters of human mortality (the indefinite extension of life through artificial cell-reparation mechanisms), the elimination of human labor due to near absolute automation (replicators producing objects, as well as other replicators to replace and upgrade themselves). All these positively charged eliminations, however, are secondary to the most terrifying potential consequence of nanotechnology gone awry: the abolition of life, the wholesale destruction of the biological.

Beyond whatever kind of warning the gray goo problem presents in relation to the real advances of nanotechnology, it allegorizes eliminative threats to life that nevertheless exist in other spheres. It absorbs threats that we may not be able to deal with directly, threats that need to be displaced in order to keep them from cutting a gash in our symbolic order—threats that are too uncomfortable, that indict us too shamefully, that demand too much of us in terms of altering our way of life to encourage anything but displacement or concealment. The cut is too deep. The notion that Drexler's apocalyptic scenario recodes a different, already active process of elimination seems a particularly plausible explanation considering the implausibility of the gray goo threat, according to the very scientist who originally posed the problem.

One of the things that the gray goo problem may stage is the very dissipative tendency that is at the core of capitalist production itself—the movement toward resource elimination as the necessary correlation to the expansion of capital. Few would claim to be anything but appalled by capital's dissipative compulsion, just as they would refuse to accept that such an impulse be naturalized as part of the intrinsic dynamic of rational economic development. The innocence that allows us to be hoodwinked in this way belongs to another time. The delusional character of a system predicated on infinite growth can't be smudged out of the picture so easily anymore. We know that such a system is not viable in the long run, that its predatory practices are indefensible, and yet on so many levels we continue to behave as though capitalism were a necessary and unshakeable system. It's a fatality that we can at most resist through the subtraction of our subjective belief in it, which we often register in private gestures, at reduced scales, with "personal initiative" and demands for "corporate responsibility." We participate, despite ourselves, in a consensual collective fantasy, frayed at its edges but holding, of plenitude and regeneration, of the miracle of the system's unendingness, assailed on every side by apocalyptic fantasies but nowhere extinguished by them, ratifying the old Jamesonean/Žižekean quip that it is easier to imagine the end of the world than the end of capitalism. In fact, it is Žižek who never tires of reminding us that in our "post-ideological" world we participate fully in the capitalist game while simultaneously telling ourselves that we don't believe in it at all. We disavow in thought and speech what we adhere to in action.

The naturalization of resource depletion, shielded as much as taxed by our disavowals, cannot help but affect cultural production. Sculpture, in its slouching toward interior design and décor—

even if it does so in a reflexive, post-Broodthaersean mood—recognizes its complicated and diminished place in a world where nearly all object production and experience is geared toward commodified urban infrastructure. This reduced ambition anticipates the desertified landscapes to come of post-resource depletion.

Last year, design research collective InfraNet Lab/Lateral Office developed a series of speculative infrastructural projects.[4] Among these was Re-Rigging, an ambitious proposal that sought to develop the offshore oil excavation infrastructure for the Caspian Sea, not yet marching at full speed due to post-1991 border and legal disputes but inevitably on its way nonetheless. The project seeks to render this infrastructure such that potentials embedded at the design stage can be actualized when the rigs eventually become derelict and are left behind (oil extraction has been given a very short lifespan there, hitting its peak between 2020 and 2030). After the oil is used up, the built structures would serve new functions as recreational sites, bird sanctuaries, and the like. What is astonishing in this is that the depletion of petroleum is naturalized as empirical fact—as if it had already happened—and design can only be relevant by factoring that into the process. This is the project's pragmatic realism. A coming decimated landscape—the end point of a process so natural that it can be accounted for before it is even set in motion—becomes a determinant factor in the architectural production of the present.

While it is true that InfraNet Lab/Lateral Office is proposing adaptive and reactive systems, laudably serving as counterpoints to the monological infrastructures of the twentieth century that end up as useless concrete carcasses, the first thing it adapts and reacts to is the will to dissipation

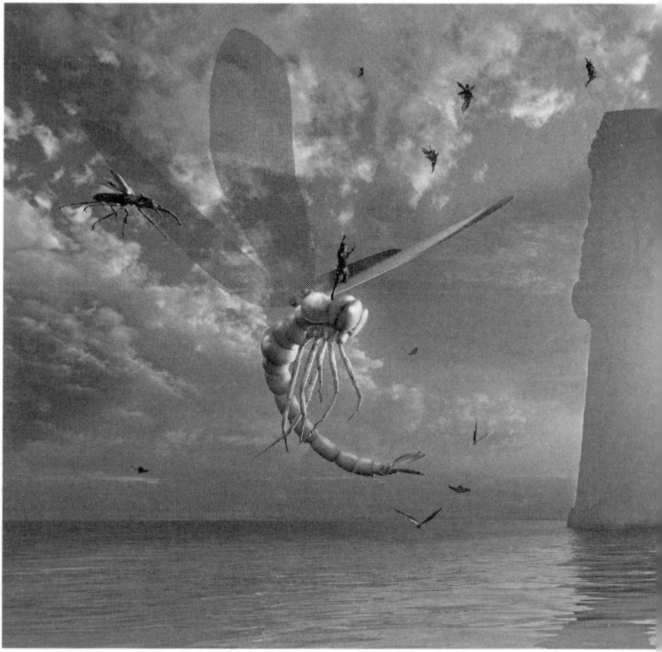

John Russell, *Faerie Poem*, 2009. Backlit digital print on vinyl.

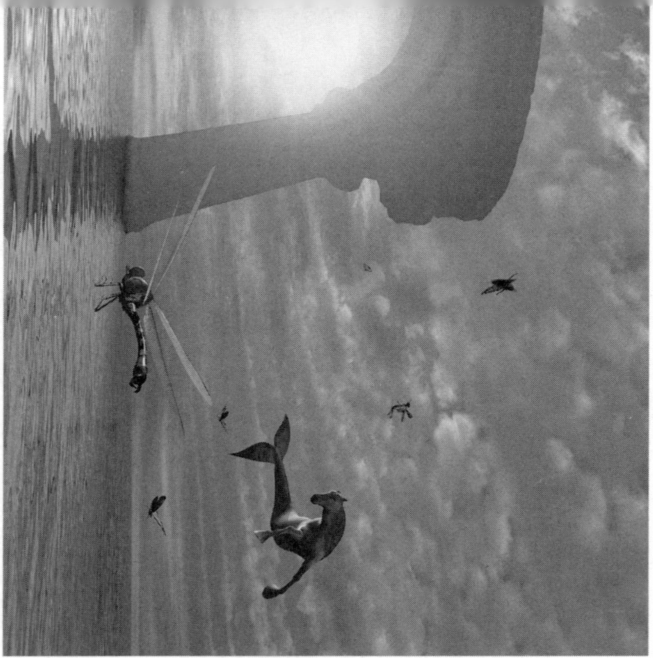

that characterizes transnational capital. This translates into a kind of site or even geographical sensitivity: infrastructure is not only conceived to exploit one aspect or resource of a place—in this case, the products of the subsea geology—but as an interface between a multiplicity of elements, conditions, and populations. In the Caspian Sea, the infrastructure proposed by InfraNet Lab/Lateral Office will look to intertwine the subsea, the activity in the sea (the need to sustain and enlarge the populations of sturgeon), and what happens in the air (the migratory patterns of birds that cut right over this body of water), while also building into the system the potential to recuperate the infrastructure after it can no longer serve its original purpose. The passive anticipation of uselessness that accompanied infrastructural building becomes active planning for post-depletion. It's preemptive design for the inevitable. In order to curtail the possibility of having only abandoned infrastructure in the end, one has to think from the other side of devastation. InfraNet Lab/Lateral Office explains it in the language of promotional brochures: "The Caspian Sea's oil rig field is retrofitted for post-oil occupation by wildlife, maverick entrepreneurs, and adventure seekers."[5]

Resource depletion, even if still in potentia, establishes "retrospectively" the horizon of possibility and necessity for current design. Inexistent, projected, the deserts to come are the regulative force that determines what will be produced. An architectural need is formulated in such a way that any call to curtail the progress of destruction is rendered romantic. This is the new normal, the way power is extracted from the only future that transnational capital proposes as conducive to its maintenance and growth. Like credit in the financial sphere, preemptive design objectifies the future before it even arrives. Preemptive design capitulates to an erosion of critical distance in order to vindicate itself as the pragmatic-ethical option: it is willing to look the bitter truth in the face and devise, in an unsentimental way, the best possible solution for the depletion to come. It doesn't look ahead in order to imagine detours, to insert "retrospectively" counterfactual possibilities into our present. It stares down that romantic option and soberly and pragmatically accepts that the only agency possible is that of the hardboiled and sober social clairvoyant: she knows what's coming, so the best she can do is hide tents and rafts and bottles of water in the houses that the hurricane will devastate. This is just a step removed from "the superstitious compulsion to make some gesture when we are observing a process over which we have no real influence."[6]

3. Last Stop

When we speak of "post-Fordism," "immaterial labor," "cognitive capitalism," "precarity," and so forth, we are certainly speaking of the material conditions and effects of capitalism as it currently functions. However, these are its conditions as it explicitly relates to us. What if we attempt to take stock of it from a different vantage point? What if we read capitalism not as it manifests itself in relation to human bodies but as its destination reveals it to be: an Alien monstrosity, an insatiable Thing that appropriates the energy of everything it touches and, in the process, propels the world toward the inorganic? After all, aren't depletion and dissolution its underlying logics, accompanying its rampant drive to growth, its myth of unending prosperity? Isn't it consistently and egregiously dragging things—natural resources, ways of life, communal values, traditional forms of social organization, symbolic systems, laboring bodies, public spheres, social safety nets, self-sufficient economies, entire populations (animal and human), the destabilizing potential of formal innovation in aesthetic production, happiness—to their terminus point, either to complete annihilation or to subsumption under a logic of general equivalence? What if we propose that capitalism has something like agency and that this agency is manifested in ecophagic material practices? Capitalism eats the world. Whatever transformations it generates are just stages in its monstrous digestive process.

Surely this is what someone like Nick Land has in mind when he proposes that "the history of capitalism is an invasion from the future by an artificial intelligent space that must assemble itself entirely from the enemy's resources."[7] It feeds on what it finds, leaving behind a metaphorical gray chemical sludge. This alien intelligence from the future seems committed to bringing about an ultimate inorganic state, the apocalypse of that final drag of everything into the post-biological, and it is working incrementally as it moves forward through history in order to realize the future it left "behind." Like a swarm of replibots run amok, capitalism feeds on this world in order to swell itself, but maybe not to swell into anything more than an enlarged, raging version of itself—like a massive hurricane, all spinning forces looking to avoid any shoreline (political and economic alternatives) that may serves as a counterforce, chasing the conditions that will allow it to speed up and grow even more. And like the replibots, its own demise, too, may be announced in the devastation it leaves behind, but it counteracts this on at least two fronts: by generating myths of interplanetary travel and post-biological "life" (the Singularity and so forth) and pushing technological unfolding down these roads; and by generating abstract financial instruments that allow it to "create value ex nihilo," as Alex Williams argues:

> What is necessary is to think the in-itself of capitalism outside of any correlation to the human. [...] For surely what all analyses of capitalism have presumed to date is the capitalist "for-us" (construed in positive or negative terms), whereas capital is ultimately a machine which has almost no relation to humanity whatsoever, it intersects with us, it has us as moving parts, but it ultimately is not *of* or *for-us*. Capital properly thought is a vast inhuman form, a genuinely alien life form (in that it is entirely non-organic) of which we know all-too-little. A new investigation of this form must proceed precisely as an anti-anthropomorphic cartography, a study in alien finance, a *Xenoeconomics*. [...] Marx's labor theory of value fails to think the capitalist in-itself, the ability to create value ex nihilo (i.e., credit, and all financial instruments constructed from variations on this theme). For Marx credit, "virtual capital," and speculation built upon it is "the highest form of madness." Instead we ought to think of credit-based "virtual" capital as the highest form of capital. This is not a mere semantic shift, but rather a revolutionary inversion of the L[abor] T[heory of] V[alue], following Deleuze & Guattari in considering capitalism-as-process, conducted upon pre-existing social forms, disassembling and reassembling them to suit its own nefarious and presently obscure ends. As process rather than concrete "thing" we must consider its true nature to be contained in its destination, rather than the primitive building blocks from which it originally

constituted itself (i.e., in the worlds of "virtual" capital rather than the alienation of human labor, which is surely merely an initial staging post).[8]

A split, at some point, is easy to imagine: capitalism continues to expand virtually, while the landscapes it once extracted resources from are left useless. The end of the world again, before the end of capitalism. The end of us. Granted some license, we can graft the slimed and dead world that the gray goo problem promises to an imaginary point at which capitalism has realized the goal inherent to its compulsion to deplete. It's the look of its destination. As is always the case with allegory, it's not that one scene replicates another, but that it recodes it in order to cast it in high-relief through imperfect but suggestive correspondences. One scene becomes a figural machine through which another one can be explained or approximated, particularly where direct representation is found wanting, where the stiff edges of verisimilitude prohibit accurate depiction, where bodies are asked to generate an understanding of their own abolishment.

4. Increased Velocity

Seeing as the ground has shifted beneath current cultural production, a question to consider is: What new options appear on the horizon for cultural production by opening an "inhuman" perspective on this gray goo capitalism? How do we do more than find the best compromise for a dissipative tendency that forcefully encodes itself in cultural objects, that works from the get-go to confiscate and annul divergent options to the kind of aesthetic artifacts that reinforce its naturalization?

Surely, there is the possibility of generating resistance, of finding new ways to counter the compulsion to expand at any cost, of articulating and producing or prefiguring new ways of living that challenge capitalism. In short, there is the possibility of refusing any perspective that puts us under erasure, that disregards a priori whatever participatory, resistant, transformational, insurrectionary, and emancipatory gestures we may still muster. There may be no need to undermine just yet what we may be able to accomplish, the ways in which we can still locate sites in which to intervene politically and/or where we can generate economic difference that challenges the logic and kinds of relations that capitalism allows, rendering visible practices that are currently discounted or repressed. This is what marks intelligent, politically infused cultural projects as relevant in a lifeworld no longer free of the tendency to absolute commodification and ruthless co-optation.

Not long ago, Franco Berardi wrote about one of the continuities between modernity and what has followed it: the idea of acceleration as an underlying principle. He proposes that, despite whatever changes characterize the social transition out of modernity, the drive to speed things up has survived the shift from the manufacturing sphere to the semiotic one. These days,

> when the main tool for production ceases to be material labor and becomes cognitive labor, acceleration enters another phase, another dimension, because an increase in semiocapitalist productivity comes essentially from the acceleration of the info-sphere—the environment from which information arrives in your brain.[9]

As is always the case with Berardi, he is interested in how these things function in relation to the human body. His metric is always anthropocentric. He finds a crisis point where the production of semiotic goods exceeds, in speed of production and management of quantity, the human brain's capacity for attention. For him, it is a question of processing time for the brain—or, rather, of the lack of this necessary time and the injunction to make things increasingly easier that follows this shortage. Everything must be easier, less meaningful, so that we can take in more of it, sacrificing robust experiences for the sake of mere informational ingestion. "More and more signs buy less and less meaning" as "our relationship to the world [...] become[s] purely functional, operational—probably faster, but precarious."[10]

Berardi's suggested resistance to this is to call for a reactivation of the relationship of language to desire, to put the body back in the circulation of signs as a way to ground this circulation again, to make it sensuous, to rein it in so that it functions within the time constraints that the brain imposes. But what of a different tactic, one that is the very opposite of this: an aesthetics that pivots on testing acceleration, in speeding things up even further, disintegrating things more ruthlessly? If we tap capitalism's dissipative compulsion as a force to be deliberately folded back into our practices, does it have anything to offer besides an acceleration of its methods? Can we draw unexpected morphologies and affects by intensifying this will to deplete? Can we push until mutations imminent to its perpetually recurring processes become manifest? Can we force random glitches in its patterns of reproduction? Can we speed up until the very notion of "making it easier" is no longer feasible, a kind of kaleidoscopic and liquid complexity spinning at desperate velocities foreclosing on it? Can we embrace the inorganic as a way to crack open pockets of resistance to it, to perturb our implacable movement toward it, to discover unexpected potentialities?[11]

Continued in "Notes on the Inorganic, Part II: Terminal Velocity."

1
K. Eric Drexler, *Engines of Creation: The Coming Era of Nanotechnology* (New York: Anchor Press, 1986), 172.

2
Robert A. Freitas Jr., "The Gray Goo Problem," excerpted version of article "Some Limits to Global Ecophagy by Biovorous Nanoreplicators, with Public Policy Recommendations" (originally 2000), KurzweilAI.net, March 20, 2001, http://www.kurzweilai.net/the-gray-goo-problem.

3
Ibid.

4
Projects were collected in Infanet Lab/Lateral Office, *Coupling: Strategies for Infrastructural Opportunism* (New York: Princeton Architectural Press, 2011).

5
Ibid., 33.

6
Slavoj Žižek, *First as Tragedy, Then as Farce* (London: Verso, 2009), 11.

7
Nick Land, "Machinic Desire," *Textual Practice* 7 no. 3 (1993): 479.

8
Alex Williams, "Xenoeconomics and Capital Unbound," *Splintering Bone Ashes* (blog), October 19, 2008, http://splinteringboneashes.blogspot.com/2008/10/xenoeconomics-and-capital-unbound.html.

9
Franco Berardi Bifo, "Time, Acceleration, and Violence," *e-flux journal*, no. 27 (September 2011), http://www.e-flux.com/journal/time-acceleration-and-violence.

10
Ibid.

11
Or: are these questions mere manifestations of our naïveté, ways of duping ourselves into participating in a fantasy or a symptom generated by a dissipative compulsion that advances regardless of how we position ourselves in relation to it? Are we surrendering more than we mean to when we take this treacherous path? Are these questions blindly groping for a kind of fetish aesthetics that allows us to have our transnational capitalism while claiming to be able to challenge it—to recover critical distance—from the inside? In other words, are they part of the general logic of our "post-ideologic" moment: a way to be radical at the level of the proposal, while acting in ways that help entrench and naturalize the structural necessities of the system at every other level? One should tread cautiously here.

Franco "Bifo" Berardi

Malinche and the End of the World

Humans have experienced an end of the world (the end of a world) before. A world ends when signs proceeding from the semiotic meta-machine grow indecipherable to a cultural community that perceives itself as a world.

A world in fact is the projection of meaningful patterns onto the surrounding space of lived experience, and the sharing of a common code whose key lies in the forms of life of the community itself.

When flows of incomprehensible enunciation proceeding from the meta-machine invade the space of symbolic exchange, our world collapses because we are unable to say anything effective about events and things that surround us.

When signs proceeding from the environment are no longer consistent and understandable within the shared code frame, when the meaning of the signs that convey effectiveness and power escapes the shared cultural code, a civilization ceases to be vital. It enters a tunnel of despair and quickly decays, then dissolves. Its members die, or lose their ability to feel like they are part of a common evolving reality. Those who survive undergo a process of integration into the code of an emerging culture, of assimilation to the colonizer's language and system of values.

From the point of view of the various indigenous cultures of pre-Columbian Mesoamerica, the Spanish colonization can be described as an end of the world (as the end of a world).

The Spaniards overcame the indigenous population thanks to their overwhelming military force, but colonization was essentially a process of symbolic and cultural subjugation. The "superiority" of the colonizers lay essentially in the operational effectiveness of their technical productions and expressions. Colonization destroyed the cultural environment in which indigenous communities had lived for centuries: alphabetic technology—the power of the written word—overwhelmed, threatened, and finally superseded the indigenous cultures. The Christian message merged with precolonization mythologies, and modern Mexican culture emerged as an effect of submission to alphabetic semiosis, but also as an effect of contamination and syncretism.

The alphabetic meta-machine is based on the externalization of memory, and on the possibility of transferring information in time and space. Thanks to this functional superiority of their semiomachine, the Europeans subdued, subsumed, and recoded the cultural universe of the natives, both in Mexico and in other areas of the continent.

What happens when a world dies, when outside flows of semiosis overpower and outperform the existing language and forms of life, and an entire world of values, expectations, and moral codes disintegrates?

Is it possible to deal with the emerging forms on the basis of the past code? Obviously not, but it is what we are currently doing, because we are unable to do otherwise. We try to interpret phenomena emerging from a hypercomplex and hyperfast system according to the normative categories that proceed from the alphabetic universe.

Malinche

The mythos of Malinche lies at the foundation of the Latin American Unconscious.

Before the arrival of the Spanish invaders, Malinche ("Malinalli" in the Nahuatl language, or "Marina" for the Spaniards), the daughter of a noble Aztec family, was given away as a slave to passing traders after her father died and her mother remarried.

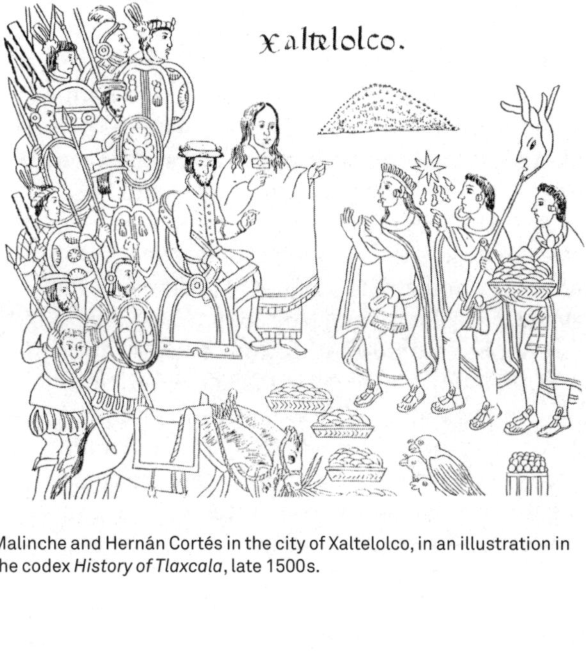

Malinche and Hernán Cortés in the city of Xaltelolco, in an illustration in the codex *History of Tlaxcala*, late 1500s.

By the time Cortés arrived, she had learned the Mayan dialects spoken in the Yucatan while still understanding Nahuatl, the language of the Aztecs. For many years, Malinche—a resourceful woman of exceptional beauty and intellect—became the lover of Cortés and accompanied him as his interpreter. She translated the words exchanged between Cortés and Moctezuma, king of the Aztec population of Tenochtitlan, and she translated the conqueror's words when he met crowds of indigenous people. She translated for Nahuatl-speaking people the words of Christian conquerors and Christian priests.

In the novel *Malinche* (2006), Laura Esquivel imagines Malinalli trapped between her own beliefs—taught to her through folktales and vivid imagery by her loving grandmother—and the Christian beliefs introduced by her master and lover. How did she manage to translate Christian mythology and ethical concepts into the mythology of Quetzalcoatl and Huitzilopochtli? What kind of symbolic transformation and re-elaboration did her translations involve? In Mexico—and South America in general—Christian culture and mythology was reshaped in a syncretic way, and ambiguity was accepted as an essential feature of the religious exchange. The translator was a traitor in a double direction: she betrayed her own people, linking up with the invaders, but she also betrayed the conquerors, her lover included. I use the word "betrayal" only in a technical sense: from the moral point of view, she owed nothing to her own people, who had sold her into slavery and treated her as a servant. Cortés chose her as his lover and collaborator, and they had a child, Martin, who was the first Mexican person.

Malinche was extremely helpful to Cortés in his conquest. In a letter preserved in the Spanish archives, Cortés said: "After God we owe this conquest of New Spain to Doña Marina" (her Spanish name). The legacy of Malinche is controversial: in contemporary Mexico, the word "malinche" is sometimes used pejoratively to describe someone who denies their heritage, someone who values other cultures above their own. Although she has been described as a traitor, historians say that when conflict exploded between the Spanish and indigenous people, Malinche played a key role in avoiding bloodshed. Her role as translator gave her the power to control information, and, most importantly, to translate concepts. Octavio Paz speaks of Malinche in *The Labyrinth of Solitude*:

> In contrast to Guadalupe, who is the Virgin Mother, the *Chingada* is the violated Mother. [...] Guadalupe is pure receptivity, and the benefits she bestows are of the same order: she consoles, quiets, dries tears, calms passions. The *Chingada* is even more passive. Her passivity is abject: she does not resist violence, but is an inert heap of bones, blood, and dust. Her taint is constitutional and resides, as we said earlier, in her sex. This passivity, open to the outside world, causes her to lose her identity: she is the *Chingada*, she loses her name, she disappears into nothingness, she *is* Nothingness. And yet she is the cruel incarnation of the feminine condition.
>
> If the *Chingada* is a representation of the violated Mother, it is appropriate to associate her with the Conquest, which was also a violation, not only in the historical sense but also in the very flesh of Indian women. The symbol of this violation is doña Malinche, the mistress of Cortés. It is true that she gave herself

> voluntarily to the conquistador, but he forgot her as soon as her usefulness was over. Doña Marina becomes a figure representing the Indian women who were fascinated, violated, or seduced by the Spaniards.[1]

Malinche is not only the expression of the mixing of cultures. She is also the expression of the rebirth of the world from the collapse of the old. She is considered a symbol of subjection but also a symbol of the emergence of a new Mexico, of a new history and a new world. But first and foremost she is the expression of the consciousness that her world is over: the world as a system of consistent cultural and semiotic references disintegrates. If the limits of a world are the limits of the language that makes this world consistent and meaningful, Malinche is the symbol of the end of a world, and also the symbol of the formation of a new semiotic space of world-projection at the intersection between two different codes. Malinche is able to transform the collapse of her world into the creation of a new language, and therefore of a new world that is neither a perpetuation of the old, nor a mere translation of the world of the *conquistadores*.

Only when someone is able to see such a collapse as the obliteration of memory and identity—in a word, as the end of the world—can a new world can be imagined. This is the lesson that Malinche teaches us.

The Cognitive Automaton and Us

At the beginning of the twenty-first century we are in a position that is similar to that of Malinche: the conqueror is here, peaceful or aggressive, infinitely superior, unattainable, incomprehensible. We have given birth to the conqueror, who emerged from our history and went away, beyond the ocean, and destroyed any form of existing life in order to create a new code, based on purity, in order to create the automaton, the rationale for never-ending automation.

The bio-info automaton is taking shape at the point of connection between electronic machines, digital languages, and minds formatted in a way that complies with its codes. The automaton's flow of enunciation emanates a connective world that conjunctive codes cannot interpret, a world that is semiotically incompatible with the social civilization that was the outcome of five centuries of humanism, enlightenment, and socialism.

I will never be able to live in peace with the automaton, because I was formatted in the old world. As Pris says in *Blade Runner*, I'm dead because I'm stupid. My body survives because I cannot find a way out. The human race is becoming an army of sleepwalkers: people suffering from Alzheimer's Disease, people taking pills to face reality, smiling, saying yes, yes ...

The automaton is the reification of the networked cognitive activity of millions of semioworkers around the globe. Only when they become compatible with the connective code can semioworkers enter into the process of networking. This implies the deactivation of conjunctive modes of communication and perception (compassion, empathy, solidarity, ambiguity, and irony), paving the way for the assimilation of the conscious organism into the digital automaton.

According to transhumanist ideology, a few decades from now the digital automaton will be able to perfectly replace human organisms. Ray Kurzweil thinks that in the near future humans and machines will become interchangeable from the point of view of cognitive efficacy. This is clearly possible, but the implication that the automaton and the human will merge—essential to the transhuman hypothesis—is false: the automaton will never be assimilable to the human being because human specificity lies in the relation between conscious rationality and the Unconscious.

From the operational point of view, the functional cognitivity of the automaton is more powerful than human cognitivity—more powerful, more effective, and obviously more destructive. But the unbridgeable difference between the conscious organism and the automaton, as complex and refined as it may be, lies in the Unconscious.

The Unconscious of the automaton is the material hardware of electromagnetic machinery that we call the Net. The human Unconscious is fleshy, marked by ambiguity, inconsequentiality, and (most importantly) death.

The automaton is pure functionality, even when it is endowed with self-regulating evolution. It will subsume human cognitive competence and subject it to its rule. The prospect that we have to face, then, is not the tender transhuman alliance between friendly, hyperintelligent machines and human beings; it is rather the final subjection of humans to the rule of nonorganic intelligent automata, whose behavior will be regulated according to criteria inscribed in them by their builder: biofinancial capitalism. The automaton will be able to evolve, yes. But the paradigm of this evolution will be inscribed into its infogenetic code by the builder. And the builder coincides with the most advanced corporations of biofinancial capitalism, like Google.

In the global landscape today, after the disappearance of egalitarian cultures, we see only two actors: the first actor is the all-pervading force of financial abstraction, the second is the proliferation of rancorous reactive identitarian bodies.

Financial abstraction is based on the faceless operativity of automatisms embedded in soulless social dynamics. Nobody is really in charge, nobody is consciously making decisions: in economic operations, logical mathematical implications have replaced the decider, and the algorithm of capital has grown independent of the individual will of the owner.

The impersonality of the financial abstraction escapes any attempt at conscious political transformation, so people who have lost control of their lives cling to a sense of illusory belonging: nation, religious faith, and ethnicity are protections against insecurity and loneliness. They are also tools of aggression used against competitors.

The connective energies of the new generation are recombined by the technofinancial automaton, and reduced to a condition of precariousness. Aggressive belonging is their only form of cohesion.

Will the general intellect be able to disentangle itself from the automaton? Can consciousness act on neurological evolution? Will language overcome the limits of the code of vanishing conjunctive cultures? Will pleasure, affection, and empathy find a way to reemerge out of their conjunctive framework? Will we translate into human language the connective language of the automated semiomachine whose buzzing is growing in our heads?

These are questions that only Malinche can answer, opening to the incomprehensible other, betraying her people, and reinventing language in order to express what cannot be said.

1
Octavio Paz, *The Labyrinth of Solitude and Other Writings* (New York: Grove Press, 1985), 85–86.

Diedrich Diederichsen

Music—Immateriality—Value

I.

Music has no value. That is both the problem as well as the foundation for a broad stream of observations to follow here on the utopian character of music. The idea that music does not have—or has *ceased* to have—any value may be assessed in different ways; it may be regarded as good or bad. Of course, one may also legitimately object to the idea that music can even drop out of the economy at all, but this depends on whether the economic valuation of music is bound to an object—such as a score or recording—or whether it is not.

A central tenet of Marxist thought is built around the distinction between exchange value and use value, the most well-known interpretation of which formulates it as a critique of exchange value's dominance over use value. However, it has been repeatedly pointed out—and with good reason—that such a glorification of pure use value has dreamed itself, ideologically, into a state in which the total immediacy of use assumes a unity that cannot exist in any society characterized by some degree of functional differentiation. Yet even such a romantic conception of use value remains a value nonetheless—a use that is not immediately realized. Value becomes an attribute of a thing that can be stored, reused, or realized sometime in the future, whether through use or exchange. For a thing to have value, it must possess a permanence or iterability with respect to how that value is realized in use or exchange. In the broadest sense, it must be a thing, an object.

There are things that die as they are used, and their description is usually couched in utopian metaphors. A famous example is the life of birds, which—as described in Matthew 6:26 and recalled to us by an old drunkard in the Hitchcock film *The*

Birds—"neither sow nor reap nor gather into barns and yet are fed." The same is true of the land of milk and honey, where things appear on the table, as they are needed, without any labor of storage or preparation. Yet even in all these examples of ideal conditions, these free and effortless processes of consumption remain dependent on a providential nature and a natural form of production. It is not we ourselves who produce all these things for our immediate use and consumption in response to our slightest wishes and whims, but other instances and authorities of an enchanted world: the gods, a magic spell, or nature. Alongside this, music's basic situation becomes even more utopian.

I pick up a musical instrument and produce a sequence of tones. These tones enchant my surroundings and me as I produce them. At some point I grow tired, the tones cease, and the enchantment passes. My favorite quotation about this phenomenon can be heard on the Radio Hilversum recording of Eric Dolphy's last concert, which took place in 1964, just before he died because no one could treat his particular type of diabetes, one that occurs only in people of African descent. Dolphy said: "When you hear music, after it's over, it's gone in the air; you can never recapture it again." What I produced has vanished without a trace; it created no value—nor, however, did it depend on a providential nature and the miracles of the land of milk and honey. It was me. I myself, using my talents and abilities—that which belongs to me as a human being and sets me apart from the animals—gave expression to something; that is, I lent inner states, which are also exclusively mine, and yet whose form is familiar to all other human beings from their own internal, subjective states, a form that was understandable to others and may thus have been beautiful. I realized myself as a human being in the dialectic between my nature as a unique individual and my nature as a social and collective being, and I did so entirely without economy, without reification, without the creation of value, without storage, costs, or profits, without the calculation of future time and hence without speculation, without interest or the creation of secondary value, and without valorization.

This is how utterly utopian music is, or rather how utopian it would be if it could exist in this way, as music in itself. And yet this notion, this awareness of music's essential independence and potential solipsism, also plays a role in every realistic, mediated idea of music. But the visual arts have also experienced a utopian dimension, whether in their past, when it lay in the power that art objects had in religious rituals, or in the cult of the original, whose auratic power resides in its indexical relation to the revered artistic genius of its creator and his or her own special connection to nature, or—as in cases like the Virgen de Guadalupe or Veronica's veil—a connection to God Himself or to His Son. Theater too has seen various projects, which, although they are not utopian, nonetheless go beyond aesthetic and edifying functions: whether it be Greek tragedy, which seeks to reconcile the audience to the limits of its life possibilities through catharsis, or the bourgeois theater as an institution of enlightenment.

In considering this series of examples, one is struck by the fact that such a utopia of music possesses a radicalism that the other ideal functions of the arts do not. While the other arts formulate maximums or optimums, it is always in relation to emerging or established social rules, and not as the *suspension* of those rules—which would be genuinely utopian. One might, then, argue that a utopia of music formulated in this way—one that could really be derived from a rejection of commodity capitalism—would be a relatively modern description of an original state. And, for good reason, we tend to be a little bit skeptical where modern descriptions of original states are concerned; precisely such utopias, which derive a mission of the arts from an original state, are often thoroughly impractical and romantically idealized. Indeed, we know this to be a decidedly reactionary figure of thought: the attacking of a stage of social differentiation from the standpoint of an archaic notion of unity, an absence of differentiation.

Yet this critique of reactionary utopianism does not fully apply to the utopia of music, and for good reason: in recent times—that is, in the twentieth century and then once again in the opening years of the twenty-first—this utopia has come much closer to being realized than ever before, at least if one is willing to spell out its social character. This utopia also has another dimension: it is, so to speak, always real in cases where one makes music for oneself and the immediate environment, in which the sociable aspect of music can be temporarily established as noneconomic—if not in its forms and formats then at least in its social gestures. “I heard his refrain as the signal changed: he was playing real good for free,” as Joni Mitchell sang of a street musician in 1969 in her song “For Free.” The street was so loud that it was impossible to hear him, but when the light changed and the traffic briefly paused, she could hear his refrain. And it was real good. And it was free.

The social dimension of this seemingly private and hermetic style of musical production, which, in spite of being social, nonetheless seeks to preserve music’s lack of value, can be found in the emergence of forms that help to realize music-making that is not defined by any previous instructions, objects, or protocols—as *ensemble* play, as collective and cooperative production. Thanks to free improvisation and aleatoric modes in a wide range of musical cultures, real practices of this kind were able to become experiential realities in the second half of the twentieth century, as were the barriers and limits of such practices—which sprang up everywhere, especially with attempts to professionalize them. Before this period, however, music that sought to escape reification—if such music even existed—neither had nor could have had any consciousness of itself and its social character, for that would have presupposed a means of storing and valorizing music that, it would seem, had not existed for rural cultures before the rise of the music industry and its technological foundations. It goes without saying that the fiddler at the fair had no conception of a liberated type of music that defied reification, but rather entered completely into the social function of his music—to impress the girls or to get free drinks.

At the same time, however, this fiddler did not produce a type of music that, in the sense described above, only existed insofar as it was actually performed. He lived in a universe where normative stipulations had even more gravity than they do in a world where conservatories judge what is correct and incorrect in the interpretation of scores. True, there was no existing material—a score or recording—that turned music into an object that could be traded and economically valorized, but another kind of force existed in this pre-economic musical state. For some time now, the American copyright activist Lawrence Lessig has traveled around the world with a lecture that opens on an image from around 1900, showing a father and his sons making music together and singing in front of a rustic dwelling. For Lessig, it depicts a golden age when music was still an activity and not pure consumption, an age he now sees returning in funny YouTube montages and other phenomena he describes as "remix culture" (presumably unaware of the term's widespread use in the context of musical remixes). Upon further inspection, however, one finds that it is less an image of free music-making than of the dominance of the patriarchal system.

The picture shows an authoritarian father explaining to his sons—perhaps even lovingly (it doesn't make *that* much difference)—what is correct and incorrect in terms of tradition. This embodied authority—the knowledge of a proper music and the proper means of producing it, imparted in unmarked gestures taken to be commonplace—represents (or at least *might* represent) a much more massive immobilization of music than any reification through a musical object. This reification at least contains its immobility in an external object, and thus represents an advance over its embodiment—however natural the romanticizers of folklore may find that embodiment. To be sure, things become different—but only slightly—when such embodied knowledge belongs to a culture of resistance, an issue I return to below.

So while we see that the notion of an absolutely valueless music—a music free of all value, valorization, or fixation—has often been projected into the past, its actual place would have to be in the present and in the future, and not just because we are speaking about utopia. Except in Arcadia, such a music has never existed as a social practice. On the other hand, it may have existed innumerable times as a mode of communication detached from society, as the song one sings to oneself, the whimsy with which one rhythmically structures one's steps, the drone that one produces with one's own body as a resonating chamber. And out of those countless individual moments that never solidified into objects, when individuals or little groups had musical experiences that had nothing to do with musical objects or any social purpose, music and music-like behavior have gained the reputation of being able to touch one's most intimate subjectivity. This pure, often solipsistic musical experience that comes prior to aesthetic experience always involves objects and external things, but does not yet belong to the order of the arts (and I say this without judgment). However, it may be regarded as the precondition for the possibility of an aesthetic experience of music.

In this way, something else emerged that might also be described as a value: a profusion of individual and collective musical experiences nourished by moments of agreement between signifiers and signifieds, moments in which one feels that one understands oneself, or feels understood by others. This is valuable in an entirely different sense, not because it is exchangeable and/or available for future realization, but rather because it has some weight on a scale of values that are only partially economic and object-like—values such as health, love, and justice. In order to be valuable in the first sense, music must always refer to its own experiences of value in the second sense: it must simulate them, touch on them, perhaps even actually make them available. But this noneconomic value must be distinguished from music's utopian absence of value. Though the two can support each other, it would also be possible to experience music's noneconomic value without the category of a valueless music that I alluded to earlier. It can be experienced with musical objects and musical commodities; and indeed one can only have aesthetic experiences as such—in which, by definition, a public dimension merges with a subjectivity—with objects in the broadest sense.

The ideology of bourgeois society, however, insists that great value in the second sense must not have any economic value in the first. And yet this same society has developed a discourse for legitimating economic value through precisely this priceless and unpurchasable character: through objects that—despite having value in the first sense—command a special price for their value in the second, noneconomic sense. This problem has been described frequently. Pierre Bourdieu has pointed out that a specific form of uselessness is also produced within the aesthetic domain to distinguish these goods from every conceivable utility, from every value in the first sense.[1] And yet the bourgeoisie pays for this noneconomic value in every economic sense. The goods are afforded an exchange value, just no use value. It is here that the utopian goods with no value meet the exchange value of that which bourgeois ideology regards as priceless and invaluable: neither has any use value, though one can in fact be bought—for a very high price. And to the extent that it can be bought, it also ceases to have no value.

There is nothing that bourgeois culture values more highly than the break with its own economic principles, provided that it is capable of valuing this break economically. This has nonetheless led to great freedoms; in particular, it has given rise to the ethic of a freedom as devoid as possible of anything that can be valued economically. While this ethic has always been ideologically contaminated, it was still extremely productive—as the avant-gardes of the twentieth century witnessed. Nevertheless, the most massive conceivable shock to this ideology and its practice has come, as it were, from the other end of the world.

II.

Pop music as a form of industrially—as well as sub-industrially—produced music first emerged in the 1950s as something that could be described neither as folklore, nor as a purely cultural-industrial commodity, nor as art. It often finds its means through discrete, individual effects that are closer to the logo—the context-independent sign of advertising—than through classical notions of music. Its musical elements are simple, and they are for the most part borrowed from local or socially and politically segregated, excluded musical styles, but these styles are not performed with local, context-specific gestures—rather, they are most often torn from those contexts with a certain economic violence. To break from contexts offering only local—and therefore very limited—validity and value and perform the music in a nonlocal manner is to risk sacrificing a loss of value in the noneconomic sense with only a modest increase in the economic sense; it is to make a gain—in global, universalist terms—that often cannot be realized economically, but ends up forming communities in a "deviation" (to borrow a concept from Heinz Klaus Metzger) from the original economic intention of the music. Pop music begins by employing the simplest possible means, which therefore tend to be inexpensive and empty—that is, hollowed out by frequent use—without concern for their traditional meanings and ritual values in an original context. While these inexpensive means are not *entirely* without economic value, they are, for all intents and purposes, completely without value from the standpoint of artistic judgment. Their economic promise concerns the modest profit that always materializes when one produces cheaply, and without the burden of lasting effects or historical evaluation.

Most of pop music is thus comprised of "worn out" musical elements—harmonic and melodic effects that have been utilized so often that they have become completely empty. Musique concrète and noises from the outside world are included as sonic logos; a physical, rhythmic insistence and a performative emphasis on the physical aspects of playing, once again with an eye to recognizability and immediate effect, are characteristic. In addition, more than any technically recorded and reproduced music before it, this inexpensive music relies on effects associated with technical reproduction; indeed, it is inconceivable without the existence of sound recording and storage media; the "studio version" is its central musical object—unlike the recording in jazz that documents a session or the recording in classical music that reconstructs a concert (and whose central musical object remains the score), and unlike the ethnographic field recording that points to a distant or vanished world. Nevertheless, the central *act* of pop music remains the moment when a real performer becomes recognizable as the representative of a studio recording—the musical object—and "liquefies" it. This liquefaction marks a critical point in the production of musical value.

The progress of musical development in the bourgeois era led to the continuous refinement of the musical object, which influenced the business of music well before the introduction of the phonograph record, but also violated notions of a musical Arcadia in a twofold sense—in addition to defining music, it also opened it up to valuation and made it possible to buy and sell copyrights. While compositions

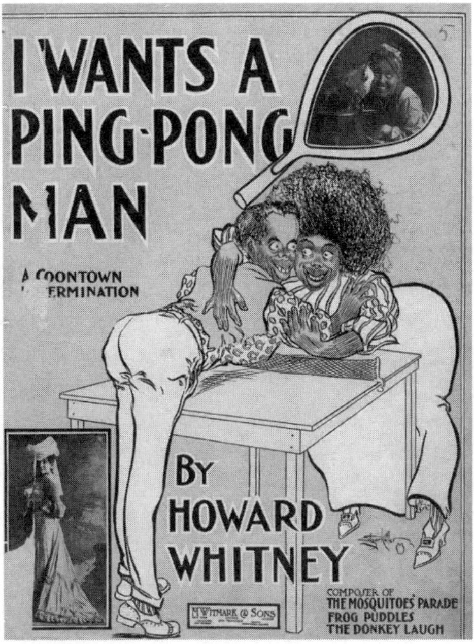

“I Wants a Ping Pong Man,” lyrics and music by Howard Whitney.

were initially commissioned works, that changed with the rise of Tin Pan Alley and the production of scores for a market. In the period following the Civil War, twenty-five thousand pianos were sold in the United States each year, and it is estimated that more than half a million young people learned to play the piano. This represented a move away from the traditional embodied authority of the father toward the authority of the musical object—in this case sheet music—which was booming on a mass scale, accompanied by the expansion of the music publishing industry. Beginning in about 1885, people began to talk about Tin Pan Alley, by which they meant 28th Street in Manhattan, where the most important music publishers had their offices. The result was not only higher print runs but also the invention of a standardized, Taylorized, Fordist method of composition based in a division of labor. Composers were essentially paid by the song: sitting in their publishers' buildings, they hammered out one danceable thirty-two-bar number after another, among them the masterpieces that are canonized today as the Great American Songbook. Already on a purely musical level, these songs were comprised of standard phrases and clichés—filled with immediate economic value and devoid of any contact whatsoever with inwardness, with the concept of a musicality that develops out of itself. They reflect an urban lifestyle, and they have a typical and interchangeable quality about them stemming from the fact that they were produced specifically in order to be exchanged.

Production standards sink even further when they cease to relate to the production of notes and begin to relate instead to the production of records, a shift that occurred after the Second World War at the latest. Records began to be marketed primarily on the radio, and then on television, and the jingles, logos, and sonic signatures that were the raw material of pop music became the sonic junk of advertising—the cheapest attention-getting noise that money can buy, the vocabulary of pop's environment, the language that it has no choice but to speak. The resulting functional music seems to have achieved the maximum possible degree of interchangeability; fleeting remnants of emotion, which come and go like leaves in the wind, seem to cling to it only temporarily.

Here, then, we would seem to have something like the nadir promised above. The economic value is small but not insignificant. The musical objects must simply be produced in sufficient quantity in order for their production to be profitable. They only have to mean a little bit to as many people as possible, but not too much to any one person. And their noneconomic value must be modest as well. Precisely this music, which is, in every sense, without value, now sparks the greatest enthusiasm, the most tremendous ecstasies that secular Western music has ever unleashed. How is this possible?

This extremely simple, yet physically compelling, effect-oriented music created its effects without any of the preconditions of traditional and ritual musical frameworks. It referred to everyday life and could easily be incorporated into it precisely because it contributed nothing to its own explanation, whether through meanings or traditional preconditions. With a crude and interchangeable set of effects, it was possible to do things with it, to use it actively—doo-wop, early rock and roll, and R&B came out of street-corner music and the nightlife and club scene, and they retained that connection even when they moved to television, where they began to mean something to masses of teenagers and others on the fringes—or the threshold—of social integration. This moment, this audience, this musical object, and these commodities represent a kind of zero point of art, a zero point of community-building and also of folklore, a zero point too in terms of noneconomic value. But this also forms a basis for the creation of a new kind of noneconomic value.

In his book *Performing Rites: On the Value of Popular Music*, Simon Frith points out that, like sports fans, users and fans of pop music have constantly produced evaluative discourses—a form of communication consisting entirely of value judgments.[2] This is liquefaction: value judgments, rankings, listings, and fetishes are instances in which musical objects are actively appropriated and dissolved, becoming musical "agglutinations" of the lowliest kind. Ever-newer masses of semi-integrated young people and minorities with money to spend discover endless opportunities to agglomerate bureaucratic lists and tables, existential and sexual applications, and risky lifestyles. At this point, there normally comes an affirmation of the more romantic forms of active reception, of existential forms of "liquefaction," of risky lives and what is often called liberation, and there is nothing wrong with that. But in 1960 and again in 1980, the bureaucratic energy of reception, which was generally unleashed by unromantic nerds, gave rise to a new knowledge. The fact that it looked bureaucratic was only a problem from the vantage point of a ritualized bourgeois aesthetic expectation: where the rich man stages edification, the poor one establishes a bureaucracy. And who would be so narrow-minded as to give one of these options precedence over the other?

In pop music after 1955, a new logic of attractiveness emerged that surpassed the attraction of the music itself on the basis of its having little economic and no artistic value (and being hence free and open to participation), functioning instead on two new bases: first, an interplay between image and sound that could never have been staged before the advent of television and the teen idol industry, and second, the interplay between indexical, phonographic recordings of actual human beings'/stars' physical traces and the recognition of those stars on actual stages. These two logics of attraction explain a great deal, and the first self-descriptions and myths produced by pop music—in particular, the cult of authenticity—sought, albeit clumsily, to describe precisely these effects: the identity of sound and image, reproduced recording and live performance—the effectuation of identity and reality.

There are still other factors at work. I will not delve into them here, but one of them is particularly important and should be mentioned. In order to introduce it, I must make a slight correction to my concept of noneconomic valuelessness. Even in pop music, there is something that corresponds to inwardness, to the solipsistic pleasure in the pure experience of playing, and playing with, music—to doing as one wishes with sounds. Even in pop music, there are elements with no economic value, but which have a very high value of a different kind—a value that is, in the broadest sense, a political one. Unless it is further qualified, the noneconomic value I introduced above knows only one kind of subject: the subject who is still intact—at least reasonably intact—and authorized to do as he or she pleases. All others, all outsiders, all those who are excluded, but also those who are based in remote communities, know of something else: a dialectic between the feeling of being protected by a given music on the one hand, and, on the other, the feeling of being emboldened—of struggling to one's feet and beginning to take steps—by that very same music. These are accumulated, unstable social experiences stored within musical forms, and they include even those forms patched together by the uninitiated and the unauthorized, by music-industry people and other outsiders, to become pop music. And it is in this sense that we have something to learn from Lagos: not the economic practices of the ghetto, not its reality, and not the romantic notion that what is especially unstable is also especially advanced, but rather something concerning the proto-aesthetic content of music and its organization.

In America in 1955, musical elements of folk, blues, and African-American and immigrant music all shared a common feature, and it may be true that post–world music today shares the same feature of an inwardness marked by violent exclusion, as well as a sense of belonging that is often no less violent. It is this commonality—audible time and again in music such as the sorrowful American country song—that I call political, however vastly removed it may be from all that generally tends to be politically instrumentalized or romanticized, such as the kitschy talk of "rebel" culture and formats of "resistance." These forms of music are absolutely proto-political. Or they are, somewhat more paradoxically, *spiritually* political. And they can be drawn in every conceivable direction when they are politicized. What is important here is that music possesses another, less ahistorical, less ideal type of noneconomic value: political value. And that value remains present in pop music.

III.

Pop music never knows what it is doing. This is true of both its thoroughly economicized mainstream components as well as its niche cultures. And it is worth pointing out that an economy that consists of nothing but niche production would be an entropic horror—one in which there would be no public realm and no aesthetic experience. But pop music constantly rediscovers the conditions of its own emergence, not in well-defined, large-scale historical movements, but in small steps and often cyclical acts of rebellion. Time and again, attempts are made to "inject" economic valuelessness—as a related phenomenon or shot of energy—into forms of pop music that have lost contact with those conditions. When there is no longer any contact with the spiritually political dimension of pop music, improvised rock music suddenly arises—and with something in mind that it tries to reconstruct. Other logics of attraction are reconstructed in this same way: where voices no longer sound as if they could possibly come from actual bodies, hip-hop emerges. That's just how it works.

But now we have a real mess on our hands. A form of valuelessness has arisen, very much in the ideal, romantic sense. But rather than allowing itself to be transferred into a higher value, it is moving on from *economic* valuelessness to infect the *noneconomic* kind as well, perhaps in order to demonstrate that no such transcendental value ever actually existed—at least not where music was made for money. Instead of dwelling on the obvious—as critical spoilsports have repeatedly done by asserting that pop music, in the long run, cannot sustain its implicit utopian and oppositional potential before proceeding to organize it industrially and bureaucratically—the logic of pop music itself (or the logic of precisely these latent political elements) has led to its own obsolescence as an economic model. It has served its purpose as a music of distancing, of niche creation, as the dance music of new temporary communities so elegantly states: that the musical object itself has become superfluous—not just technically, through file-sharing, but conceptually and economically as well.

The rave was already an event without an object: people did not go home and begin to collect the records they'd heard that night. One might argue that this was in itself a success. As indeed it was, but as tends to happen with utopian enclaves in a world that is otherwise unchanged, they invert to become their opposite. Freedom creates poverty. In a world in which the object has disappeared as a reference point, other logics take effect—logics of a vastly more liberated form of entrepreneurship: the exploitation of bodies, performance, and "liveness" replaces the exploitation of a labor that had previously produced objects, objects whose conditions of production could be negotiated. The realization of a world without musical objects has assimilated aesthetic experience in a utopian and dialectical sense, but because it has done so only partially and temporarily, it has also brought about a regression to a stage that precedes aesthetic experience altogether.

At the same time, however, the specific forms of active reception associated with pop music—and not its contents or noneconomic values—have become the new standard of its culture and industry. We no longer live in a society of spectacle but in one of participation. Active consumption—by so-called "prosumers"—are the bread and butter of contemporary sociability; the specific stubbornness of the fan, the permeability of the barrier between

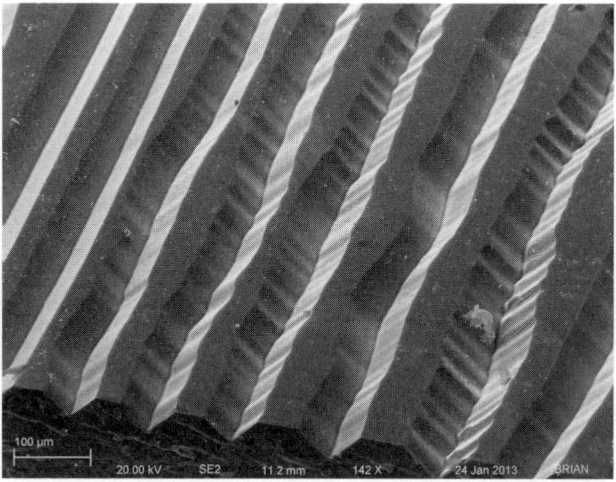

Detail of vinyl record incisions.

audience and stage—all essential components of the pop music culture of the last fifty years—are now standard staging formats. They are prescribed, they are hegemonic, they are stressful, and they drain energy from precisely those forces and forms of empowerment that pop music is normally thought to support. The musical utopia of economic valuelessness and the concept of a greater, non-economic value then attach themselves to the logic of virtuosity—as Paolo Virno calls it—as a normative model of production, of labor without work.[3]

What is to be done? Pop music cannot be rescued; something new must be invented to take its place, and music may or may not have a role to play in whatever that turns out to be. One cannot set out to invent such a thing, just as pop music itself simply emerged, as it were, in places far from the forward march of progress, in a development that was historically necessary, as we know today, but was unpredictable for its contemporaries. It did not arise where enlightened people tried something new, but where others acted quickly and from a sense of spiritual urgency. We must remain open to the possibility of something similar happening again. But pop music was only able to come into being by repeatedly coming into contact with radical artistic forces, as when John Cale and La Monte Young developed The Dream Syndicate from the spirit of the Everly Brothers, or Tony Conrad suspected that the solipsistic drone might be used as an anticapitalist weapon. So while one can no longer reconstruct pop music in a purposeful and systematic way, one can still move forward with the neo-neo-avant-garde work of utopian practices or their derivatives—perhaps in a more complex and radical manner, while touching on other arts that have similar problems—at the admittedly high price of creating niches, provided that one also remain in contact with the world of cheap and worn-out forms that have preserved something of people's actual lives, however unrecognizable they may have become. These do not necessarily have to be musical forms. What is needed, however—not for economic reasons, but for political and cultural ones—are reference points for everyone. The niche has become neither a utopia nor a permanent state of affairs, but rather the end.

Translated from the German by James Gussen.

1
See Pierre Bourdieu, *Distinction: A Social Critique of the Judgement of Taste*, trans. Richard Nice (Cambridge, MA: Harvard University Press, 1987).

2
See Simon Frith, *Performing Rites: On the Value of Popular Music* (Cambridge, MA: Harvard University Press, 1998).

3
Paolo Virno, "Virtuosity and Revolution: The Political Theory of Exodus," in *Radical Thought in Italy: A Potential Politics*, ed. Paolo Virno and Michael Hardt (Minneapolis: University of Minnesota Press, 2006), 189–212.

Rasmus Fleischer

How Music Takes Place: Excerpts from "The Post-digital Manifesto"

How to decide what music to listen to? Presented with boundless access, this is the perpetual question today. The standard response is to propose the use of automated systems of recommendation. Instead of spending all that time choosing music ourselves, we could just let software identify patterns in the statistical data we have left in our trail. Next, this software goes on to offer us radio stations specially tailored to our individual preferences, stations that often prove themselves shockingly adept at opening our ears to music we didn't even knew we liked. In spite of this, the underlying principles of these recommendation systems remain quite primitive. "Customers Who Bought This Item Also Bought ..." is the basic functionality, familiar from online bookstores. At the center of it all we find the individual, whose preferences are to be compressed and reduced into a statistical profile.

Why assume that preferences come firmly lodged in the individual? The transitory bodily relations to music are constantly being reshaped, suggesting that what we usually call "personal taste" might be better understood as an aggregate of the supra- and the sub-personal. The everyday musical choices we make are influenced by factors like time of day, day of week, or season of the year. Other factors include weather, metabolism, intoxication, and the almost random way in which various sensory inputs seem to trigger associations with our earlier personal musical experiences. But above and beyond anything else, it is the people around us who exert the biggest influence on our musical choices—in our relations, through our desires. It is never the case that people who get together automatically and iteratively start to adjust their presumed internal preferences until a mix arrives that makes everyone happy. In real-life situations calling for musical selection, direct democratic ideals must remain inapplicable.

1.

Music unfolds in the charged field separating the opposing poles of responsibility and irresponsibility. If there is no one present who is willing to step forward and assume responsibility for what is played, then it can scarcely be held that there is any music taking place at all. In such a situation, it would be more accurate to say that the room is being drowned in Muzak. And, on the other hand, if full responsibility were assumed by everyone—something verging on the hypothetical—no one would dare make a sound. The situation turns into silence, albeit a musical one. In musical improvisation, aiming for such a state of full and collective responsibility might be possible. And if that aim ever gets fulfilled, the music will have ended, with everybody present reverently holding their breath.

In the impulse to set the tone, to proceed from silence into the beginning of a new tune, there will also inherently be a backing off from individual responsibility. The first riffs of a saxophonist, the first beat of a drummer, the first track laid down by a DJ—these are all actions that cannot be justified on their own merits, precisely because they are (and must be) clichés. In order for music to begin, its initiators must temporarily cloak themselves in something recognizable. Here, the overflow of associations generated by any given musical genre makes for a lot of material for cloaking. The musician might choose to hide behind the name of a famous composer, behind stage clothes, or behind the mythic persona of an artist. In those first few bars of music, there must always be a relinquishing of responsibility, even if only momentarily.

Responsibility only makes its appearance at the moment when one individual starts to imitate the other. This might happen through a body swaying to the rhythm, or the voice which joins in on the chorus. The cliché, now turned into a musical springboard, presents itself as a profusion of possible associations; trying to imitate them all inside an event anchored in time and duration is simply impossible. Repetition therefore becomes something more than a source of clichés; in every repetition there is selection, and in every selection there is difference. This is what makes it possible for music to rise above the level of the cliché.

These lessons, derived from the musical situation, might successfully be applied to another situation in which the concept of responsibility becomes central: politics. The turn of the nineteenth century saw the instigation of the parallel construction of parliaments and concert houses, functioning as political and musical temples for the rising bourgeoisie. The philharmonic (conductor–orchestra–audience) mirrors the democratic (chief of state–parliament–citizen); both are images of an idealized distribution of responsibilities, and both promise the future abrogation of all dissonances in one final chord of harmony.

The introduction of ever more efficient forms of mass media meant dramatic changes for the worlds of politics and music. During the twentieth century, these new technologies came to serve as dominant filtering systems that managed the new surplus of opinions, presenting the end consumer with a processed selection that consisted of a worldview accessible to the single individual. However, by the year 2000 it became obvious that mass media was struggling to maintain its position in this system. Now it is up to us to construct new technologies of selection and to make sense of this surplus of opinions.

That which we call politics will always involve, much like music, some kind of oscillation between responsibility and irresponsibility. If no one assumes personal responsibility for his or her actions, this could hardly be called politics; a better name for it would be administration. Most of what the media reports on as "politics" is predicated on the systematic shunning of responsibility, and the conjured phantasms (like "public opinion" or "the economy") can therefore hardly be considered worthy of the name.

If all of us did the very opposite of this—taking full responsibility and acknowledging our complicity in the course of world events—the result would be a situation that could only be understood as a kind of revolution. Revolution not in the sense of some sudden outburst of militant action, but simply as a sort of electric, tremulous calm: nothing happens, nothing is planned, and no work is carried out—a concept in line with the idea of the general strike championed for so long by anarcho-syndicalists. It is a singularity beyond politics, but yet, as it subsides, it reveals politics turned on its head.

If revolution is conceived like this, it appears more like the consequence of a highly contagious sense of responsibility. Put this in contrast to the culture of the self-proclaimed revolutionaries who remain content with doing nothing more than dumping responsibility for the afflictions that plague us at the doorstep of others. "You are evil, therefore I am good": the fundamental formula of ressentiment. This refusal of responsibility turns music into Muzak and replaces political agency with the banality of evil. No political party program could ever help guide us to the opposite shore, to revolution. But there is something truly revolutionary in the musical insight that responsibility could be something else than submission to "the common good."

2.

May Day. Every year an echo of the previous. "Attending rallies, that's *so* yesterday!" go the groans of the haters. "Why even bother taking to the streets today, given the capacity of digital media?" In this argument, rallies get treated as if they were a kind of mass media: their sole purpose being to communicate a message, either to the external public or to the authorities in power. Similar ideas are often held by the organizers of rallies themselves, as shown by the tendency to either see rallies as a chance to cultivate their cult of the megaphone, or as an opportunity to stage something nice for the cameras.

From a post-digital viewpoint, a May Day rally becomes something different. Marches should not be classified as mass media; they are methods for handling a surplus of opinions through a process of selection rooted in material presence. Textually mediated politics—the type you would find at the annual meeting, in the op-ed, on the internet forum—does not require the same degree of prioritizing. If you need to satisfy some inner or outer contradiction or opposition, just insert an additional turn of phrase somewhere. A political rally, on the other hand, is an event constrained by time and space. Chants are restricted to one at a time. Flags are rationed to one per participant. Collective priorities are set, and as a result a common style is affirmed.

However, this selection—the color of the flags, the phrasing of the slogan—is not the only thing signaling the politics of a march. In fact, it is not even the most important one. The composition of a march constitutes a politics of its own, and if we turn our attention to the case of the loudspeaker membranes, this becomes acutely visible. Are there activists to regale the crowd with megaphones, or is kick-starting the chants left to energetic protesters? The presence of megaphones will unconditionally turn a protest into a manifestation of dictatorship, no matter what messages they emit. It is for the minority to dictate, literally, the message. It is for the masses to read it back.

The question is brought to a head in the use of music in political protests. Here we find, on the one hand, a cultivation of traditions going back to the days before electrically amplified music was invented. The performances of brass bands and choirs become performances of dialectical music: the earth will rise on new foundations, by way of dissonances dissolved in a final chord of harmony. Here, every piece of music carries with it a message that appeals to reason. The brass band can be traced to a military musical tradition, and is regimented according to the principle of the division of labor: each individual specializes in one task or instrument. The choir, on the other hand, amounts to a humanism that bases its politics on the naked human voice.

The percussionists' mobilization of the body differs in that they do away with any detours through reason. Rhythm might be able to create the preconditions necessary for both dancing and marching, but it can never aim for dialectical resolution. While melodies necessarily come with durations and ends, rhythms must incessantly keep on repeating themselves. The difference in potential amplitude might vary hugely between any two percussive instruments, but nowhere is there

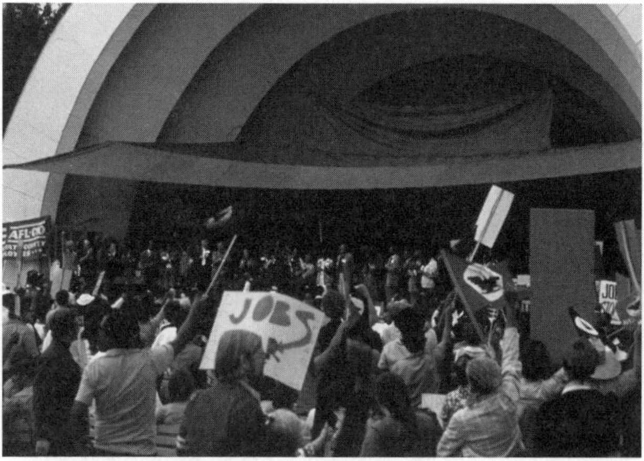

This 1973 protest against inflation and unemployment took place at a band shell at Lake Shore, Chicago. Reverend Jesse Jackson is shown speaking.

any hierarchy between lead part and backing part, which is typical for melodic music. If the politics of percussion open up to the utopian, then these portals already have their presence in the acting out of collective mobilization.

Organizers of political rallies rarely show themselves to have more sense than shop owners when it comes to the deployment of music. Clumsy attempts at playing "something for everyone" end up in a stale and soupy mix lacking taste. Movements that have committed themselves to attracting people of all ages and backgrounds often get carried away by the idea of music as an instrument of inclusion and never consider the fact that there will always be a corresponding degree of exclusion.

Musical direct democracy can never be anything more than a pipe dream, to put it bluntly. If all participants play one song each, this would simply be serial dictatorship. No truly meaningful musical experiences can come out of such practices. The responsibility of serving as a local musical dictator should be conferred on the DJ, but we must reserve our right to leave for new premises, where other DJs are the temporary dictators of music. Serial dictatorships can't be preferable to multiple parallel dictatorships scattered in space. This explains why derelict factories and squats usually prove themselves so beneficial to the cultural life of cities. A post-digital sensibility of music comes with an inherent questioning of the ownership of the spaces where music takes place.

3.

Somehow I was part of a group that found itself acquiring an old city bus. Totally ignorant of the inner workings of engines and keen on taking a trip, we then proceeded to restore it. Inside the bus, there was an unusually persistent feeling that digitalization had made it all the more important to "be there." And there we were, twenty-three of us, ready to occupy space, ready to sacrifice time. None of us knew everyone else, but everyone knew someone. Those connections that already existed had mostly been formed through the internet. Now, manifested in the post-digital, this loose patchwork of online friendships was processed into a more sharply delineated group. If you grow tired of an online conversation, logging off or switching windows is just a click away. Getting off a bus in motion and in the middle of a highway, well, this is something different altogether. All this had the effect of intensifying the presence we felt inside the vehicle.

Presence serves selection. It corresponds to certain needs, triggered by the surplus of both music files and of friends on the net. Sometimes it feels like the list of friends on the social network site stretches into eternity. Everyone always turns out to have some sort of connection to everyone else; six degrees of separation. There is immense potential in digitally mediated friendships, but it is only when these are materialized in the post-digital—when selection becomes a pressing issue—that friendships can be said to *happen*. There are no physical rooms with room enough for an unlimited number of bodies. Being physically present does not allow for tabbing to the next chat window in order to get away from a tedious conversation. You might choose to leave, to go somewhere else and strike up a new conversation there. This is still not the same thing as typing into a new blank chat window, because there is an already existing situational context we must take into consideration before we act.

Something similar could be said of the cassette tape player. If a song starts to go stale, we just push the fast-forward button or flip the tape to be instantly thrown into the midst of a new track. We are spared the parade of aborted intros that distinguishes the anxious skipping of the digital.

The tape recorder introduces a degree of unpredictability into music, a randomness different in nature than the algorithmic shuffling of the MP3 player. When you switch unlabeled tapes, you can never be sure what you will hear next. A fair guess is that it might be something that someone nearby liked ten or twenty years ago—at least if all the music available is stuffed in an old gym bag, stored on exactly a hundred tapes, all scavenged from closets and storage rooms. This was the situation in our trusty old bus, in which there was an unvoiced understanding that digital music players were off-limits. This decision had followed from the simple fact that internet access would be more than scarce during the voyage. Certain situations demand that you commit yourself to your set goals: maximum information, or maximum presence? We went for the latter. Thus, we turned ourselves into a mobile, albeit slow, laboratory of materializing internet culture during a summer week's drive from Sweden down to Italy.

Crossing the Alps in a bus manufactured in 1977 and originally intended for city traffic has all the trappings of a seriously risky enterprise. It can't be said that there is any less risk in squeezing together twenty-three people—most of whom know each other only vaguely through some chat channel—and having them live in highly cramped conditions in a bus for a week. Anything else would be a lie—especially considering the total lack of any sort of prearranged division of responsibilities. In some situations, such muddiness might lead to a dilution of presence and the scattering of the group to the four winds. On other occasions there might be a material framework acting as a glue during events, making the question of responsibility unavoidable, and thus intensifying presence. The maximum level of intensification (and consequently also the capacity to be lit up, let down, or let in) is reached if getting there and back again turns out to be time-consuming, arduous, or even impossible. As we increasingly come to experience music as synonymous with effortless digital skipping from track to track there is also a corresponding growth in the richness of the strenuous exertions that have to be endured before breaking through to the spaces where music might happen.

In the post-digital, almost any barrier to the boundless flood of music can be turned into a resource for the production of presence: basements lacking room for no more than a certain number of people; time running out and limiting the number of songs in a session or on a tape; loudspeakers incapable of delivering sound levels above a certain decibel or outside of a set spectrum of frequencies; instruments featuring no more than thirty-two keys; cops breaking up the party; backs that break when trying to carry that one extra kilo of vinyl; geographical distances; disk space; grit. All these levees, these barriers that determine how music happens—they feed the post-digital with the traction needed for the production of memorable events.

The family just seating themselves in front of the television, eager to watch this evening's episode of "So You Think You Can Dance," is just as involved in the post-digital as the thousand ravers dancing through the night inside the abandoned factory. Both cases represent examples of musical events giving rise to a production of presence, a process constrained by the specific situational limitations that events impose on themselves. If it so happens that the intensity inside the factory is stronger, this is not because the crowd involves more people than the living room. Rather, the intensity of the experience is caused by the crowd having accumulated greater potential for experiencing a collective crossing of some barrier or threshold. Conversely, it would be unfair to blame a less intense TV experience on bad programing alone. In the bus, we felt the presence of an urgency and intensity exceeding the sum of the individual contributions of all of the twenty-three passengers. This intensity of presence was specific to the intermingling of two distinct technologies: the bus and the cassette tape.

Our methodology could certainly (and with some justification) be accused of nostalgia. According to the transportational logic governing the tourism industry and the art world alike, traveling is what you do in order to present yourself at an end destination. Travel is thus reduced to nothing more than the distance you have to cover in order to get from point A to point B. This has the consequence of making air travel seem a more rational choice than going by bus. According to the logic of high fidelity so keenly propped up by the consumer electronics industry, sound quality is just a question of either being good or bad. In light of such logic, cassette tapes would unarguably seem the inferior alternative when compared to digital audio formats.

The question becomes, then: Why should hanging on to tapes be considered reactionary when the same does not apply to forming a rock band? The intermittent staging of spectacles that are supposed to represent a "return to the roots of rock'n'roll" seems to be a favorite pastime of the record industry. It should be kept in mind that the

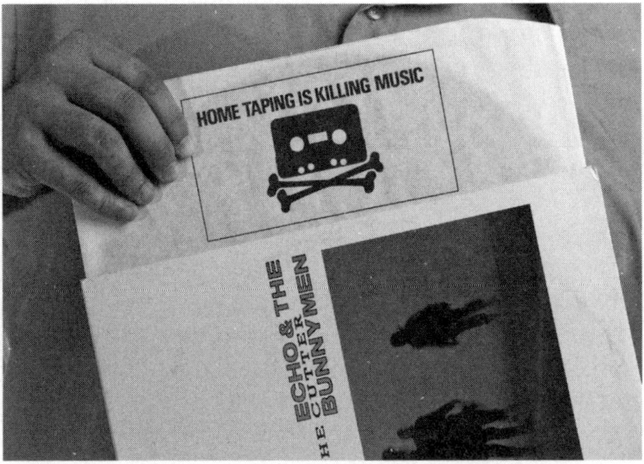

“Home Taping Is Killing Music” was the slogan of a 1980s anti-copyright infringement campaign by the British Phonographic Industry.

format of the rock band in itself represents a set of restrictions on musical possibilities. In terms of the production of presence, there is nothing to say that such constellations necessarily outrun or equal what others, given the right time and the right place, achieve using nothing but a boom box and a bag of tapes.

It is precisely because the bus trip took our common experiences of the digital superabundance of information as a starting point that our vision of the post-digital as a countermovement appeared with such clarity and force. This experiment proved extraordinary in that it taught us so much about the limits of materiality; about bigger and smaller collectivities; about high as well as low frequencies; about the future, and about the past.

4.

In ancient Greece, the seven- or eight-stringed lyre was not just the symbol of music: it *was* music. Music, in its turn, was not seen as just a manifestation of the harmony of the spheres. The cosmos was itself music, music was mathematics, and the lyre a magical artifact capable of transmuting those principles into sensations that could be experienced by mortals. The lyre itself has since been replaced by other stringed instruments, such as the guitar or the piano, whose tunings are based on alternative mathematical principles.

To us, arguing that a piano is music would seem slightly absurd. Before we can begin to talk about music, there must first be someone sitting down in front of it and selecting which of its eighty or so keys to play. From music as a thing, to music as an activity. What if the same shifting of perspectives could be applied to the post-digital? We have only to approach MP3 files as not being much different than ordinary musical instruments. The file does not equal music, but it contains certain musical potentials, which can become realized as soon as someone sits down and starts playing with it. Playing an MP3 file on a device means that a specific configuration of both hardware and software is mobilized, situated in time and space, in the presence of a limited selection of people. If you randomly bang on all the keys of a piano, you can expect to produce music to the same degree that shuffling a playlist containing all the songs ever recorded would pave the way for music to take place.

This line of thinking could, to some extent, be said to represent a devaluation of the status of recorded music—which is certainly the case, at least in comparison to the soaring heights that resulted from the CD bubble of the '90s. It does not, however, exclude any difference in musical quality between recorded objects. Rather, we now have the opportunity to reformulate our criteria for quality assessment: a great song that is captured, fixed, and stored—and it is irrelevant if it is encoded into an MP3 file or written on a music sheet—will harbor greater potential for being realized as great music, just like a well-built and well-tuned piano will harbor greater musical possibilities than a piano recently recovered from the garbage dump.

But given the right hands and the right situation, even the most miserable wretch of a piano is capable of producing fantastic music. Analogously, a great singer might pull off a fantastic performance of a song that up until then had been written off as terrible. The same thing goes for the possibilities open to the remix artist who works with low-quality recordings. The thing is that raw materials like these (in the form of notation or recordings) will put greater demands on artistic skill by virtue of placing greater constraints on musical maneuvering. On the other hand, this basic idea of enforcing constraints on musical options is what every musical instrument really is about—to apply specific tunings to stringed instruments is just one of many ways to express this idea.

The development of new musical instruments seems to have ground to a complete halt during the heyday of autonomous music, back when the natural position of the composer was at the top of the pyramids of aesthetics and copyright legislation. New music meant new compositions—not new instruments. The modernist avant-garde composer also seemed content with the available selection. Pianos were certainly prepared, and scores were written that imposed on the musicians the most grueling and exotic playing techniques. But the performances still involved the same old instruments. With the emergence of electrified music, however, the barriers that kept composer, musician, instrument builder, and sound technician apart slowly started to crumble. Performance-wise, there might not have been many new additions for audiences to remark on (same old electric guitars), but what they got to hear was the sound of a constantly mutating constellation of effect modules and boxes.

If viewed from a distance, all unique combinations of instrument and sound effects start to resemble something more like meta-instruments. The same thing happens if we consider hardware and software, and the different ways in which they can be configured to produce sounds. The development of the musical means of production finds its expression in innovations made at this meta-instrumental level, and these show themselves for the most part to be the results of collective experimentation without any identifiable single author.

The effect of the easy access to digital copies of music production software is to significantly lower not only the threshold for production, but the costs of distribution as well. In this way, the digital superabundance seems to practically feed on itself.

This essay is an edited selection from Rasmus Fleischer's book *Det postdigitala manifestet*, published in Swedish in 2009. This is its first English translation, thanks to Mikael Kopimi Altemark.

Jon Rich

Facebook: A Court of Ignorant, Cruel Judges

A Lebanese friend who happens to be a writer was telling me recently that he didn't appreciate the comments posted in response to some of his articles on the internet. He happens to work at a well-known journalistic institution whose website has been suspended in a 1990s internet vortex due to some bureaucratic complications. Although his colleagues often complain about the woeful obscurity of their writing on this website compared to other less serious yet more influential media outlets, he secretly relished the anonymity imposed by a somewhat slow-moving and antiquated form of delivery.

It was not long ago that my friend told me this, but we are living in fast-paced times. In this state of temporal compression, a worrying trend has emerged in which a writer's success has come to be measured by the number of views and comments elicited by his or her writing. Those same writers have, in a matter of a few years, adopted a new publishing ethos in which they post their thoughts, opinions, and writings on the plethora of blogging sites currently available. The generation of bloggers, many of whom started out as newspaper writers and later moved to electronic publishing, didn't stop there—they expanded their commenting activity to their personal Facebook pages.

In pure numbers, the results have been astonishing. Journalists who used to write long-form, in-depth articles—quality notwithstanding—in the traditional newspaper format started to cut their articles shorter with every piece published online, until they reduced their output to short anecdotes approaching the 140 character limit of a tweet. This produces a structure that is not so different from a snapshot of a celebrity; it doesn't communicate much more than a hint at something unquantifiable. And since "hinting" is all the readers have to go by, a whole industry of entertainment reporting has sprung to life, spawning writers with authoritative voices who have the final say in what the change in Brad Pitt's hairstyle means for his relationship with Angelina Jolie. Needless to say, such "factual" interpretations are nothing more than wild rumors.

There is a plague afflicting writing and writers these days, one that makes them Google themselves to check the number of articles mentioning them by name. They have no time to read every single piece of written material that mentions them, so they focus on the statistics. As a result, they managed to venture into the same forest that they were, as writers and artists, trying to discern from the trees: "*Avatar* broke box office records," "Aristotle was mentioned millions of times on the internet," "Lady Gaga has more Likes on her Facebook page than Barack Obama"—translated into a declaration of what a great film *Avatar* is, how Aristotle is the most important thinker, how Lady Gaga is far more important then Frank Sinatra and Barack Obama combined.

It's no wonder that this way of neglecting the qualitative aspect of experience and looking purely at quantities is misleading and unfair, as Karl Marx has already explained.[1] The slippery slope the journalists and writers have been sliding down has turned them away from writing and toward advertising. No longer is there any point in delving into Althusserian structural analysis. The official goal or mission is to poll the public in order to validate one's point of view and gain legitimacy among others. In a sense, this makes the public the judge and juror and the Supreme Rulers/Kings/Khalifs who order the court jesters around to entertain them. They have no time for philosophers and truth-seekers who aspire to reinvent the rules and find values and morals in them.

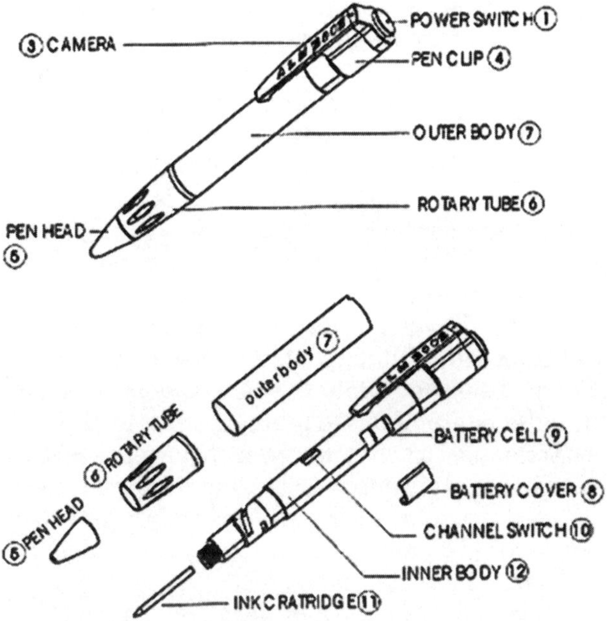

Technical drawing of a pen camera, a devise increasingly used in Syria as a means to document and upload images of the war. YouTube has created a special channel for this “citizen news” footage.

In these times of temporal compression, all of this feels like a memory from the distant past. It's possible that a day will come when we give praise to the age of the punch line, when writers will be remade as celebrities and the audience as judges. In early 2010, the writer Bilal Khbeiz published an article with the evocative title "In Praise of Books: When Authorities Close a Prison, They Foil a Revolution!" in the Lebanese cultural periodical *Juthour* (Roots). In the article, Khbeiz studied the anonymous commenters who post under published articles on the web and saw in them the rise of a new totalitarianism that favors collective sloganeering over individual opinion. In the same article, he created clear boundaries between readers and writers, with readers as totalities and writers as discrete entities.

Based on this distinction, one could say that Karl Marx and Friedrich Nietzsche are writers and Vladimir Lenin and Adolf Hitler are readers because the latter interpret based on a simplistic, totalitarian understanding of what the former have respectively written. The same applies, in frightening terms, to the Islamic extremists of today and the judges of the inquisition in medieval Europe. Osama bin Laden and Ayman Zawahiri, in their reading of the Islamic tradition, show extreme narrow-mindedness and limited imagination—no different from other average readers—when they squeeze the richness of Islam and its traditions into a tiny box inside their heads. They reduce it to broad-stroke headlines that divide people into two groups: believers and infidels. This makes them no different than the perpetrator of the Wisconsin massacre at a Sikh temple—an even worse case, since the shooter couldn't even tell the difference between a Sikh and a Muslim. A member of a white supremacist group, he considered anything outside the limits of his understanding to be hostile territory. Anyone who is different is deemed evil and worthy of contempt. Since the murderer sees an enemy in everyone who is alien to him, killing members of the Sikh faith by misidentifying them as Muslims doesn't change the truth about the event: a Muslim is no more alien to him than a Sikh is. The perpetrator sees Islam in the face of the Evil Foreigner, so Sikhs become inadvertently Muslim for being nonwhite and non-Christian. However, the bigger tragedy lies not in the blindness of the perpetrator but in that of the victims' families, who didn't flinch while declaring, "We are not terrorists, we're Indian Sikhs, not Muslims."

It's not a stretch to view this incident as a uniquely modern event, especially when it contradicts Hegel's famous objection to generalization as an exercise in blindness: at night, all cows are black.[2]

The Wisconsin massacre, as alarming as it was, looks less so when seen in the context of recent developments in Syria and the political and popular reactions to them. The adamant declarations that the Syrian opposition is an extremist Islamist opposition led by al-Qaeda completely ignores the fact that there are other facets of the opposition that are affiliated with secular, democratic ideals. But that is not the problem—the real problem is putting words into the mouths of the dead. The Syrian regime uses tanks and airplanes to pound cities and murder their inhabitants based on a nefarious assumption shared by other countries and factions—using as a pretext for retaliation the killer's own doubts and fears rather than the intent or opinion of the victim. A conscript in the army will kill those who he thinks are enemies before they kill him. Therefore, every Syrian victim is seen, in the minds of the killers and their allies, as a dead extremist based on the proof that the majority of casualties belong to the same sect. This enables the killers to commit the crime and reconstitute their victims as extremists postmortem. It is in this way that the Syrian regime resembles the Wisconsin murderer who perpetuated generalization and blindness by judging an entire group as one cohesive block of extremism. In the meantime, an individual cannot escape deadly retribution because he or she is already condemned to being either a terrorist or in the process of becoming one.

Attempts to debunk this assumption by pointing out the presence of Syrian democrats, secularists, or non-Sunni denominations among the opposition are discredited by the regime that separates individuals from their groups to label them as spies or collaborators with outside forces. The choice to become a spy is an individual one that negates belonging to a group. The Syrians are a "people," and a Syrian spy is an outsider and an enemy. Syrian Sunnis are members of that group desiring to think differently, and are thus isolated spies. This renders individuality equivalent to being a spy, and thus anyone who is different is fair game.

Killing in Syria is an ignorant act that redefines Sunnism the way bin Laden defines it, dissociating it from figures like Sheikh Muhammad Abduh and his teachings, in fact going as far as denying his existence. Such fascist claims have been addressed by the Syrian opposition in the way they presented themselves to the world and through public statements highlighting non-Sunni members who are tolerant, diverse, and secularist. The international news media fell into that trap the same way the Syrian opposition did. In August of 2012, the *Washington Times* published a report quoting an Alawi opposition member claiming that the Free Syrian Army refused to meet with him because of his sect. This was immediately denied by Abdulbasit Seeda, the Chairman of the Syrian Opposition National Council, who pointed out that there are Alawi army officers who wanted to defect and join the Free Army.

The challenge goes much deeper than this: one of the secularist opposition members currently in exile told me in a private conversation that most of the nonviolent activists who lit the spark of the current revolution have fled the country. Such is to be expected in a civil war where only the fighters survive and the only way to move forward is to see the other as an enemy and a killer. The only remaining collective consciousness is one of unbridled cruelty. The only voice to be heard is that of armed fighters, and it casts aside politicians, who end their public life as exiles, refugees, traitors, or in death. From their exile, the pacifist activists would defend the allegiance of the victims and their right to affiliate with Sunnis, constructing one argument after another in favor of the rise of the victims against their oppressors using the same labels that their oppressors have branded them with. A newborn Sunni child is an extremist by nature because the regime says so. The message of the victim mirrors that of the oppressor by claiming that the living have the right to become extremists in order to resist the ignorance of their killers. It is a counter-generalization—now championed by the victims—that envisions an individual who hails from a region, tradition, or sect as an ignorant person who uses ignorance to kill, and who is worthy of killing. This explains the thousands of killers in Syria who practice collective blindness either as victims or as perpetrators. Everyone becomes a killer.

Technology has served the Assad regime very well in many areas, judging by the speed with which the conflict became a sectarian civil war. A glance at the recent history of civil wars in the region reveals that the Lebanese civil war took a relatively long time to descend into pure violence. The war lasted for fifteen years and consumed generations of politicians and leaders before its blind fascist end. The war in Algeria started where it ended in Lebanon, with public condemnations and the justification of the murder of anyone having a different opinion than that of the warlords. The Iraqi war managed, a few years later, to do away with the need to invent pretexts to justify killing. In a few years and despite the size difference between Iraq and Lebanon, the Iraqis succeeded in destroying any tie—tribal, sectarian, or otherwise—that could bring them together.

Things developed much faster in Syria. Today, the Assad army will not hesitate to destroy entire historical neighborhoods in Aleppo, Damascus, Homs, and Hama in order to smoke out the alleged terrorists. It's hard to contemplate the wanton destruction of a habitat that has been populated continuously for more than four thousand years. What if the barbarians succeeded in flattening Rome and its monuments? And how different is the disciplined Assad army from the lunatic Taliban who demolished the Buddhist statues in Bamiyan or the crazy Malians who destroyed tombstones and shrines for being idols?

It's very possible that advancements in telecommunications caused the acceleration toward indiscriminate destruction. Since its beginning, the Syrian revolution has succeeded in creating unparalleled imagery that has taken everyone by surprise. The activists have led demonstrations against the regime knowing full well that they would be killed

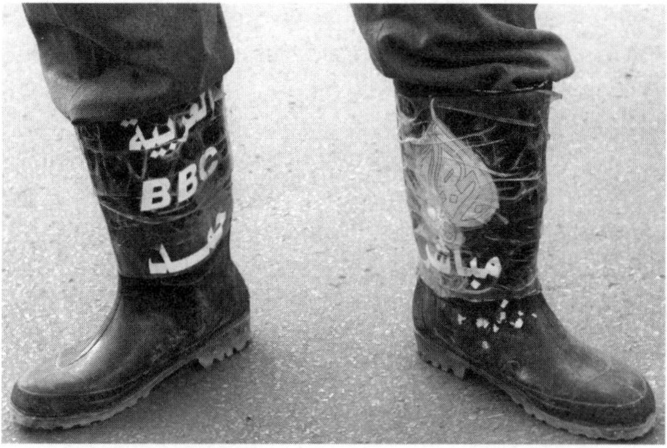

A pro-regime protester in Syria carries the names of the Qatar-based Al Jazeera network BBC Arabic and the emir of Qatar on his boots.

by the regime's soldiers. They carry their mobile cameras to film their own deaths or those of their comrades. These images have been a tremendous achievement that will forever be remembered. Sadly though, they have been accompanied by a desolate landscape devoid of writing and analysis. The proponents of the regime question the authenticity of the images with claims that they never took place in Syria. This misinformation aims at turning damning evidence into rumors based on the assumption that the Syrian people want to trust the regime. So in fact anyone could assert that images clearly representing an event are all lies and fabrication created by professional actors.

Adding to how fast things develop on the ground, the abundance of images of death and blood creates less room for deep analysis and more room for reactionary commenting, leading to the exodus from blogging to the extreme use of Facebook—a much larger difference than that between blogging and the careful, painstaking writing of Marx's *Capital*. A Facebook comment leaves the reader with no choice but to either like it or leave it. You only receive feedback from people who already like you. The objectors simply go to their own page and issue statements that garner the "liking" of their own fans. Death is denied when a Facebook activist can never prove it. They either join the page of their own sect or support group, "liking" each other's comments, or forever hold their peace.

The widespread use of Facebook has created the "final statement" that replaces the messy exchange on a blog, which in turn replaced the in-depth thinking that exists in books, effectively recreating the Facebook user as a judge. Whether they like it or not, Facebook users find themselves in the position of a superstar or a prophet, needing to utter profound statements and expecting the cheers of the crowd. As it becomes easier and easier for people to connect, this loop tragically kills conversations and exchanges them for the proclamations of ignorant judges who know nothing of the world but their own personal narratives and verdicts.

1
Karl Marx, *Critique of Hegel's Philosophy of Right* (1843).

2
G. W. F. Hegel, *Phenomenology of Spirit*, trans. A. V. Miller (Oxford: Oxford University Press, 1977), 9.

Geert Lovink

What Is the Social in Social Media?

Headlines, 2012: "Next time you're hiring, forget personality tests, just check out the applicant's Facebook profile instead" – "Stephanie Watanabe spent nearly four hours Thursday night unfriending about 700 of her Facebook friends—and she isn't done yet" – "Facebook apology or jail time: Ohio man gets to choose" – "Study: Facebook users getting less friendly" – "Women tend to have stronger feelings regarding who has access to their personal information" (Mary Madden) – "All dressed up and no place to go" (Wall Street Journal) – "I'm making more of an effort to be social these days, because I don't want to be alone, and I want to meet people" (Cindy Sherman) – "30 percent posted updates that met the American Psychiatric Association's criteria for a symptom of depression, reporting feelings of worthlessness or hopelessness, insomnia or sleeping too much, and difficulty concentrating" – Control your patients: "Do you hire someone in the clinic to look at Facebook all day?" Dr. Moreno asked. "That's not practical and borders on creepy." – "Hunt for Berlin police officer pictured giving Nazi salute on Facebook" – "15-year-old takes to Facebook to curse and complain about her parents. The disgusted father later blasts her laptop with a gun."

The use of the word "social" in the context of information technology goes back to the very beginnings of cybernetics. It later pops up in the 1980s context of "groupware." The recent materialist school of Friedrich Kittler and others dismissed the use of the word "social" as irrelevant fluff—what computers do is calculate, they do not interfere in human relations. Holistic hippies, on the other hand, have ignored this cynical machine knowledge and have advanced a positive, humanistic view that emphasizes computers as tools for personal liberation.

This individualistic emphasis on interface design, usability, and so on was initially matched with an interest in the community aspect of computer networking. Before the "dot-com" venture capitalist takeover of the field in the second half of the 1990s, progressive computing was primarily seen as a tool for collaboration among people.

In a chapter entitled "How Computer Networks Became Social," Sydney media theorist Chris Chesher maps out the historical development of computer networks, from sociometry and social network analysis—an "offline" science (and a field of study that goes back to the 1930s) that examines the dynamics of human networks—to Granowetter's theory of the strengths of weak links in 1973, to Castells's *The Network Society* in 1996, to the current mapping efforts of the techno-scientists that gather under the umbrella of actor-network theory.[1] The conceptual leap relevant here concerns the move from groups, lists, forums, and communities to the emphasis on empowering loosely connected individuals in networks. This shift happened during the neoliberal 1990s and was facilitated by growing computing power, storage capacity, and internet bandwidth, as well as easier interfaces on smaller and smaller (mobile) devices. This is where we enter the Empire of the Social. It must also be said that "the social" could only become technical, and become so successful, after the fall of the Berlin Wall in 1989, when state communism no longer posed a (military) threat to free-market capitalism.

If we want to answer the question of what the "social" in today's "social media" really means, a starting point could be the notion of the disappearance of the social as described by Jean Baudrillard, the French sociologist who theorized the changing role of the subject as consumer. According to Baudrillard, at some point the social lost its historical role and imploded into the media. If the social is no longer the once dangerous mix of politicized proletarians, of the frustrated, unemployed, and dirty clochards that hang out on the streets waiting for the next opportunity to revolt under whatever banner, then how do social elements manifest themselves in the digital networked age?

The "social question" may not have been resolved, but for decades it felt as if it was neutralized. In the West after World War II, instrumental knowledge of how to manage the social was seen as necessary, and this reduced the intellectual range of the question to a somewhat closed circle of professional experts. Now, in the midst of a global economic downturn, can we see a renaissance of the social? Is all this talk about the rise of "social media" just a linguistic coincidence? Can we speak, in the never-ending aftermath of the 2008 financial crisis, of a "return of the social"? Is there a growing class awareness, and if so, can it spread electronically? Despite widespread unemployment, growing income disparities, and the Occupy protests, it seems unlikely that we will see a global networked uprising. Protests are successful precisely because they are local, despite their network presence. How can the two separate entities of work and networked communication connect?

We can put such considerations into a larger, strategic context that the "social media question" poses. Do all these neatly administrated contacts and address books at some point spill over and leave the virtual realm, as the popularity of dating sites seems to suggest? Do we only share information, experiences, and emotions, or do we also conspire, as "social swarms," to raid reality in order to create so-called real-world events? Will contacts mutate into comrades? It seems that social media solves the organizational problems that the suburban baby-boom generation faced fifty years ago: boredom, isolation, depression, and desire. How do we come together, right now? Do we unconsciously fear (or long for) the day when our vital infrastructure breaks down and we really need each other? Or should we read this Simulacrum of the Social as an organized agony over the loss of community after the fragmentation of family, marriage, and friendship? Why do we assemble these ever-growing collections of contacts? Is the Other, relabeled as "friend," nothing more than a future customer or business partner? What new forms of social imaginary exist? At what point does the administration of others mutate into something different altogether? Will "friending" disappear overnight, like so many new media-related practices that vanished in the digital nirvana?

The container concept "social media," describing a fuzzy collection of websites like Facebook, Digg, YouTube, Twitter, and Wikipedia, is not a nostalgic project aimed at reviving the once dangerous potential of "the social," like an angry mob that demands the end of economic inequality. Instead, the social—to remain inside Baudrillard's vocabulary—is reanimated as a simulacrum of its own ability to create meaningful and lasting social relations. Roaming around in virtual global networks, we believe that we are less and less committed to our roles in traditional community formations such as the family, church, and neighborhood. Historical subjects, once defined as citizens or members of a class possessing certain rights, have been transformed into subjects with agency, dynamic actors called "users," customers who complain, and "prosumers." The social is no longer a reference to society—an insight that troubles us theorists and critics who use empirical research to prove that people, despite all their outward behavior, remain firmly embedded in their traditional, local structures.

The social no longer manifests itself primarily as a class, movement, or mob. Neither does it institutionalize itself anymore, as happened during the postwar decades of the welfare state. And even the postmodern phase of disintegration and decay seems over. Nowadays, the social manifests itself as a network. Networked practices emerge outside the walls of twentieth-century institutions, leading to a "corrosion of conformity." The network is the actual shape of the social. What counts—for instance, in politics and business—are the "social facts" as they present themselves through network analysis and its corresponding data visualizations. The institutional part of life is another matter, a realm that quickly falls behind, becoming a parallel universe. It is tempting to remain positive and portray a synthesis, further down the road, between the formalized power structures inside institutions and the growing influence of informal networks. But there is little evidence of this Third Way approach coming to pass. The PR-driven belief that social media will, one day, be integrated is nothing more than New Age optimism in a time of growing tensions over scarce resources. The social, which used to be the glue for repairing historical damage, can quickly turn into unstable, explosive material.
A total ban is nearly impossible, even in authoritarian countries. Ignoring social media as background noise also backfires. This is why institutions, from hospitals to universities, hire swarms of temporary consultants to manage social media for them.

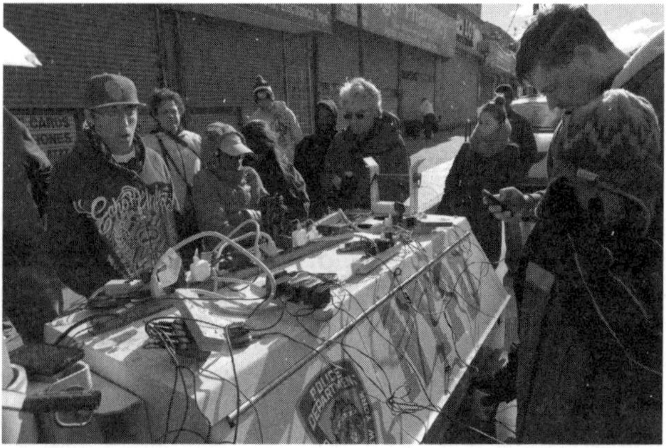

New York city police supply a generator so that victims of Hurricane Sandy can charge their cell phones.

Social media fulfill the promise of communication as an exchange; instead of forbidding responses, they demand replies. Similar to an early writing of Baudrillard's, social media can be understood as "reciprocal spaces of speech and response" that lure users to say something, anything.[2] Later, Baudrillard changed his position and no longer believed in the emancipatory aspect of talking back to the media. Restoring the symbolic exchange wasn't enough—and this feature is precisely what social media offer their users as an emancipatory gesture. For the late Baudrillard, what counted was the superior position of the silent majority.

In their 2012 pamphlet *Declaration*, Michael Hardt and Antonio Negri avoid discussing the larger social dimensions of community, cohesion, and society. What they witness is unconscious slavery: "People sometimes strive for their servitude as if it were their salvation."[3] It is primarily individual entitlement in social media that interests these theorists, not the social at large. "Is it possible that in their voluntary communication and expression, in their blogging and social media practices, people are contributing to instead of contesting repressive forces?" For us, the mediatized, work, and leisure can no longer be separated. But what about the equally obvious productive side of being connected to others?

Hardt and Negri make the mistake of reducing social networking to a media question, as if the internet and smartphones are only used to look up and produce information. Concerning the role of communication, they conclude that "nothing can beat the being together of bodies and the corporeal communication that is the basis of collective political intelligence and action." Social links are probably nothing but fluff, a veritable world of sweet sassiness. In this way, the true nature of social life online remains out of sight, and thus unscrutinized. The meeting of the social and the media doesn't have to be sold as some Hegelian synthesis, a world-historical evolution; however, the strong yet abstract concentration of social activity on today's networked platforms is something that needs to be theorized. Hardt and Negri's call to refuse mediation will have to move further. "We need to make new truths, which can be created by singularities in networks communicating and being there." We need both networking and encampment. In their version of the social, "we swarm like insects" and act as "a decentralized multitude of singularities that communicates horizontally."[4] The actual power structures, and frictions, that emerge out of this constellation have yet to be addressed.

The search for the social online—it seems a brave but ultimately unproductive project to look for the remains of nineteenth-century European social theory. This is what makes the "precarious labor" debate about Marx and exploitation on Facebook so tricky.[5] What we need to do instead is take the process of socialization at face value and refrain from well-meaning political intentions (such as the "Facebook revolutions" of the 2011 Arab Spring and the movement of the squares). The workings of social media are subtle, informal, and indirect. How can we understand the social turn in new media, beyond good and evil, as something that is both cold and intimate, as Israeli sociologist Eva Illouz described it in her book *Cold Intimacies*?[6] Literature from the media industry and the IT industry tends to shy away from the question posed here. Virtues such as accessibility and usability do not explain what people are looking for "out there." There are similar limits to the (professional) discourse of trust, which also tries to bridge the informal sphere and the legal sphere of rules and regulations.

The "obliteration of the social" has not led to a disappearance of sociology, but it has downgraded the importance of social theory in critical debates. A "web sociology" that has freed itself of the real/virtual dichotomies, not limiting its research scope to the "social implications of technology" (such as, for example, internet addiction), could play a critical role in developing a better understanding of how "class analysis" and mediatization are intertwined. As Illouz wrote to me in response to this question: "If sociology has traditionally called on us to exert our shrewdness and vigilance in the art of making distinctions (between use value and exchange value; life world and colonization of the life world, etc.), the challenge that awaits us is to exercise the same vigilance in a social world which consistently defeats these distinctions."[7] Albert Benschop, the Amsterdam pioneer of web sociology and editor of SocioSite.net, proposes that we overcome the real/virtual distinction altogether. He makes an analogy to the Thomas theoreme, a classic theory in sociology, when he says, "If people define networks as real, they are real in their consequences." For Benschop, the internet is not some "secondhand world." The same could be said of the social. There is no second life, with different social rules and conventions. According to Benschop, this is why there is, strictly speaking, no additional discipline necessary.[8] The discussion about the shape of the social relates to all of us; it should not be cooked up—and owned—solely by geeks and startup entrepreneurs. As Johan Sjerpstra puts it:

> Welcome to the social abyss. We can no longer close our eyes for the real existing stupidity out there. We're in it all together. Pierre Levy, please help us out: where is the collective intelligence now that we need it?[9]

The social is not merely the (digital) awareness of the Other, even though the importance of "direct contact" should not be underestimated. There needs to be actual, real, existing interaction. This is the main difference between old broadcast media and the current social network paradigm. "Interpassivity," the concept that points at a perceived growth of the delegation of passions and desires to others (the outsourcing of affect) as discussed, for instance, by Pfaller, Žižek, and Van Oenen, is a nice but harmless concept in this (interactive) context.[10] To question the current architectures and cultures of social media is not to be motivated by some kind of hidden, oppressed offline romanticist sentiment. Is there something like a justified feeling of overexposure, not just to information in general but to others as well? We all need a break from the social circus every now and then, but who can afford to cut off ties indefinitely? In the online context, the social requires our constant involvement, in the form of clicking. We need to make the actual link. Machines will not make the vital connection for us, no matter how much we delegate. It is no longer enough to build on your existing social capital. What social media do is algorithmically expand your reach—or at least they promise to.

Instead of merely experiencing our personal history as something that we reconcile with and feel the need to overcome (think of family ties, the village or suburb, school and college, church and colleagues from work), the social is seen as something

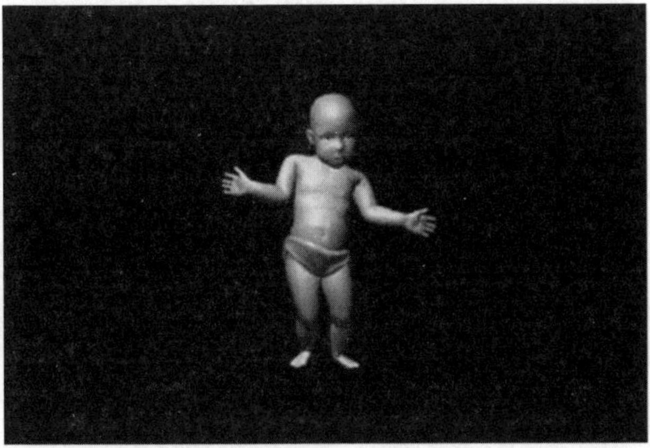

Still from the animation "Baby Cha-Cha." The video was considered to be one of the first to go viral at the end of the 1990s.

that we are proud of, that we love to represent and show off. Social networking is experienced in terms of an actual potentiality: I *could* contact this or that person (but I won't). From now on I will indicate my preferred brand (even without being asked). The social is the collective ability to imagine the connected subjects as a temporary unity. The power of connection is felt by many, and the simulations of the social on websites and in graphs are not so much secondary experiences or representations of something real; they are probes into a postliterate world ruled by images.

Martin Heidegger's dictum "We don't call, we are being called" runs empty here.[11] On the internet, bots will contact you regardless, and the status updates of others, relevant or not, will pass before your eyes anyway. The filter failure is real. Once inside the busy flow of social media, the Call to Being comes from software and invites you to reply. This is where the cool and laid-back postmodern indifference of quasi-subversive attitudes comes to an end. It is meaningless not to bother—we are not friends anyway. Why stay on Facebook? Forget Twitter. These are cool statements, but they are now beside the point. The user is no longer in a "state of stupor." The silence of the masses that Baudrillard spoke about has been broken. Social media has been a clever trick to get them talking. We have all been reactivated. The obscenity of common opinions and the everyday prostitution of private details is now firmly embedded in software and in billions of users.

The example Baudrillard used was the opinion poll, which he said undermines "the authentic existence of the social." Baudrillard replaced the sad vision of the masses as an alienated entity with an ironic and object-centered vision. Now, thirty years deeper into the media era, even this vision has become internalized. In the Facebook age, surveys can be done continuously—without people's direct participation in questionnaires and the like—through data mining. These algorithmic calculations run in the background and measure every single click, touch of the keyboard, and use of a keyword. For Baudrillard, this "positive absorption into the transparency of the computer" is even worse than alienation.[12] The public has become a database full of users. The "evil genius of the social" has no other way to express itself than to go back to the streets and squares, guided and witnessed by the multitude of viewpoints that tweeting smartphones and recording digital cameras produce. In the same way that Baudrillard questioned the outcome of opinion polls as a subtle revenge of the common people on the political/media system, we should question the objective truth of the so-called Big Data originating from Google, Twitter, and Facebook. Most of the traffic on social media originates from millions of computers talking to each other. Active participation of 10 percent of the user base is high. These users are assisted by an army of dutiful, hardworking software bots. The rest are inactive accounts. This is what object-oriented philosophy has yet come to terms with: a critique of the useless contingency.

The social media system no longer "plunges us into a state of stupor," as Baudrillard said of media experience decades ago. Instead, it shows us the way to cooler apps and other products that elegantly make us forget yesterday's flavor of the day. We simply click, tap, and drag the platform away, finding something else to distract us. This is how we treat online services: we leave them behind, if possible on abandoned hardware. Within weeks we have forgotten the icon, bookmark, or password.

We do not have to revolt against the media of the Web 2.0 era, abandoning it in protest because of allegedly intrusive privacy policies; rather, we can confidently discard it, knowing it will eventually join the good old HTML ghost towns of the '90s.

Here is Baudrillard parsing the situation back in the old media days: "This is our destiny, subjected to opinion polls, information, publicity, statistics: constantly confronted with the anticipated statistical verification of our behavior, absorbed by this permanent refraction of our slightest movements, we are no longer confronted with our own will." He discusses the move toward obscenity that is made in the permanent display of one's own preferences (in our case, on social media platforms). There is a "redundancy of the social," a "continual voyeurism of the group in relation to itself: it must at all times know what it wants. [...] The social becomes obsessed with itself; through this auto-information, this permanent auto-intoxication."[13]

The difference between the 1980s, when Baudrillard wrote these theses, and thirty years later can be found in the fact that all aspects of life have opened up to the logic of opinion polls. Not only do we have personal opinions about every possible event, idea, or product, but these informal judgments are also valuable to databases and search engines. People start to talk about products of their own accord; they no longer need incentives from outside. Twitter goes for the entire specter of life when it asks, "What's happening?" Everything, even the tiniest info spark provided by the online public, is (potentially) relevant, ready to be earmarked as viral and trending, destined to be data-mined and, once stored, ready to be combined with other details. These devices of capture are totally indifferent to the content of what people say—who cares about your views? That's network relativism: in the end it's all just data, their data, ready to be mined, recombined, and flogged off. "Victor, are you still alive?"[14] This is not about participation, remembrance, and forgetting. What we transmit are the bare signals indicating that we are still alive.

A deconstructivist reading of social media shouldn't venture, once again, to reread the friendship discourse ("from Socrates to Facebook") or to take apart the Online Self. No matter how hard it is to resist the temptation, theorists should shy away from their built-in "interpassive" impulse to call for a break ("book your offline holiday"). This position has played itself out. Instead, we need cybernetics 2.0—initiatives such as a follow-up to the original Macy conferences (1946 to 1953), but this time with the aim of investigating the cultural logic inside social media, inserting self-reflexivity in code, and asking what software architectures could be developed to radically alter the online social experience. We need input from the critical humanities and the social sciences; these disciplines need to start a dialogue with computer science. Are "software studies" initiatives up to such a task? Time will tell. Digital humanities, with its one-sided emphasis on data visualization, working with computer-illiterate humanities scholars as innocent victims, has so far made a bad start in this respect. We do not need more tools; what's required are large research programs run by technologically informed theorists that finally put critical theory in the driver's seat. The submissive attitude in the arts and humanities toward the hard sciences and industries needs to come to an end.

And how can philosophy contribute? The Western male self-disclosing subject no longer needs to be taken apart and contrasted with the liberated cyber-identity or "avatar" that roams around the virtual game worlds. Interesting players in the new media game can be found across the globe, from Africa to Brazil, India, and East Asia. For this, an IT-informed postcolonial theory has yet to be assembled. We should look today's practices of the-social-as-electronic-empathy right in the eyes. How do you shape and administer your online affects? To put it in terms of theory: we need to extend Derrida's questioning of the Western subject to the nonhuman agency of software (as described by Bruno Latour and followers of his actor-network theory). Only then we can get a better understanding of the cultural policy of aggregators, the role of search engines, and the editing wars on Wikipedia.

With its emphasis on Big Data, we can read the "renaissance of the social" in the light of sociology as the "positivist science of society." As of yet there is no critical school in sight that could help us to properly read the social aura of the citizen as user. The term "social" has effectively been neutralized in its cynical reduction to data porn. Reborn as a cool concept in the media debate, the social manifests itself neither as dissent nor as subcultural. The social organizes the self as a techno-cultural entity, a special effect of software, which is rendered addictive by real-time feedback features. In the internet context, the social is neither a reference to the Social Question nor a hidden reminder of socialism as a political program. The social is precisely what it pretends to be: a calculated opportunity in times of distributed communication. In the end, the social turns out to be a graph, a more or less random collection of contacts on your screen that blabber on and on—until you intervene and put your own statement out there.

Thanks to Facebook's simplicity, the online experience is a deeply human experience: the aim is to find the Other, not information. Ideally, the Other is online, right now. Communication works best if it is 24/7, global, mobile, fast, and short. Most appreciated is instantaneous exchange with "friended" users at chat-mode speed. This is social media at its best. We are invited to "burp out the thought you have right now—regardless of its quality, regardless of how it connects to your other thoughts."[15] The social presence of young people is the default here (according to the scholarly literature). We create a social sculpture, and then, as we do with most conceptual and participatory artworks, we abandon it, leaving it to be trashed by anonymous cleaners. This is similar to the faith inherent in all social media: it will be remembered as an individual experience of online community in the post-9/11 decade. And happily forgotten as the next distraction consumes our perpetual present.

It is said that social media has outgrown virtual communities (as described by Howard Rheingold in his 1993 book of the same name), but who really cares about the larger historical picture here? Many doubt whether Facebook and Twitter, in their current manifestations as platforms for the millions, still generate authentic online community experiences. What counts are the trending topics, the next platform, and the latest apps. Silicon Valley historians will one day explain the rise of "social networking sites" out of the ashes of the dot-com crisis, when a handful of survivors from the margins of the e-commerce boom-and-bust reconfigured viable concepts of the Web 1.0 era, stressing the empowerment of the user as content producer. The secret of Web 2.0, which kicked off in 2003, is the combination of (free) uploads of digital material with the ability to comment on other people's efforts. Interactivity always consists of these two components: action and reaction. Chris Cree defines social media as "communication formats publishing user generated content that allow some level of user interaction," a problematic definition that could include most of early computer culture.[16] It is not enough to limit social media to uploading and self-promotion. It is the personal one-to-one feedback and small-scale viral distribution elements that are essential.

As Andrew Keen indicates in *Digital Vertigo* (2012), the social in social media is first and foremost an empty container; he adduces the exemplary hollow platitude that says the internet is "becoming the connective tissue of twenty-first century life." According to Keen, the social is becoming a tidal wave that is flattening everything in its path. Keen warns that we will end up in an antisocial future, characterized by the "loneliness of the isolated man in the connected crowd."[17] Confined inside the software cages of Facebook, Google, and their clones, users are encouraged to reduce their social life to "sharing" information. The self-mediating citizen constantly broadcasts his or her state of being to an amorphous, numb group of "friends." Keen is part of a growing number of (mainly) US critics warning us of the side effects of extensive social media use. From Sherry Turkle's rant on loneliness, Nicholas Carr's warnings on the loss of brain power and the ability to concentrate, to Evgeny Morozov's critique of the utopian NGO world, to Jaron Lanier's concern over the loss of creativity, what unites these commentators is their avoidance of what the social could alternatively be, were it not defined by Facebook and Twitter. The problem here is the disruptive nature of the social, which returns as a revolt against an unknown and unwanted agenda: vague, populist, radical-Islamist, driven by good-for-nothing memes.

The Other as opportunity, channel, or obstacle? You choose. Never has it been so easy to "auto-quantify" one's personal surroundings. We follow our blog statistics and our Twitter mentions, check out friends of friends on Facebook, or go on eBay to purchase a few hundred "friends" who will then "like" our latest uploaded pictures and start a buzz about our latest outfit. Listen to how Dave Winer sees the future of news: "Start a river, aggregating the feeds of the bloggers you most admire, and the other news sources they read. Share your sources with your readers, understanding that almost no one is purely a source or purely a reader. Mix it all up. Create a soup of ideas and taste it frequently. Connect everyone that's important to you, as fast as you can, as automatically as possible, and put the pedal to the metal and take your foot off the brake."[18] This is how programmers these days loosely glue everything together with code. Connect persons to data objects to persons. That's the social today.

1

Chris Chesher, "How Computer Networks Became Social," in Chris Chesher, Kate Crawford, and Anne Dunn, *Internet Transformations: Language, Technology, Media and Power* (forthcoming from Palgrave Macmillan in 2015).

2

Jean Baudrillard, "The Masses: Implosion of the Social in the Media," *New Literary History* 16, no. 3 (1985): 1, http://www.jstor.org/stable/468841.

3

All quotes here in and in the next paragraph are from Michael Hardt and Antonio Negri, *Declaration* (New York: Argo-Navis, 2012), 18–21.

4

Ibid., 35 (both quotes).

5

See the exchange "The $100bn Facebook question: Will capitalism survive 'value abundance'?" on the nettime e-mail list, early March 2012. Brian Holmes writes there in various postings: "What I have found very limiting in the discourse around so-called web 2.0 is the use of Marx's notion of exploitation in the strict sense, where your labor power is alienated into the production of a commodity and you get an exchange value in return." ... "For years I have been dismayed by a very common refusal to think. The dismaying part is that it's based on the work of European history's greatest political philosopher, Karl Marx. It consists in the assertion that social media exploits you, that play is labor, and that Facebook is the new Ford Motor Co." ... "The 'apparatus of capture,' introduced by Deleuze and Guattari and developed into a veritable political economy by the Italian Autonomists and the Multitudes group in Paris, does something very much like that, though without using the concept of exploitation." ... "Social media do not exploit you the way a boss does. It emphatically _does_ sell statistics about the ways you and your friends and correspondents make use of your human faculties and desires, to nasty corporations that do attempt to capture your attention, condition your behavior and separate you from your money. In that sense, it does try to control you and you do create value for it. Yet that is not all that happens. Because you too do something with it, something of your own. The dismaying thing in the theories of playbour, etc, is that they refuse to recognize that all of us, in addition to being exploited and controlled, are overflowing sources of potentially autonomous productive energy. The refusal to think about this—a refusal which mostly circulates on the left, unfortunately—leaves that autonomous potential unexplored and partially unrealized."

6

Eva Illouz, *Cold Intimacies: The Making of Emotional Capitalism* (Cambridge: Polity Press, 2007).

7

Private e-mail correspondence, March 5, 2012.

8

Albert Benschop, "Virtual Communities: Networks of the Future," trans. Connie Menting, October 1997, http://www.sociosite.org/network.php.

9
Ibid.

10
See Robert Pfaller, *Ästhetik der Interpassivität* (Hamburg: Philo Fine Arts, 2008); and Gijs van Oenen, *Nu even niet! Over de interpassieve samenleving* (Amsterdam: Van Gennep, 2011).

11
See Avital Ronell, *The Telephone Book* (Lincoln: University of Nebraska Press, 1989).

12
Baudrillard, "The Masses," 5.

13
Ibid., 210.

14
Standard phrase uttered by Professor Professor, a Bavarian character who speaks English with a heavy German accent in the BBC animated series *The Secret Show* from 2007.

15
Anand Giridharadas, "A New, Noisier Way of Writing," *New York Times*, February 24, 2012, http://www.nytimes.com/2012/02/25/us/25iht-currents25.html?_r=1.

16
Read more at Chris Cree, "Definition of Social Media," *Success Creeations*, May 14, 2008, http://successcreeations.com/438/definition-of-social-media/#ixzz1nJmIQl1c.

17
Andrew Keen, *Digital Vertigo* (New York: St. Martin's Press, 2012), 13.

18
See David Winer, "What News Must Do," *Scripting*, February 24, 2012, http://scripting.com/stories/2012/02/24/whatNewsMustDo.html.

Brian Kuan Wood

"I Must First Apologize…": In Conversation with Joana Hadjithomas and Khalil Joreige

It was probably only a few years ago that we still thought, wow, these communication networks are a very convenient means of sending money and messages across long distances. Communication would bring us all together, make the world shrink, and eliminate distances once and for all. But all this time, other technologies were being developed by more advanced, more cunning parties who knew this was a fiction, and that actually long distances will never be conquered by some silly global unity, but can only be capitalized on by money-laundering schemes, offshore finance, and online scams that actually rely on the remoteness of two parties in order to construct floating solidarities based in mutual benefit, pseudo-anonymity, and the imagination of the other.

Opening at the Villa Arson in Nice in July 2014, and later on at Home in Manchester, then at the MIT List Visual Arts Center in Boston, "I Must First Apologize..." is the title of Lebanese filmmakers and visual artists Joana Hadjithomas and Khalil Joreige's exhibition of works resulting from having collected, archived, and studied more than four thousand advance-fee frauds and scam e-mail messages since 1999. These e-mails are a cyber iteration of an old genre that dates back to the eighteenth century known as "the Jerusalem letter." The same structure applies today: a person claims to possess a large sum of money that s/he needs to transfer urgently and promises a substantial percentage of this money to the person who will help. Of course, this transfer never takes place.

But what does take place is a dramaturgy of various political and economic imaginaries whereby the history of the past few years of advanced communication is retold through semi-fictitious and highly personalized accounts of its conflicts, wars, uprisings, shifts in global economy, financial value fluctuations, raw materials, religious extremism, political changes, and even ecological disaster. Also known as "the Nigerian scam," since a notable number have originated from the country, these frauds have been surprisingly efficient as hundreds of millions of dollars are extracted each year, sometimes leading to murder and suicide. But for Hadjithomas and Joreige, the de facto protocols in these bits of communication are also perhaps the deepest inscription of a new weird political cartography based in emotional blackmail and the use of narration and fabulation to manufacture common experiences.

Brian Kuan Wood How did you first become interested in scammers?

Joana Hadjithomas One of the first scam e-mails we received was in 1999. The story was touching and well documented, and I found myself hesitating in a kind of troubled place between fiction and reality. We didn't understand it very well, but we just kept it. Then we received others. We didn't know what to do with them, but we saved them. We thought they were saying something about the state of the world. As we received more, we started to become interested in how they used micro-narrative devices.

Khalil Joreige When we started to archive the scam e-mails, it was because they fit something that we recognized. They fit into a tradition of narration, so they also deal with this storytelling, with the construction of things. These scams base themselves on a plausible reality rooted in news or real events or conflicts. They construct their frauds by borrowing the identities of real people. They often include a link to a website in order to demonstrate the reality of an event, including names, historical facts, or news websites. I don't know if you remember, but the early scams had a lot of CNN and YouTube links. For almost eleven years we kept reading these woeful texts that you usually send directly to the trash, and then we suddenly wondered whether you can take them from the trash and make something out of them. Perhaps something poetic could be created. If people embody the scams, will the scams then embody the imaginary they create—an imaginary without images, usually?

JH There was also another layer that was interesting. Written in the first person and structured like monologues, the scams often usurp famous individuals' identities, posing as the children or wives of politicians, or of notorious dictators and claiming to possess a large sum of money that he/she needs to transfer urgently. But they all use a small anecdote, a detail that just makes you feel that it can be true. They often come from people who are very familiar with the political situation they claim to be victim to.

BKW That's the hook that gives it credibility.

JH Yes. And it comes as an alternative to the official history.

KJ This is how we read them, as symptoms.

JH The people writing the scams usually claim to be related to a prominent figure. One comes across Yasser Arafat's wife, Suha; or the former Tunisian first lady; Gaddafi's lawyer; Mubarak's eldest son; PKK leader Öcalan's brother; Liberian president Charles Taylor's wife; the son of Guinea-Bissau's General Assumane Hanis; the children of the Ivorian Colonel Coulibaly; Nenita Villaran, the widow of the former minister of finance of the Philippines; the secretary of Khodorkovsky, the Russian billionaire; but also American army officers in Iraq, anonymous widows who really existed, or the children of cocoa merchants, gold-mine owners ... It is always someone in the backstage of history that is writing.

BKW It reminds me of how often one encounters in literature the folding of grand narratives into personal, private narratives. It marks the timeless tension between the private and the public. A grand narrative is usually a political narrative, and then you have the interior life of a person's mind, or a family, which both is and isn't reducible to the terms of the grand narrative. The private life slips alongside the grand narrative, and often even reflects it, but it isn't the same thing. Private life does not represent the dominant ideology, but it does represent its holes, its shortcomings, its mistakes, and so on.

JH We were always interested in anecdotes or stories kept secret for not reflecting the official history, or what you might call the grand narrative. It happens in theater too. It evokes what you see in classical plays—you always have the best friend, the servant, who tells the story in another way.

BKW But in literature this is always used as a poetic device. What is so interesting about the scams is that these same poetics are used for economic and emotional extraction. They're applied as a tool. This narration, actually, is not just the way that literature works. It's also the way that the mind works in an economy based on identification.

KJ The narrations that unfold in these scams are part of a literary tradition known as the Jerusalem letter, and previously known as the Spanish prisoner. Jerusalem letters originated in France at the end of the eighteenth century, and have widely influenced present-day scams. They tell stories of lords and their servants (usually the narrators) fleeing the events of the French Revolution, and similarly appeal to the victim through a sort of scenario or life story of the person whom the money belongs to, justifying how he has obtained the money and why he needs help. The stories in the actual scams seem familiar to us. They borrow elements from theater as well as the narrative structures of cinema; for example, the narrative arc of Hollywood films. They also suppose an existing narrative that determines your expectations of the one they provide. We're interested in how scam e-mails work within this preexisting imaginary and what kind of propositions and productions of meanings they offer. Our project *The Lebanese Rocket Society* is about an event that really happened, but that no longer fits into how we perceive ourselves. That is, today a space project in Lebanon in the '60s does not fit our imaginary. So everyone forgot it and thought it was a fiction. And in these e-mails, the stories that are fake—they become credible and efficient because they conform to a common imaginary. The scams often prove very effective. Several hundred million dollars are transferred every year to scammers and their bank accounts.

JH What kind of faith makes us believe in images and in tales? When you go to the theater or to the cinema it's very clear that it is just a play, a film. What makes you choose to believe? This choice was interesting for us to think about. The scam e-mails always play on your belief that you are exceptional, that you are the only one who can be trusted. They establish an individual relation in a process that is totally collective—a mass mailing, but with a totally individual mode of address.

KJ There is a desire to be part of the story.

JH And there is also a preconceived idea of what makes stories credible or not. For example, corruption is taken to be much more plausible in certain parts of the world than others: Africa, Asia, the Middle East, and Russia. Politically, it's strange. Scammers could say, for instance, that there is corruption in France, in London, in the States.

> **BKW** But then it wouldn't register in the same way. So it's not that they create their own imaginary. They actually ride on an existing imaginary that's already been produced by world events, and by the way they're reported.

JH They have to fit their imaginary of corruption into a preexisting one. And they try to reinforce it, while in the end creating something new also. What was really funny was that so many of them were translated on Google Translate, with bizarre sentences and mistakes. In trying to fit the existing imaginaries, they inadvertently create another language altogether.

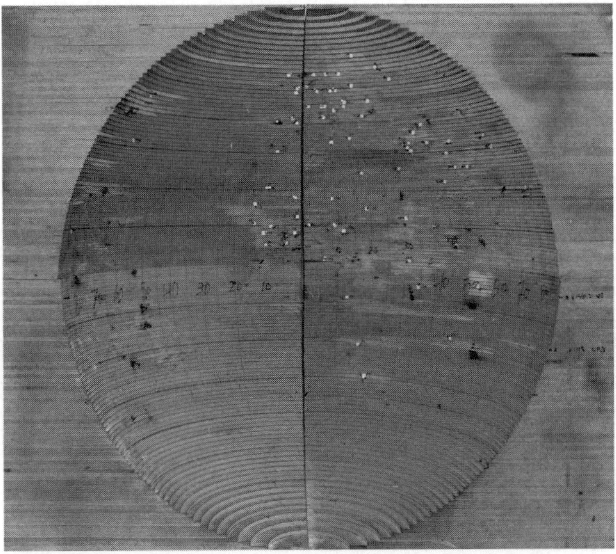

Joana Hadjithomas & Khalil Joreige, *A Matrix*, 2014. Wood sculpture, soundtrack.

KJ In carefully reading all four thousand e-mails in our archive, we saw, little by little, a sort of map emerging, a strange history of our contemporary time: the conflicts, wars, shifts in the global economy, financial values, raw materials, religion, politics, terrorism, and even ecological concerns. These virtual archives outline a cartography of conflicts, an image of the state of the world. In our installation *The Geometry of Space* we map the scams in order to track the circulation and geographic itineraries of the e-mails. The locations and countries that appear in a selection of over two hundred e-mails per year are used to identify these itineraries, whose coordinates (latitude and longitude) coincide with different events around the world. The sculpture gives shape to a globe, a physical reality to the virtual network as well as to the chronicle of events tabulated over a year of scams.

JH From political changes in Africa to the earthquake in Haiti, to certain well-known news items (such as a scandalous divorce or bankruptcy) to the latest events in Libya, Syria, or Egypt, scammers are on the lookout for all kinds of conflict, natural catastrophe, or military coups, using the names of exiled or fugitive dictators and so forth. Some e-mails exploit financial knowledge, referring to the exchange rates of cocoa, aluminum, steel, gold, and oil, or to banking institutions and their recent financial crises.

KJ In the last five years, something really new started happening with religion in scam e-mails. For example, dealing with a lot of born-again Christians or Muslims who don't want their family to inherit money because they are not good Christians or Muslims.

JH They claim to know that you are a good Muslim, a good Christian, and they want to offer you money for that very reason. At a certain point, we imagined them becoming a novel, or a kind of universe, because you would receive an e-mail from, for example, the son of Coulibaly. And then, you would receive an e-mail from his nephew. And then, you'd receive an e-mail from a guy telling you, be careful, I'm a special agent and you are being scammed, and we are offering you compensation. And then you have Ban Ki-moon writing to tell you to be careful of this compensation. They were echoing each other, with the same characters reappearing with something else to say.

BKW If you think you understand the situation, you take for granted that the scammer is a poor guy from Nigeria who is just doing a job and trying to get money. But then if you see the amount of money that they are actually able to gather, you realize their resources are vast. And they're scamming posh people in the UK, US, and Western Europe, people who are idle and sitting at home, doing nothing. But then, as with circular plotlines, in one instance the scam-baiters turned out to be scammers too, selling fake artworks on the market. The scam-baiters try to scam real scammers, and you can't tell who had the real power and who is doing what to whom.

JH You have many levels. When we were preparing the two installations *A Letter Can Always Reach Its Destination* and *The Rumor of the World*, we asked thirty-nine people to each recount one scam, to try to embody those scams, give a face to this immaterial, virtual, trash content. And, to our amazement, we discovered that one of those nonprofessional actors, named Fidel, used to be a scammer! And when we interviewed him on the subject, Fidel kept repeating: "If you're not greedy, why would you answer such an e-mail?" If the victim answers the e-mail, he or she is saying, I am greedy, I want money. And the scammers want money too. Secondly, the victim is always considered naive and unaware of what's happening. But it's often not the case. These victims are a lot closer to us than one can imagine. Scams play on something totally different, a kind of inner hope, a faith that we have in each one of us.

Then you have the scam-baiters, a group of individuals, mainly in the United States, fighting global scammers. Adopting a form of role-play, they attempt to scam the scammers, answering the e-mails and pretending to play along in order to waste the scammers' time, to trap them, to swindle them in turn. It can reach an extreme stage when the scam-baiters ask the scammers for proof of their "good faith" or motivation. They might ask for videos, pictures, paintings, artifacts, sometimes art objects, conversations, sometimes physical or symbolic movements. It can even go as far as tattoos or even physical abuse. In order to give them alleged proof of their existence, scammers may find themselves painting a picture of a dog, sculpting one of their computer keyboards, or having their arm tattooed. Most often, they are humiliated or can be found humiliating others to prove their commitment to the scam-baiters. The scammers want money, but the scam-baiters, they don't want money. They really just want to scam the scammer. They claim they are taking justice into their own hands, because international law is not working efficiently. The scam-baiters consider the acts of the scammers trophies, and exhibit them in what they call the Trophy Room. And it was really incredible to see how they scam a scammer whom one would think should be able to smell a scam himself. The scam-baiters say, "Look, I can't give you money, but I'm proposing something else. And that something else has to do with art. I'm an art dealer, and if you make a sculpture for me, we might have a business relationship."

KJ Or: "I can only transfer money to members of my church." So the scammer has to become part of this church. And this church can be completely bizarre, like the Church of the Sacred Butterfly, with a kind of fraternity logic. Very strange. They make scammers fill out questionnaires and dress up. The correspondence between the scammer and the scam-baiter is usually very long. It's a new kind of suspense novel. It becomes a narrative.

BKW And a strange parallel art market.

JH Of course. The Trophy Room evokes a virtual museum. The proof of trust is art. But who's the artist? Is it the scam-baiter who is sending the scammer a picture to paint, to sculpt? Or is it the scammer? Maybe the scammer even pays someone to do the sculpture.

BKW Art is in a very confusing state now. You have, for example, no new art movements since the '90s. And one remembers Francis Fukuyama's end-of-history argument from 1989, which claims that, with the triumph of liberal democracy over state communism, politics also ends. Instead, now we have economic regimes and flows of information, and it becomes extremely hard to map what is moving over the lines, because we are accustomed to old social and political codes where you have the police or the state on one side and the people on the other side. But I think you have really landed on something that might be a basic material in the weird exchanges we are having today. Not knowing who's on which side places the issue of trust at the center of any exchange. It always reminds me of a work by Yoko Ono from 1966, *Play It by Trust*, where both sides of the chessboard are white pieces, so the game can only be a negotiation to decide what the game is supposed to be in the first place.

KJ This is, for us, really important. It shifts completely the category of the victim. It also has something to do with the relation to art we were interested in. For example, in the film *Khiam*, we filmed six detainees who had been recently freed from the Khiam detention camp, located in the area occupied by Israel and its proxy militia, the army of South Lebanon. When they evoked the experience of detention and especially the relation they developed to art, Sonia, Afif, Soha, Rajae, Kifah, and Neeman—who spent about ten years in prison—recall the camp and narrate how they managed to survive, and more importantly to resist. They did this through the creation and the clandestine production of a needle, a pencil, a string of beads, a chess game, a sculpture. Faced with a total lack of elementary and necessary objects, they developed and exchanged astonishing artistic production techniques. But they are not artists. And as soon as they leave the detention camp, they will go back to their normal life. And they are not artists anymore.

JH They never did an artwork afterward. But for them, what they produced in the camps is art.

KJ So, this relation to what is art goes back to the condition that makes something appear as art, at a certain moment.

JH When we read the memoirs of criminal investigator Eugène François Vidocq, who, in the eighteenth century, identified the Jerusalem letters, the ancestor to these online scams with the same exact structure, narrative, etc., we were interested to see him claiming that these letters/scams appear at very particular historical moments. They only appear at moments of turmoil, such as the French Revolution, because you no longer know where power is located. And we think it is the words themselves that are being reconfigured. So scams appear in certain conditions, maybe because they fill a gap. They can play on your emotions and say: I am the servant of a marquis, and the marquis is dead now and I have his money. They use this moment of confusion. We have always thought about the period in '75–76 in Lebanon, at the beginning of the civil wars, where all the powers were mixed. There was no strong state, no strong army. Militias everywhere, and the power was totally diffuse, nothing was really structured. After that, the situation was reconfigured—each militia gained a district, and there were distinct powers again. But there was a moment of confusion at first, and in this moment of confusion a lot of things can happen. And maybe in art, we are living in one of those moments. The relation to the market is so present, and artwork is money. We are artists that come from totally different situations in a region and specially a country where for years there was no real market for contemporary art.

We built our practice in that way and felt more like researchers than anything else, moving between art and cinema.

KJ It's also a way for us to interrogate the status of the arts. The scenography for *The Trophy Room* refers to the one that architect Lina Bo Bardi produced in the São Paulo Museum of Art in 1968, designed for André Malraux's Le Musée Imaginaire (or, Museum without Walls), in a gesture toward art history, the status of the artwork, its production, circulation, and diffusion today. At the same time, the place on the internet where the scam-baiters' trophies are exhibited is called "419: The Trophy Room." And what is a trophy? A trophy is something the winner gets. I fight with you, and I get a trophy because I am the winner.

BKW It's a sign of conquest.

JH But then many of those trophies are difficult to see in terms of winning. Often you don't know who wins. It's so confused.

BKW Most of the trophies are jokes as well.

JH In a way, at first, they can be fun. But then you see this guy tattooing himself, and suddenly it's very cruel. The game can become very violent, and it can question our place as spectators. It also reproduces a colonial mentality still present in the relation between North and South, and replays our relation to authority and to the other—how the South presents itself, or the North, how the North presents the South, or itself. The trophies are physical objects, giving a concrete form to this fool's play and to the lies. In doing this, such a game unwittingly becomes a form of artistry, either by default or by accident. Not only do the objects prove that something exists, but they also take on an aesthetic and poetic power. They show a complex world where greed and desire question traditional ethics.

BKW This goes back to the way narratives and narration become a very central form of command when the terms of exchange are unclear. It becomes a question of who controls narratives, and how the narrative is produced. What registers does a narrative access in order for it to hold together? It's really interesting, as filmmakers, also, that you do that.

KJ It is very related to our relationship with cinema. Of course, "I Must First Apologize..." is really a film. We conceived the whole exhibition as a film that unfolds in the shape of installations, sound, video, sculptures, and drawings, deconstructing the data and transforming it to produce images and representations. One encounters recurring lead characters, and minor ones, scammers, victims, scam-baiters, parallel edits, original settings, essential props, scenarios, and virtual fictions—all echoing a relation about belief, desire, giving a physicality to things that are not present.

JH At the same time it is like in our films, when we integrate a certain reality and suddenly things occur, things happen and displace expectations completely. It was an incredible coincidence to meet Fidel when we were working with the nonprofessional actors, and to have one who suddenly started adding a lot of parts to his script and reenacting his scam so well. We were really surprised. Fidel said, very naturally, "I was a scammer before," and he agreed to talk about his previous life. He wrote some of these scams.

KJ Fidel was a scammer in Nigeria. And then his sister asked him to stop, because it was not acceptable for her. And so he moved to Beirut, where he's a trainer and does some striptease on the side. But when we started to interview him, all his references were to cinema. He would say, "If you want to believe in a film, the actors should be good. You have to believe in the story."

JH "A scam has to be well produced. You cannot, for example, do a scam that is badly produced. You need to have good props. You have to have the right shoes, the right watch. You have to have a good car."

KJ "You have to prepare a set." For example, if the scammer makes an appointment and a rendez-vous, he won't be there alone. He will put another actor in the restaurant, who will come and say hi to confirm the status of the scammers and his play. If he's a well-known businessman, and the scammer is sitting with him, a member of his group will come and interfere.

JH It's staged.

KJ So it's all about small details that will build these worlds, and that will make you believe in these worlds. For us, it's also a question of how you can start to believe in a fiction. Those stories, and the scam, represent the kinds of stereotypes in which you can believe. But when you follow some of the lives of the actors in the scams, it all seems real. Some characters have such a singular story that it is nearly unbelievable, but true. You could never invent it in fiction. It's too fabulous.

BKW A documentary, the real, can be too complex to communicate across long distances. It's too much of a fabulation. Often you can only use fiction.

KJ This debate is very complex for me. It was, for example, at the center of our film *I Want to See*, with Catherine Deneuve and Rabih Mroué. We refer to this Godard sentence in *Notre Musique* where he says, showing two pictures, that when it comes to 1948, the Israelis remember through fiction and the Palestinians through documentary. This sentence was very polemical, but we understand it in the sense that, when the weight of reality is too heavy, you cannot imagine a fiction.

BKW Fiction is for the victors and documentary is for the victims.

KJ But you can read it in another way, for those who are on the outside of the story. It's a very Benjaminean way of thinking about it. If the victor controls the narrative, the victims only have the small events, or the ways of resisting this dominant narrative.

JH And you have this idea that when you have history, then you also have fiction. But if you don't have access to history, how can you have fiction? We were interested in this opposition, and in how, as Khalil was saying, when "reality" is so heavy, it may be impossible to create a "fiction." And we believe the access to fiction to be totally necessary. It's the access to fiction that takes you out of the prison of an efficient history that binds you to the role of being a victim. The victim usually is shown with no singularity, no face, no name, no history. It's a status. So how can you identify with a status? You cannot. You can't know much about it. As it is usually presented to you, the victim's story becomes impossible for you to access.

KJ For us, it is important here to shift the gaze, to try to give the person a face, a name, a history again.

JH When we filmed *I Want to See*, we thought of the best way for people to see ruins again, because they are portrayed so often on television that people don't see them anymore. So if we put a fictional body, like Catherine Deneuve, in places where reality is so heavy after such a terrible war—the 2006 war in Lebanon—what might happen? It might create something that you recognize but that doesn't fit together. And this encounter between two things that are known but that are not suppose to meet creates something unknown that can force you to think about what you are seeing.

KJ It mutually destroys the fiction and the documentary. These categories are not stable anymore. We continuously have to reconfigure what is a fiction and what is so-called reality. So you have to generate other things, like something that's happened, suddenly, such as an accident, like meeting Fidel. In a video in the exhibition called *(DE)SYNCHRONICITY*, we filmed four sequence shots, each representing a different internet cafe in four different locations in Lebanon. From one cafe to the next, from one scam to the next, people encounter one another physically and virtually. Sixteen actors in total, including Fidel, the repentant scammer, come and go, in an

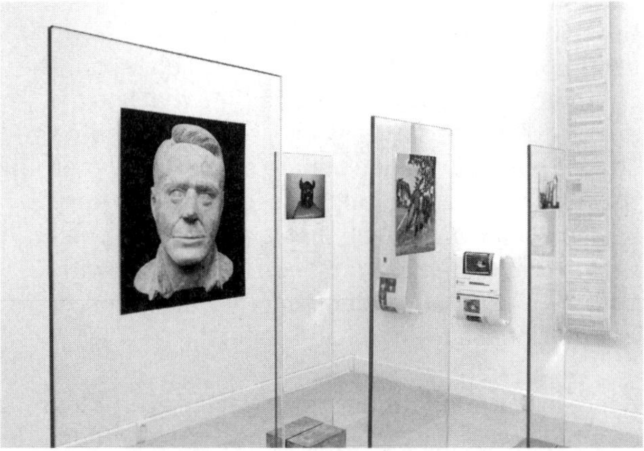

Joana Hadjithomas & Khalil Joreige, *The Trophy Room*, 2014. Cement, glass, and photographs. Dimensions variable.

orchestrated synchronization among the pedestrians and the cars captured live. Some disappear quickly. Others pass each other in a strange synchronicity, walking through one screen to another and another again before disappearing.

JH This installation has to do with how you are linked to a temporal territory more than a geographical one. When you begin mixing these different temporalities, you are at the same time reduced to a place: your laptop, your mobile, anything like this, where you can be localized. It's a shift from a geographical idea of territory to this concept of the contemporary, in the sense of a time that you are sharing. The internet is exactly the place where you share time, but you don't share space. It's something that we've been exploring, this idea of a territory that is not geographical, that is not topographical, that extends, that has not been interpreted with borders of a fiction or documentary, or places, or art, an additional continent, and so forth.

KJ In the installation *It's All Real* it's very clear how the actors we met are themselves a product of this mobility: Sasha is half Russian and half Nigerian, and lives in Beirut. Omar is half Gambian. His mother is from Sri Lanka, but he was raised by a woman from Seychelles after the death of his mother. Younes is half Filipino, half Gambian, and both parents were born in Beirut. If they want to go somewhere else, they don't have papers or money. They are all stuck in Beirut. It's like a parallel world, full of people you usually don't really see or hear. So it's a mobility that is immobilized, stuck in the present. And it has a lot to do with the internet. You are not moving. And sometimes you even feel you are stuck. It is a process of hysterical presence, something that we have been developing for a long time in our films. It's hysterical in the sense of repeating itself.

BKW I keep thinking of what Fidel said. You are greedy. I am greedy. This seems to be a sort of law of dislocation—greed. Maybe one still wants to kind of think of it as wanting money or precious commodities. But greed can also be for companionship, or something else.

JH Addiction. What is so present in all these relationships between victim, scam, and scam-baiter is addiction. You see it in the correspondence. Fidel says, "It is a story that never ends," because it's a story about love. The victim is the ghost of this story, of the exhibition, it's all about her, but you never see her and yet she's everywhere. In an entirely unexpected coincidence, we learned of someone close to us personally falling victim to one of these scams, and this person firmly refuses advice, repeating: "No, my situation is different, it's not the same." Just like some love stories or some addiction. For this person, it's not the same as for others. Just like a number of scam victims who believe they were chosen specifically by a stranger for being "the only remaining trustworthy person." This relation is about love, about a totally individual relation that a person can have or think they can have.

KJ It's also always a promise to have a better life. This is a totally nonrational belief. A continuous nonrational belief, like love.

BKW It seems that beneath a lot of the lying and believing there is a general sense of vulnerability, of not actually being able to change one's circumstances. Even for the one who is the hunter, the scammer. They can only hunt if they are in a vulnerable position to begin with.

KJ It might be about being cynical and non-cynical. Some people who believe that nothing is true, that everything is a scam, are closed to all kinds of surprises in life. If you are cynical, you won't be able to follow those surprises. Some accidents will never happen to you.

BKW Likewise, if the scammer is cynical and just wants the money quick, then they can't enter into the game, the dance. They can't go deep enough.

KJ Because they don't play into the narrative. I heard a very strange story. A woman told me about how her aunt had been scammed. She was sixty-five. And all her life, her brothers, from a very well-known family of bankers, had forced her to make certain choices. They had a lot of money. And this woman might have in some way been willingly scammed, in order to take revenge on her family.

JH It's very interesting, this idea that she was already a victim to her family. And allowing herself to be scammed gave her a way to totally explode the frontiers of right and wrong, to take revenge on her own family, to liberate herself. Her family would go and tell her to please stop. And she would answer: "You cannot stop me. You cannot stop me. I'm being scammed."

Hans Ulrich Obrist

In Conversation with Julian Assange

After traveling more than three hours from London on Sunday, February 27, 2011, I arrived at Ellingham Hall, the Georgian mansion near the eastern coast of England that Vaughan Smith offered Julian Assange to use as his address for bail during his UK extradition hearings. In the living room of the picturesque home he described to me as a "golden cage" we drank many cups of coffee and spoke until 3 a.m. about his life, his nomadism, his early beginnings and the invention of WikiLeaks, his time in Egypt, Kenya, Iceland, and other places, his scientific background, and the theoretical underpinnings of WikiLeaks.

Hans Ulrich Obrist How did it all begin?

Julian Assange I grew up in Australia in the 1970s. My parents were in the theater, so I lived everywhere—in over fifty different towns, attending thirty-seven different schools. Many of these towns were in rural environments, so I lived like Tom Sawyer—riding horses, exploring caves, fishing, diving, and riding my motorcycle. I lived a classical boyhood in this regard. But there were other events, such as in Adelaide, where my mother was involved in helping to smuggle information out of Maralinga, the British atomic bomb test site in the outback. She and I and a courier were detained one night by the Australian Federal Police, who told her that it could be said that she was an unfit mother to be keeping such company at 2:00 a.m., and that she had better stay out of politics if she didn't want to hear such things.

I was very curious as a child, always asking why, and always wanting to overcome barriers to knowing, which meant that by the time I was around fifteen I was breaking encryption systems that were used to stop people sharing software, and then, later on, breaking systems that were used to hide information in government computers. Australia was a very provincial place before the internet, and it was a great delight to be able to get out, intellectually, into the wider world, to tunnel through it and understand it. For someone who was young and relatively removed from the rest of the world, to be able to enter the depths of the Pentagon's Eighth Command at the age of seventeen was a liberating experience. But our group, which centered on the underground magazine I founded, was raided by the Federal Police. It was a big operation. But I thought that I needed to share this wealth that I had discovered about the world with people, to give knowledge to people, and so following that I set up the first part of the internet industry in Australia. I spent a number of years bringing the internet to the people through my free speech ISP and then began to look for something with a new intellectual challenge.

HUO So something was missing.

JA Something was missing. This led me to using cryptography to protect human rights, in novel ways, and eventually as a result of what I was doing in mathematics and in physics and political activism, things seemed to come together and show that there was a limit to what I was doing—and what the rest of the world was doing. There was not enough information available in our common intellectual record to explain how the world really works. These were more the feelings and process, but they suggested a bigger question, with a stronger philosophical answer for explaining what is missing. We are missing one of the pillars of history. There are three types of history. Type one is knowledge.

Its creation is subsidized, and its maintenance is subsidized by an industry or lobby: things like how to build a pump that pumps water, how to create steel and build other forms of alloys, how to cook, how to remove poisons from food, etc. But because this knowledge is part of everyday industrial processes, there is an economy that keeps such information around and makes use of it. So the work of preserving it is already done.

HUO It's kind of implicit.

JA There is a system that maintains it. And there's another type of information in our intellectual record. (This is a term I interchange freely with "historical record." When I say "historical record," I don't mean what happened a hundred years ago, but all that we know, including what happened last week.) This second type of information no longer has an economy behind it. It has already found its way into the historical record through a state of affairs which no longer exists. So it's just sitting there. It can be slowly rotting away, slowly vanishing. Books go out of print, and the number of copies available decreases. But it is a slow process, because no one is actively trying to destroy this type of information.

And then there is the type-three information that is the focus of my attention now. This is the information that people are actively working to prevent from entering into the record. Type-three information is suppressed before publication or after publication. If type-three information is spread around, there are active attempts to take it out of circulation. Because these first two pillars of our intellectual record either have an economy behind them, or there are no active attempts to destroy them, they do not call to me as loudly. But, this third pillar of information has been denied to all of us throughout the history of the world. So, if you understand that civilized life is built around understanding the world, understanding each other, understanding human institutions and so forth, then our understanding has a great hole in it, which is type-three history. And we want a just and civilized world—and by civilized I don't mean industrialized, but one where people don't do dumb things, where they engage in more intelligent behavior.

HUO Do you mean a more complex behavior?

JA Right, more complex and layered behavior. There are many analogies for what I mean by that, but I'll just give a simple one, which is the water ritual. If you sit down with a friend, and there's a pitcher of water on the table, and there are two glasses, then you pour the other person's water before your own. This is a very simple ritual. But, this is better than the obvious step, which is to pour your own water before the other person's. If we can see a few steps ahead, the water ritual is a more intelligent way to distribute water at a table. That's what I mean by civilization—we gradually build up all these processes and understandings so we don't need to make bad moves with each other or the natural world. So with regard to all this suppressed information, we've never had a proper understanding of it because it has never entered our intellectual record, and if we can find out about how complex human institutions actually behave, then we have a chance to build civilized behavior on top of it. This is why I say that all existing political theories are bankrupt, because you cannot build a meaningful theory without knowledge of the world that you're building the theory about. Until we have an understanding of how the world actually works, no political theory can actually be complete enough to demand a course of action.

HUO So that clearly maps out how you came to where you are today. Since many people now refer to you as one of their heroes, I was wondering who inspired you at the beginning.

JA There have been heroic acts that I have appreciated, or some systems of thought, but I think it's better to say that there are some people I had an intellectual rapport with, such as Werner Heisenberg and Niels Bohr. That comes when you're doing mathematics. The mathematics of Heisenberg and Bohr is a branch of natural philosophy. They developed a system or epistemology for understanding quantum mechanics, but encoded within this intellectual tradition are methods to think clearly about cause and effect. When reading mathematics you must take your mind through each intellectual step. In this case, the steps of Heisenberg or Bohr. Because good proofs are very creative, it takes the full energies of your mind to reach through one step to another. Your whole mind must be engaged in a particular state of thought, and you realize that this mental arrangement is the same as the author's at the moment of writing, so the feeling of mental similarity and rapport becomes strong. Quantum mechanics and its modern evolution left me with a theory of change and how to properly understand how one thing causes another. My interest was then in reversing this thought process and adapting it to another realm. We have an end state that we want, and I looked at all the changes that are needed to get to this end state from where we are now. I developed this analogy to explain how information flows around the world to cause particular actions. If the desired end state is a world that is more just, then the question is: What type of actions produce a world that is more just? And what sort of information flows lead to those actions? And then, where do these information flows originate? Once you understand this, you can see it is not just starting somewhere and ending elsewhere, but rather that cause and effect is a loop; here we are today, and we want to create an end state as a result of action. We act and by doing so bring the world into a new state of affairs, which we can consider our new starting point, and so this process of observe, think, act continues.

HUO Science, mathematics, quantum theory—all of these come together in your work. If one reads about your beginnings before WikiLeaks, one finds that you were not only instrumental in bringing the internet to Australia, but that you were also one of the pioneering, early hackers. You co-authored this book called *Underground: Tales of Hacking, Madness and Obsession on the Electronic Frontier*. I'm curious about your hacker background, and this book as well, since it seems to be a sort of fundament on which a lot of things were based afterwards.

JA In my late teenage years, up until the age of twenty, I was a computer hacker and a student in Melbourne. And I had an underground magazine called *International Subversive*. We were part of an international community of underground computer hackers. This was before the internet connected continents, but we had other ways of making international connections. So each country had its own internet, of a sort, but the world as a whole was intellectually balkanized into distinct systems and networks.

HUO Like The WELL in the States.

JA Right, that kind of thing, or ARPANET, which connected universities in the States. And something called x.25, run by the telecommunications companies, that banks and major companies used to link systems together. We, the underground community, sometimes bumped into each other deep inside these computer networks. Or we would meet at underground watering holes like QSD in France or ALTOS in Germany. But it was a very small community, with perhaps only twenty people at the elite level that could move across the globe freely and with regularity. The community was small and involved and active just before the internet, but then crossed into the embryonic internet, which was still not available to people outside of university research departments, US military contractors, and the pentagon. It was a delightful international playground of scientists, hackers, and power. For someone who wanted to learn about the world, for someone who was developing their own philosophy of power, it was a very interesting time. Eventually our phones were tapped and there were multiple, simultaneous raids that resulted in close to six years of legal proceedings. The book covers my case, but I deliberately minimized my role so we could pull in the whole community, in the United States, in Europe, in England, and in Australia.

HUO Did it also create kind of a connection between all these different local scenes?

At that time, you were also known as an ethical hacker.

JA Right, though I actually think most computer hackers back then were ethical, since that was the standard of the best people involved. Remember, this was an intellectual frontier, and it had very young people in it. It needed young people for the degree of mental adaptation necessary. Because it was an intellectual frontier, we had a range of people who were very bright, though not necessarily formally educated.

HUO When you worked as a hacker, were you inspired by anarchistic ideas?

JA I wasn't personally. The anarchists' tradition revolving around figures like Pierre-Joseph Proudhon and Peter Kropotkin was not something on my horizon. My personal political inspirations were people like Aleksandr Solzhenitsyn, anti-Stalinists in *The God That Failed*, and US radical traditions all the way up to the Black Panthers.

HUO Liberation movements.

JA Yes, the various liberation movements—in their emotional tone and force of will, not in intellectual content. That tradition really spread into some other things I did later, like the Cypherpunks, in 1993 and '94. 1994 was probably the peak of the Cypherpunk micro movement. Cypherpunk is a wordplay on Cyberpunk; the latter was always viewed as nonsense by real computer hackers—we were the living Cyberpunks while others were just talking about it, making artistic pastiche on our reality. We viewed the better books as a nice showing of the flag to the general public, but like most causes that are elitist and small, we had contempt for bowdlerized popularizations. The Cypherpunks were a combination of people from California, Europe, and Australia. We saw that we could change the nature of the relationship between the individual and the state using cryptography. I wouldn't say that we came from a libertarian political tradition as much as from a libertarian temperament, with particular individuals who were capable of thinking in abstractions, but wanting to make them real. We had many who were comfortable with higher mathematics, cryptography, engineering, or physics who were interested in politics and felt that the relationship between the individual and the state should be changed and that the abuse of power by states needed to be checked, in some manner, by individuals.

HUO Is this the fundament of WikiLeaks?

JA Yes and no. There are many different intellectual strands that ended up in WikiLeaks that are unrelated to ideas swirling around the Cypherpunk community. But the use of mathematics and programming to create a check on the power of government, this was really the common value in the Cypherpunk movement.

HUO And you were one of the protagonists?

JA I was. There wasn't really a founding member or a founding philosophy but there were some initial principles, people like John Young, Eric Hughes, and Timothy C. May from California. We were a discussion group like the Vienna school of logical positivism. From our interactions certain ideas and values

Publish or Perish

When asked during the interview to write a mathematical formula for WikiLeaks, Julian Assange wrote simply “Publish or Perish.”

took form. The fascination for us was simple. It was not just the intellectual challenge of making and breaking these cryptographic codes and connecting people together in novel ways. Rather, our will came from a quite extraordinary notion of power, which was that with some clever mathematics you can, very simply—and this seems complex in abstraction but simple in terms of what computers are capable of—enable any individual to say no to the most powerful state. So if you and I agree on a particular encryption code, and it is mathematically strong, then the forces of every superpower brought to bear on that code still cannot crack it. So a state can desire to do something to an individual, yet it is simply not possible for the state to do it—and in this sense, mathematics and individuals are stronger than superpowers.

HUO Could this have been an epiphany that then led to WikiLeaks?

JA Well, there is no singular epiphany. WikiLeaks is many different ideas pulled together, and certain economies permit it to be cheap enough to realize. There are some epiphanies, such as my theory of change, an understanding of what is important to do in life, an understanding of what information is important and what is not, ideas having to do with how to protect such an endeavor, and many small technical breakthroughs that go along the way. They're building blocks for my final view about what form things should take. It is a complex construction, like a truck, which has wheels, cranks, and gears, all contributing to the efficiency of the whole truck, and all of which need to be assembled in order for the truck to get to the destination that I want it to get to by a certain time. So to some degree the epiphany is not in the construction of this vehicle, because there are many little epiphanies in each part, but rather it is that there is a destination that this truck should go to and a way to get out of there.

HUO There's a path?

JA Yes, there's a path, and therefore there needs to be a truck that will go down this path. Then, it becomes a matter of assembling all the pieces necessary for this truck, which is a complex machine, technically and logistically, in terms of political presentation and cause and effect, and as an organization, and how I interact, personally, with all this. It's not a simple thing. I actually think that anyone who has built an institution around an idea will tell you this—that there are some ideas about where you want to go, but in order to get there you need to build an institution. In my case, I built—and got other people to help me build—both the machine and the institution.

HUO Because it's such a complex thing, I suppose it's not possible for you to just sketch it on a piece of paper.

JA No, this would be like sketching democracy—something that's not possible to draw. There are all these different parts, and each has their own drawing. It's the ensemble of all these parts that makes WikiLeaks work like it does. But perhaps there are some economic epiphanies. There's a universe of information, and we can imagine a sort of Platonic ideal in which we have an infinite horizon of information. It's similar to the concept of the Tower of Babel. Imagine a field before us composed of all the information that exists in the world—inside government computers, people's letters, things that have already been published, the stream of information coming out of televisions, this total knowledge of all the world, both accessible and inaccessible to the public. We can as a thought experiment observe this field and ask: If we want to use information to produce actions that affect the world to make it more just, which information will do that? So what we ask for is a way to color the field of information before us, to take a yellow highlighter and mark the interesting bits—all the information that is most likely to have that effect on the world, which leads it toward the state we desire. But what is the signal that permits us to do that? What can we recognize when we look at the world from a distance? Can we somehow recognize those things that we should mark as worthy candidates to achieve change? Some of the information in this tremendous field, if you look at it carefully, is faintly glowing. And what it's glowing with is the amount of work that's being put into suppressing it. So, when someone wants to take information and literally stick it in a vault and surround it with guards, I say that they are doing economic work to suppress information from the world. And why is so much economic work being done to suppress that information? Probably—not definitely, but probably—because the organization predicts that it's going to reduce the power of the institution that contains it. It's going to produce a change in the world, and the organization doesn't like that vision. Therefore, the containing institution engages in constant economic work to prevent that change. So, if you search for that signal of suppression, then you can find all this information that you should mark as information that should be released. So, it was an epiphany to see the signal of censorship to always be an opportunity, to see that when organizations or governments of various kinds attempt to contain knowledge and suppress it, they are giving you the most important information you need to know: that there is something worth looking at to see if it should be exposed and that censorship expresses weakness, not strength.

HUO So within that complex field of information this signal is actually a very clear sign.

JA Yes, within that complexity. Censorship is not only a helpful economic signal; it is always an opportunity, because it reveals a fear of reform. And if an organization is expressing a fear of reform, it is also expressing the fact that it can be reformed. So, when you see the Chinese government engaging in all sorts of economic work to suppress information passing in and out of China on the internet, the Chinese government is also expressing a belief that it can be reformed by information flows, which is hopeful but easily understandable because China is still a political society. It is not yet a fiscalized society in the way that the United States is for example. The basic power relationships of the United States and other Western countries are described by formal fiscal relationships; for example, one organization has a contract with another organization, or it has a bank account, or is engaged in a hedge. Those relationships cannot be changed by moderate political shifts. The shift needs to be large enough to turn contracts into paper, or change money flows.

HUO And that's why you mentioned when we last spoke that you're optimistic about China?

JA Correct, and optimistic about any organization, or any country, that engages in censorship. We see now that the US State Department is trying to censor us. We can also look at it in the following way. The birds and the bees, and other things that can't actually change human power relationships, are free. They're left unmolested by human beings because they don't matter. In places where speech is free, and where censorship does not exist or is not obvious, the society is so sewn up—so depoliticized, so fiscalized in its basic power relationships—that it doesn't matter what you say. And it doesn't matter what information is published. It's not going to change who owns what or who controls what. And the power structure of a society is by definition its control structure. So in the United States, because of the extraordinary fiscalization of relationships in that country, it matters little who wins office. You're not going to suddenly empty a powerful individual's bank account. Their money will stay there. Their stockholdings are going to stay there, bar a revolution strong enough to void contracts.

HUO It was around 2007 that WikiLeaks began developing contacts with newspapers. When was the first major coup?

JA We had published a number of significant reports in July 2007. One was a detailed two-thousand page list of all the military equipment in Iraq and Afghanistan, including unit assignments and the entire force structure. That was actually important but, interestingly, too complex to be picked up by the press, and so it had no direct impact. The first to be "recognized by the international press" was a private intelligence report by Kroll, an international private intelligence agency. This was produced by their London office, at great expense to the new Kenyan government, who were trying to find out where Daniel arap Moi and his cronies had smuggled the Kenyan treasury to. They managed to trace some three billion dollars worth of money, looted from Kenya, to London banks, Swiss banks, a ten-thousand-hectare ranch in Australia, properties in the US, companies in London, and so on.

HUO And that changed the Kenyan elections.

JA It swung the electoral vote by 10 percent, changing the predicted result of the election and leading to a rather extraordinary series of events, which ended with an overhaul of the structure of the government and the Kenyan constitution.

HUO So one could say that, for the first time, WikiLeaks produced reality?

JA Yes. Remember that in the theory of change I outlined, we have a starting point. We have some observations about reality, like where Daniel arap Moi stashed all his money. Then that information came to us, and then we spread it around in a way designed to maximize impact. And it entered the minds of many people, and caused them to act. The result was a change in the Kenyan election, which then went on to produce many other changes.

HUO And what would you say was the next big production of reality after that?

JA Some of them are harder to track. An election is fairly easy, because either the government or the opposition is elected. In Kenya, we saw a situation somewhere in the middle, where the opposition was elected, but the government wouldn't give up power, resulting in a power struggle. The next big disclosure was the two sets of the main manuals for Guantánamo Bay. We got one from 2003, which is the year after Guantánamo Bay started taking detainees. It revealed a new banality of evil. The Pentagon tried to say, "Oh, well, that was 2003. That was under General Miller." And the next year there was a different commander, so supposedly everything changed for the better. But courage is contagious, so someone stepped up to smuggle us the 2004 manual. I wrote a computer program to compare every single letter change between the 2003 Guantánamo Bay manual and the 2004 manual. We pulled out every goddamn difference and showed that the manual had gotten significantly worse; more despotic as time had advanced.

HUO To what extent do you think WikiLeaks prompted the current wave of protests in the Middle East?

JA Well, we tried. We don't know precisely what the cause and effect was, but we added a lot of oil to the fire. It's interesting to consider what the possible interactions are, and it's a story that hasn't really been told before. There's a great Lebanese newspaper called *Al Akhbar* who in early December of last year started publishing analyses of our cables from a number of countries in North Africa, including Tunisia, and also our cables about Saudi Arabia. As a result, *Al Akhbar*'s domain name was immediately attacked—redirected to a Saudi sex site. I didn't think there was such a thing, but apparently there is. Then, after *Al Akhbar* recovered they received a massive denial of service attack, and then much more sophisticated computer hackers came in and wiped them out entirely—their entire cable publishing operation, news stories, analyses, completely wiped out. The Tunisian government concurrently banned *Al Akhbar*, and WikiLeaks. Then, computer hackers who were sympathetic to us came and redirected the Tunisian government's own websites to us. There's one particular cable about Ben Ali's regime that covers his sort of internal, personal opulence and abuse, the abuse of proceeds. The *New Yorker* had an article describing that this was actually reported by an American ambassador.

HUO Right, that he had seen a cage with a tiger and abuses of power.

JA Right, so some people have reported that the people in Tunisia were very upset to hear about these abuses in this cable, and that inspired them to revolt. Some parts of that may be true, though two weeks later there was also a man who set himself on fire, the twenty-six-year-old street vendor, reportedly because of a dispute over a license in the market. And this took the rage to the streets. But my suspicion is that one of the real differences in the cables about Tunisia came in showing that the United States, if push came to shove, would support the army over Ben Ali. That was a signal, not just to the army, but to the other actors inside Tunisia, as well as to the surrounding states who might have been considering intervening with their intelligence services or military on behalf of Ben Ali. Similarly, some of the revelations about the Saudis caused Saudi Arabia to turn inward to deal with the fallout of those relations. And it is clear that Tunisia, as an example, then set off all the protests in the rest of the Middle East. So when we saw what was happening in Tunisia, we knew that Egypt was on the borderline, and we saw these initial protests in Egypt as a result of Tunisia.

We really tried very hard to get out lots and lots of cables, hundreds of cables, to show the abuses of Mubarak and so on, to give the protestors some additional fuel, but also to remove Western support for Mubarak. Now we also have Libya bordering Egypt. Working with the *Telegraph* in the UK, we pushed out 480 cables about Libya, revealing many abuses, but also intelligence about how the Libyan regime operated—we removed some of that Western support for the Libyan regime, and perhaps some of the support from the neighboring countries. The approach we took, and continue to take, with the demonstrations in the Middle East, has been to look at them as a pan-Arab phenomenon with different neighboring countries supporting each other in different ways. The elites—in most cases the dictatorial elite—of these countries prop each other up, and this becomes more difficult if we can get them to focus on their own domestic issues. Information produced by the revolutionaries in Egypt on how to conduct a revolution is now spreading into Bahrain. So this is being pushed out. We have pan-Arab activists spreading, and there exists Western support for these opposition groups, or for the traditional dictatorial leadership. And that support can be affected by exposing not just the internal abuses of power on the part of the regime, but also by exposing the nature of the relationship between the United States and these dictatorships. When the nature of this is exposed, we have a situation much like what actually happened with Joseph Biden, the vice president of the United States, who last year called me a "hi-tech terrorist." This year, he said that Mubarak was not a dictator, but presumably a democrat, and that he should not stand down. Look at how the behavior of Washington changed with regard to Mubarak just before he fell. After we released these cables about the relationship between the United States and Mubarak in foreign military subsidies and the FBI's training of torturers in Egypt, it was no longer possible for Biden to make these kinds of statements. It became completely impossible, because their own ambassadors were saying, just the year before, that Suleiman and Mubarak had been extremely abusive to the Egyptian people in so many ways—and that the United States had been involved in that abuse, in some way. So, if you're able to pull out regional support and Western support, and the underground activists are good, and are sharing and spreading information with each other, then I think we can actually get rid of quite a few of these regimes. Already we're seeing that Yemen and Libya might be the next to go.

HUO And you've got cables there as well.

JA Yes, there was a big one we did for Yemen, which revealed that the president had conspired with the United States to have the US bomb Yemen and say that the Yemeni Air Force did it. So that was a big revelation that we released in December of last year. Although the president is still there, he has been handing out tremendous concessions as a result. That's been happening throughout the Arab world now—some of them are literally handing out cash, and land, and offering cabinet posts to some of the more liberal forces in the country. They've been pulling election timetables forward, saying they'll resign at the next election—many interesting and important types of concessions. So, although I think we will see a few more go down, in the end it actually doesn't really matter whether the leader is removed or not. What matters is that the power structure of the government changes. If you make the concessions that the people want, you're actually nearly all of the way when you want to be a just and responsible elite.

HUO Constitutional monarchies?

JA Right, they can keep their monarch. In practice, you may have a society that is closer to what people want, a society that's much more civilized. But let me first qualify all that I've just said. I've received reports from people who have been on the ground in Egypt, in Bahrain, and have come over and briefed me personally on what's happening. And it seems very good that, for example, when Mubarak was removed he was the head of a patronage network that extended down into every position in Egypt, to the chief of the lawyers' syndicate to the groceries industry, to particular people in the army, and so forth. So every institution and every city council had its own mini-revolution after Mubarak was removed. I think that this change in the power structures underneath will, to a large degree, confine and constrain whoever assumes power later. Still, with these revolutions we have to be careful not to end up with something like the Orange Revolution, where you had liberal forces, but ones that were being literally paid by the United States and Western Europe. They opened up and liberalized Ukraine in important ways, but the result was that opportunists inside the country rose up and opportunists outside the country came in and really destroyed the social fabric of the country, leading within five years to a backlash that installed

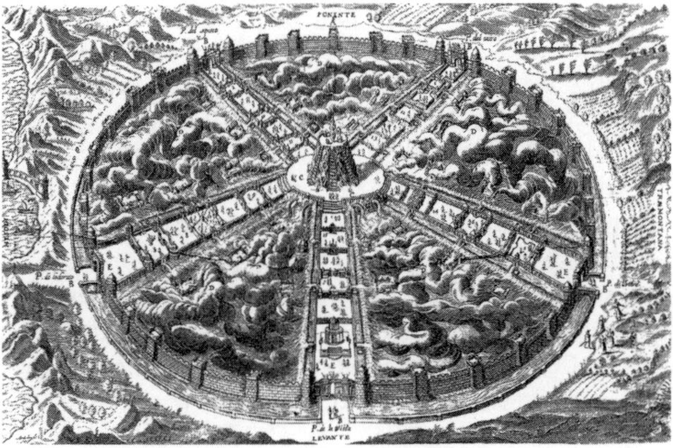

Bartolomeo Del Bene, *Civitas Veri* (*City of Truth*), 1609.

a much more Soviet-style president with close ties to Russia. These situations still need monitoring. One of the documents used by the revolutionaries in Cairo is quite interesting to consider. After Mubarak fell, we witnessed an extraordinary change in rhetoric from Hillary Clinton and the White House, from "Mubarak is a great guy and he should stay," to "Isn't it great what the Egyptian people have done? And isn't it great how the United States did it for them?" Likewise, there is an idea that these great American companies, Facebook and Twitter, gave the Egyptian people this revolution and liberated Egypt. But the most popular guide for the revolutionaries was a document that spread throughout the soccer clubs in Egypt, which themselves were the most significant revolutionary community groups. If you read this document, you see that on the first page it says to be careful not to use Twitter and Facebook as they are being monitored. On the last page: do not use Twitter or Facebook. That is the most popular guide for the Egyptian revolution. And then we see Hillary Clinton trying to say that this was a revolution by Twitter and Facebook.

HUO What about Iran? Does WikiLeaks have releases connected to Iran?

JA Yes. There have been more demonstrations there recently, so we've been releasing material on Iran consistently since December. And the reason it has been consistent is quite interesting. Media partners that we've worked with—such as *Der Spiegel*, the *New York Times*, the *Guardian*, *El País*, and *Le Monde*—have already been inclined to produce stories critical of Iran, so they trawled through the cables to find bad stories about Iran and have been publishing them since December at a tremendous pace. Beyond publishing the underlying cables, we haven't actually done any of our own work on Iran. But this is actually because the Western mainstream press is, as far as I can tell, inspired to produce bad stories about Iran as a result of geopolitical influences. So we didn't need to assist, while with Egypt we had to do all the work. We'd given these Western papers all the material, and they didn't do a goddamn thing about Egypt. However, this changed later on when we partnered with the *Telegraph*, who listened closely to our predictions.

HUO When you began working with what you call "media partners," was that a new strategy of concerted action of some sort?

JA It was a concerted action for a number of reasons. We've partnered with twenty or so newspapers across the world, to increase the total impact, including by encouraging each one of these news organizations to be braver. It made them braver, though it did not entirely work in the case of the *New York Times*. For example, one of the stories we found in the Afghan War Diary was from "Task Force 373," a US Special Forces assassination squad. Task Force 373 is working its way down an assassination list of some two thousand people for Afghanistan, and the Kabul government is rather unhappy about these extrajudicial assassinations—there is no impartial procedure for putting a name on the list or for taking a name off the list. You're not notified if you're on the list, which is called the Joint Priority Effects List, or JPEL. It's supposedly a kill or capture list. But you can see from the material that we released that about 50 percent of cases were just kill—there's no option to "capture" when a drone drops a bomb on someone. And in some cases Task Force 373 killed innocents, including one case where they attacked a school and killed seven children and no bona fide targets, and attempted to cover the whole thing up. This discovery became the cover story for *Der Spiegel*. It became an article in the *Guardian*. A story was written for the *New York Times* by national security correspondent Eric Schmitt, and that story was killed. It did not appear in the *New York Times*.

HUO I'm very interested in the whole idea of projects that are unrealized for having been censored, for being too big, or for other reasons. What are your unrealized projects or dreams?

JA There are so many. I'm not sure it's quite right to say they're unrealized because a lot will hopefully be realized, or are in the process of being realized. We're still too young to look back and say, oh, this is something we never managed to do. But there is one thing we tried to do and failed at, and it's very interesting. So, it was my view early on that the whole of the existing Fourth Estate was not big enough for the task of making sense of information that hadn't previously been public. To take our most recent case as an example, all the journalists in the world would not be enough to make complete sense of the four hundred thousand documents we released about Iraq, and, of course, they have other things to write about as well. I always knew this would be the case. I was very confident about having enough source material. So what we wanted to do was to take all that volunteer labor that is spent on writing about things that are not terribly important, and redirect it to material that we released, material that has a real potential for change if people assess it, analyze it, contextualize it, and push it back into local communities. I tried very hard to make that happen, but it didn't. I had looked at all these people writing Wikipedia articles, and all these people writing blogs about the issue du jour, whatever that was, especially in relation to war and peace. And I thought about the tremendous amount of effort that goes into that. When some of these bloggers are asked why they don't do original stories, and why they don't have opinion pieces and analysis of media output, they say, "Well, we don't have original sources so we can't write original material." So, surely, rather than write a Wikipedia article on something that would have no political influence, the opportunity to write about a secret intelligence report revealed to the world at that very moment would surely be irresistible, or so I thought.

But I'll give you an example to explain what I found instead. I released a secret intelligence report from the US Army Intelligence on what happened in Fallujah in the first battle of Fallujah in 2004, and it looked like a very good document—secret classification labels all over it, nice maps, color, a good, combined military and political description of what had happened, even *Al Jazeera*'s critical involvement. And there was analysis of what the US should have done, which was to conduct a political and psychological shaping operation before they went in. In the case of Fallujah, some US Military contractors had been grabbed and hanged in the town, and the US response gradually became an invasion of the town. So, rather than being a carefully preplanned operation, it had been a continual escalation. They hadn't set up the necessary political and media factors to support the military objective. It was an extremely interesting document, and we sent it to three thousand people. Nothing appeared for five days. Then, a small report by a friend of mine, Shaun Waterman at UPI, appeared as a newswire, and then another one by a guy, Davis Isenberg, who spends half his time at the Cato Institute, but published this for the *Asia Times*. But before the UPI report, there was nothing by any bloggers, by any Wikipedia-type people, by any leftist intellectuals, by any Arab intellectuals, nothing. What's going on? Why didn't anyone spend time on this extraordinary document? My conclusion is twofold. First, to be generous, these groups don't know how to lead the intellectual debate. They've been pacified into being reactive by the presence of the mainstream press. The front page of the *New York Times* says something and they react to that. Find what is newsworthy and tell the public that it is newsworthy. That's the generous interpretation, but I think the main factor, however, for those who are not professional writers, and perhaps many who are, is simply that they use their writing to advertise their values as conforming to those of their paper. The aim of most nonprofessional writers is to take the cheapest possible content that permits them to demonstrate their value of conformity to the widest possible selection of the group that they wish to gain the favor of.

So if one were a European leftist, why wouldn't going through that secret Fallujah document, assessing it, and writing about it properly advertise one's own values to their group? Well, actually, it would. But the cost/reward ratio doesn't work. The cost is that they would have to read and understand a thirty-page document, and then write about it in a way that would get this new information into their group and prove that it was important. But the *New York Times* and other mainstream press vehicles already do that, and they've also created the market for a response. One only needs to read a single article in the *New York Times* and issue a riposte or agreement. The frame and the audience have already been primed.

HUO Do you have dreams for the future?

JA Yes, many. I'll tell you about one, which is interesting. Orwell's dictum, "He who controls the present controls the past, and he who controls the past controls the future," was never truer than it is now. With digital archives, with these digital repositories of our intellectual record, control over the present allows one to perform an absolutely untraceable removal of the past. More than ever before, the past can be made to completely, utterly, and irrevocably disappear in an undetectable way. Orwell's dictum came about as result of what happened in 1953 to the Great Soviet Encyclopedia. That year, Stalin died and Beria fell out of favor. The Great Soviet Encyclopedia had a page and a half on Beria from before he fell out of favor, and it was decided that the positive description of Beria had to go. So, an addendum page was made and sent to all registered holders of this encyclopedia with instructions specifying that the previous page should be pasted over with the new page, which was an expanded section on the Bering Strait. However, users of the encyclopedia would later see that the page had been pasted over or ripped out—everyone became aware of the replacement or omission, and so we know about it today. That's what Orwell was getting at. In 2008, one of the richest men in the UK, Nadhmi Auchi—an Iraqi who grew rich under one of Saddam Husain's oil ministries and left to settle in the UK in the early 1980s—engaged in a series of libel threats against newspapers and blogs. He had been convicted of corruption in France in 2003 by the then magistrate Eva Joly in relation to the Elf Aquitaine scandal.

HUO She was the investigating judge. I remember reading about it when living in France at the time. It was in the daily news every day.

JA Right. So Nadhmi Auchi has interests all over the world. His Luxembourg holding company holds over two hundred companies. He has companies under his wife's name in Panama, interests in Lebanon and the Iraqi telecommunications market, and alleged involvement in the Italian arms trade. He also had a $2 billion investment around Chicago. He was also the principle financier of a man called Tony Rezko, who was one of Obama's most important fundraisers, for his various prepresidential campaigns, such as for the Senate. Rezko was also a fundraiser for Rob Blagojevich, the now disgraced governor of Illinois. Rezko ended up being convicted of corruption in 2008. But in 2008, Barack Obama was involved in a run against Hillary for the presidential nomination, so the media turned their attention to Barack Obama's fundraisers. And so attention was turned to Tony Rezko, who had been involved in a house purchase for Barack Obama. And attention was then turned to where some of the money for this house purchase might have come from, and attention was then turned to Nadhmi Auchi, who at that time had given Tony Rezko $3.5 million in violation of court conditions. Auchi then instructed Carter-Ruck, a libel firm in the UK, to go after stories mentioning aspects of his 2003 corruption conviction in France. And those stories started to be removed, everywhere.

HUO So they were literally erased from the digital archive?

JA Yes. The *Guardian* pulled three of the stories. The *Telegraph* pulled one. And there are a number of others. If you go to the former URLs of those stories you get a "page not found." It does not say that it was removed as the result of a legal threat. As far as we can tell, the story not only ceased to exist, but ceased to have ever have existed. Parts of our intellectual record are disappearing in such a way that we cannot even tell that they have ever existed.

HUO Which is very different from books, or newspapers, when some copies always survive.

JA Right. It's very different from newspapers, and it's very different from the Great Soviet Encyclopedia. The current situation is much, much worse than that. So what is to be done? I want to make sure that WikiLeaks is incorruptible in that manner. We have never unpublished something that we have published. And it's all very well for me to say that, but how can the public be assured? They can't. There are some things that we have traditionally done, such as providing cryptographic hashes of the files that we have released, allowing for a partial check if you have a copy of a specific list of cryptographic hashes. But that's not good enough. And we're an organization whose content is under constant attack. We have had over one hundred serious legal threats, and many intelligence and other actions against us. But this problem, and its solution, is also the solution to another problem, which is: How can we globally, consistently name a part of our intellectual history in such a way that we can accurately converse about it? And by "converse" I don't mean a conversation like we're having now, but rather one that takes place through history and across space. For example, if I start talking about the First Amendment, you know what I mean, within this current context of our conversation. I mean the First Amendment of the United States. But what does that mean? It's simply an abstraction of something. But what if the First Amendment was only in digital form, and someone like Nadhmi Auchi made an attack on that piece of text and made it disappear forever, or replaced it with another one? Well, we know the First Amendment is spread everywhere, so it's easily checkable. If we are confused in our conversation and unsure of what we're talking about, or we really want to get down to the details, it's in so many places that if I find a copy, it's going to be the same as the copy you find. But this is because it's a short and very ancient and very popular document. In the cases of these Nadhmi Auchi stories, there were eight that were removed, but actually this removal of material as a result of political or legal threats, it's happening everywhere. This is just the tip of the iceberg. And there are other forms of removal that are less intentional but more pernicious, which can be a simple matter of companies going under along with the digital archives they possess. So we need a way of consistently and accurately naming every piece of human knowledge, in such a way that their name arises out of the knowledge itself, out of its textual, visual, or aural representation, where the name is inextricably coupled to what it actually is. If we have that name, and if we use that name to refer to some information, and someone tries to change the contents, then it is either impossible or completely detectable by anyone using the name.

And actually, there is a way of creating names in such a way that they emerge from the inherent intellectual content of something, with no extrinsic component. Now, to make this a bit clearer, look at URLs as a name for something. There is the text for the King James Bible in Project Gutenberg, as a URL. It is the short, convenient name for this—we pass it around, and it expands to the text of the King James Bible. The problem with URLs is that they are authority names. A URL goes to some company or organization, and the name is completely controlled by the company or organization, which means that Project Gutenberg could conceivably copy the Talmud over the King James Bible but the "URL name" would remain the same. It is simply up to the whim of whoever controls that domain name.

HUO It's private.

JA Exactly. We all now suffer from the privatization of words, a privatization of those fundamental abstractions human beings use to communicate. The way we refer to our common intellectual record is becoming privatized, with different parts of it being soaked up into domain names controlled by private companies, institutions, or states. And we could have a sort of deliberate, pernicious change, like someone replacing "King James Bible" with "Talmud." Of course, that is unlikely to happen, but it is more likely that these companies will simply stop caring about that information. It no longer becomes profitable, or the company goes under. Or you have an important archive, and powerful figures are simply removing bits of history. So I've come up with this scheme to name every part of our intellectual history, and every possible future part of our intellectual history. And you can actually see the desire to do this as already being expressed in impoverished forms. When you look at something like TinyURL, or bit.ly, or one of these URL shorteners, you see that they are creating a short name from a longer and less comprehensible name, which is a URL. And those longer names are also short names or abstractions of whole texts, like the King James Bible.

We can also see it with dot-coms. Why shouldn't URLs be company, type of company, then, say, Coca-Cola? It could be us.beverages.company. Coca-Cola, right? But instead we just have coca-cola.com. We just go straight there with one word. And so, in our human language, we use words in such a way that we don't need to constantly provide a map with everything we say. Instead of having a big tree, it's a flat name space. Similarly, services like TinyURL are popular because it's just enough to get there. So my scheme is to pull out of every transmissible piece of intellectual content and intrinsic name that is mathematically bonded with that content. There's no registration, no server, no company that controls the coupling between a particular name and a piece of information. For example, for Project Gutenberg, a number of domain name registrars and Project Gutenberg itself couple the URL to King James Bible. And when you pass around that URL, you are actually passing around a dependence on the authority of the whole domain name system, and the dependence on the authority and the longevity of Project Gutenberg itself.

HUO So it becomes a kind of digital robustness.

JA That's right, and the idea is to create an intellectual robustness. So if you think about citations when using URLs, if we make an intellectual work, we stand on the shoulders of giants, which we all do, and we cite our influences in some way—not necessarily in a formal academic sense, but we simply refer to them by linking to the original thing you were looking at. URLs are an example of how we become intellectually dependent on this citation mechanism. But if that citation mechanism is actually like plasticine, and it is decaying all around us—if oligarchs and billionaires are in there ripping out bits of history, or connections between one part of history and another, because it interferes with their agenda—then the intellectual constructs that we are building up about our civilization are being built on something that is unstable. We are building an intellectual scaffold for civilization out of plasticine.

HUO So in that sense it's actually regressive compared to the book. One can't remove parts of a published book in the same way once the book is out in the world.

JA Exactly. So this new idea that I want to introduce to protect the work of WikiLeaks can also be extended to protect all intellectual products. All creative works that can be put into digital form can be linked in a way that depends on nothing but the intellectual content of the material itself—no reliance on remote servers or any organization. It is simply a mathematical function on the actual intellectual content, and people would need nothing other than this function.

HUO So that's your dream, that this could be implemented somehow.

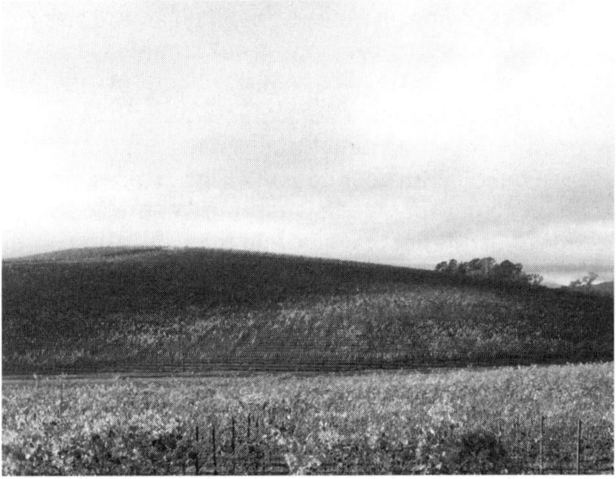

Goldin+Senneby, *After Microsoft*, 2007. Photo from installation. A few years after it was depicted in a Microsoft desktop image, the Sonoma Valley in California suffered a phylloxera bug infestation.

JA I think it's more than a dream, actually. It's been realized. It will be a new standard that, I hope, will apply to every intellectual work, a consistent way of naming every piece of intellectual creation, anything that can be digitized. And so, if we have a blog post, it will have a unique name. And if the post changes, the name will change, but the post and the name are always completely coupled. If we have a sonata and a recording of it, then it has a unique name. If we have a film in digitized form, then it has a unique name. If we have a leaked, classified document that we release, it has a unique name. And it's not possible to change the underlying document without changing the name. I think it's very important—a kind of indexing system for the Tower of Babel, or pure knowledge.

HUO I also suppose most people don't know about the danger that the archive can just be eliminated, no?

JA No, they don't, because the newspapers try to keep it all quiet. And everyone else tries to keep it quiet. If they don't, they will look weak, and they'll look like they've betrayed their readership by removing something their readership was interested in. And they'll encourage further attacks, because someone was successful in the first one. It is actually quite extraordinary that in the UK libel law, mentioning that you have removed something can be argued to be libelous. We saw this in a really flagrant case, where I had won the Index on Censorship Award for fighting against censorship.

HUO I was on the jury for it this year. I read that WikiLeaks won the Freedom of Expression award two years ago.

JA Oh really? Right, so after I won this, Martin Bright wrote a blog post in the *New Statesman* saying it was nice to meet Julian, and so on and so forth. And the next part of his blog post mentioned that these articles about Nadhmi Auchi's conviction for corruption have been disappearing. And here are the titles—he just put their titles in, as they were in the newspapers. A legal attack was then made on that particular blog post, the particular one that said we had won an award for anticensorship. And it was then censored. The list of articles was removed, and then the whole post was removed. That's how I became interested in Nadhmi Auchi, and we managed to find all these articles and get hold of a huge Pentagon report on Auchi's activities. And we managed to have the issue raised in Parliament, where they had a ninety-minute discussion on libel. But there's another big story: that Martin Bright lost his job at the *New Statesman*.

This text is an excerpt from Hans Ulrich Obrist, "In Conversation with Julian Assange, Part I," *e-flux journal*, no. 25 (May 2011).

Metahaven

Captives of the Cloud, Part III: All Tomorrow's Clouds

> A Massive, Expanding Surveillance State With Unlimited Power And No Accountability Will Secure Our Freedom by Hans Christian Andersen.
> —twitter.com/pourmecoffee[1]

> Violence arms itself with the inventions of Art and Science in order to contend against violence.
> —Carl von Clausewitz[2]

> Infrastructure is the technology that determines whether we live or die. Your infrastructure will kill you—if it fails, you fail.
> —Smári McCarthy[3]

The internet began as a place too complicated for nation-states to understand; it ended up, in the second decade of the twenty-first century, as a place only nation-states seem to understand. This has left omnipresent cloud giants Google and Yahoo!, in their own words, "outraged." They are helpless bystanders to US spy agencies as they extraterritorially, without permission, and aided by the Brits, break into data-center cables just to find out if the next bin Laden is out there posting kitten videos on YouTube. In response, Germany and Switzerland cash in on "secure" clouds; Russia fortifies its digital walls, incarcerates Pussy Riot, and offers asylum to Edward Snowden. Ecuador, which hosts Julian Assange in its London embassy as a political refugee, is to rebrand itself as a "haven for internet freedom."[4] These recent developments show the deep divide between the perspectives of various governments often claiming to restore national sovereignty over data space, and the very nature of the network itself, which is by definition transnational and borderless.

Internet and Society: The Dots Fight Back

General Keith Alexander was the director of the US National Security Agency. In his previous position as the head of the US Army Intelligence and Security Command, Alexander had an architectural firm decorate his so-called "Information Dominance Center" to look like the Starship Enterprise control room. This helped him gain political enthusiasm for spying. As *Foreign Policy* notes, "Lawmakers and other important officials took turns sitting in a leather 'captain's chair' in the center of the room and watched as Alexander, a lover of science-fiction movies, showed off his data tools on the big screen."[5] Alexander stepped down from his position after a taxing year at the helm of the spyboat. Before Edward Snowden gave thousands of the agency's top-secret documents to the press, Alexander used to publicly appear in full military attire. Sometimes he tried to win sympathy by taking the stage in a black T-shirt. In Las Vegas in 2012, Alexander urged digital troublemakers to join the NSA; he also pleaded that his agency operated lawfully and transparently. "We are overseen by everybody," he said.[6] But that was 2012. There were Patriot Act abuses, National Security Letters, and overzealous US prosecutors going after the Pirate Bay, Megaupload, WikiLeaks, and Chelsea Manning. As early as 2002, Mark Klein, an AT&T technician, witnessed an NSA-controlled wiretapping room in full operation in a data center in San Francisco. Later, a handful of US senators warned the media about a secret interpretation of the Patriot Act.[7] Nobody listened.

Then came Edward Snowden. As the magnitude of the NSA's surveillance of global internet and phone communications systems was being revealed, Keith Alexander changed his public relations tactics accordingly, appearing as an obedient, invisible bureaucrat. At Def Con 2013, Alexander presented his mission: "connecting the dots." Hoovering up everything from everyone up to three degrees of separation, or "hops," away from a known suspect in order to avert the next 9/11.[8] Columbia University law professor Eben Moglen called it, plainly, "spying on humanity."[9] Alexander was simply following an organization-wide, 9/11-centered PR memo given out as a script to its representatives.[10] Meanwhile, the NSA boasted that its surveillance had thwarted fifty-four terrorist attacks. However, that number lacked a real basis in fact, as the website ProPublica concluded after research.[11]

Keith Alexander's spaceship-style ops room sparks the same dark pleasure as the happy smile that sits on a hand-drawn NSA diagram about infiltration into Google and Yahoo![12] Alexander—the man who plotted to ruin the reputation of Islamic "radicalizers" by publicly revealing their porn site visits—is, after all, the pseudo-amicable human incarnation of neo-Stalinism.[13] The NSA uses corruption with martial agility. "Overseen" by opaque FISA courts, whose deliberations and decisions are secret, it has built a giant, data-slurping behemoth facility in Utah: a Walmart holding everyone's indeterminate digital past. Lost in a Berlusconian *bunga bunga* party, the NSA dreamed that its operations could go unseen forever. When asked by Congress if the NSA collected data on millions of Americans, the Director of National Intelligence, James Clapper, politely replied under oath: "No, sir ... not wittingly."[14] Clapper later apologized for misleading Congress by giving the "least untruthful answer."[15]

In one cunning operation, the NSA wielded its power to influence the technical standards on which the internet itself relies, including the pseudo-random number generators that occupy our computers' microchips. As Yochai Benkler asserts, the NSA "undermined the security of the SSL standard critical to online banking and shopping, VPN products central to secure corporate, research, and healthcare provider networks, and basic email utilities."[16] Jennifer Granick calls the NSA "an exceedingly aggressive spy machine, pushing—and sometimes busting through—the technological, legal and political boundaries of lawful surveillance."[17] Half-hearted attempts by the Obama administration to curb the agency's powers do little to reverse the situation. A newly appointed oversight committee is, as Benkler notes, stocked with insiders of the national security shadow world, even as the president claims, in awe-inspiring legalese, that it consists of "independent outside experts." Surprise: the Obama-appointed chief curator of the committee is James Clapper himself.[18] According to *Slate*, the proposed post-Snowden NSA reform bill, spearheaded by Democratic Senator Dianne Feinstein, "for the first time *explicitly authorizes*, and therefore entrenches in statute, the bulk collection of communications records, subject to more or less the same rules already imposed by the FISA Court. It endorses, rather than prohibits, what the NSA is already doing."[19] Showing his deep understanding of the privacy concerns of ordinary people, President Obama ordered an end to the NSA's spying on the IMF and the World Bank.[20]

Global Standards

Initially known for its quirky minimalism and math, Google has been working hard on its emotional impact on the public. Its vice president for marketing said in 2012 that "if we don't make you cry, we fail. It's about emotion, which is bizarre for a tech company."[21] Free e-mail, chat, and social networking are the Coke and McDonalds of the internet. But they don't promise Americanness. They promise connections. The largest cloud services are global standards. They are "natural," thus dominant focal points in the network, offering the largest potential social reward and likelihood of connection. "Network power" obscures less popular alternatives. The ultimate container of network power is the mobile app, which bypasses the shared internet and its protocols entirely. Instead, users are permanently within the corporation's digital walls rather than in and out of it through their web browser.[22]

Google's top executives Eric Schmidt and Jared Cohen published *The New Digital Age*, a trailblazing book about their political ideas, and how Google interacts with American power abroad. WikiLeaks's Julian Assange finds that in this paper-bound TED speech, a

> liberal sprinkling of convenient, hypothetical dark-skinned worthies appear: Congolese fisherwomen, graphic designers in Botswana, anticorruption activists in San Salvador and illiterate Masai cattle herders in the Serengeti are all obediently summoned to demonstrate the progressive properties of Google phones jacked into the informational supply chain of the Western empire.[23]

Indeed, every transaction on a Google server is an event under American jurisdiction.

Solutionism

The seizure of the internet by public-private technocrats, cloud providers, and secret services is an example of what Evgeny Morozov calls "solutionism."[24] Solutionism takes problems from social and political domains and recalibrates them as issues to be dealt with by technology alone. It brings them under the control of programmers, systems managers, Silicon Valley entrepreneurs, and their political avatars. Privacy and civil liberties are brushed aside: technological bypasses to political, social, and legal problems present themselves everywhere as progress. Who rules the internet on whose behalf, as ridiculously archaic as the question may sound, is a political and legal issue hijacked by solutionism. Milton Mueller phrases it slightly differently, as "who should be 'sovereign'—the people interacting via the Internet or the territorial states constructed by earlier populations in complete ignorance of the capabilities of networked computers."[25]

It is uncertain whether sovereignty is attainable at all; whether it, *as a concept*, holds up against the network, with its winner-takes-it-all technologies. Security expert Bruce Schneier says we must "take back" the internet: "Government and industry have betrayed the internet, and us. [...] We need to figure out how to re-engineer the internet to prevent this kind of wholesale spying. We need new techniques to prevent communications intermediaries from leaking private information."[26]

"No Water = No Data Center"

Infrastructure gets political when things don't work. As long as they do, no questions are asked. Drinking water is instantly political when nothing comes out of the faucet. Scarcity is a big politicizer. The broken internet grapples with an opposite problem: it bathes in an overabundance of apps and services, which thrive on the deterritorialization, expropriation, and extortion of life and data.

Benjamin Bratton calls this "microeconomic compliance."[27] It is probably the most convenient model of exploitation that has ever existed.

The people on the internet live in territories. They have citizenship. But this feedback loop doesn't activate political agency. What, after all, really *is* the connection between these things—"indifference, weariness and exhaustion from the lies, treachery and deceit of the political class" perhaps, as Russell Brand aptly stated?[28] Snapchat and Instagram are vehicles of social (and geopolitical) lure, endlessly more attractive than our tacit complicity with the machinery of representative politics. No one talks about political revolution, but the "Twitter Revolution" makes headlines in mainstream media. The only problem with our digital tools is their underlying standardization. We have an exhausted political machine on the one hand—"citizenship" forced into tiresome, backward rituals of participation. And on the other hand, we have the splendor and immediacy of love, friendship, connection, and technology built on microecononomic and geopolitical compliance. It seems an all too easy win for the latter. People have not considered the internet as a democratically governable structure. Decisions on the internet are delegated to a giant "don't be evil" mix.

Carne Ross, a former British diplomat and founder of Independent Diplomat, is looking for a solution beyond technology. "The balance between the individual and state needs to be more fundamentally altered," argues Ross. "New rules, in fact new kinds of rules, are needed. What is required is nothing less than a renegotiation of our contract with the state, and with each other."[29] Ross's proposal is not technical or bureaucratic. It is political in the most personal sense. Its problem is that it

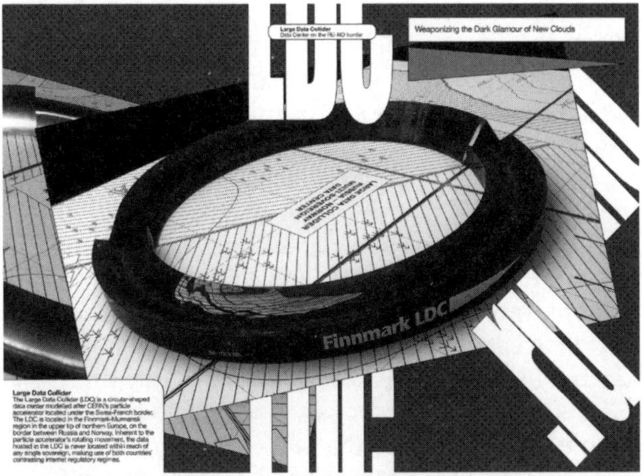

"Weaponizing the Dark Glamour of New Clouds." The search is on for critical borders [...] where noncompliant life is possible once again. The search is on for physical shelters [...] a castle, a ship, a mountain lair. We are weaponizing the dark glamour of new clouds! The Large Data Collider (LDC) is a circular-shaped data center modelled after CERN's particle accelerator located under the Swiss-French border. The LDC is located in the Finnmark-Murmansk region in the upper tip of northern Europe, on the border between Russia and Norway. Inherent to the particle accelerator's rotating movement, the data hosted in the LDC is never located within reach of any single sovereign, making use of both countries' contrasting internet regulatory regimes.

draws on decision making and enforcement structures that don't yet exist. People can look out for their common good only when they share common space and interest. They can work out their own polity better than central governments can, as Ross argues in his book *The Leaderless Revolution,* which promotes benign anarchism. Indeed, it is unclear how a renegotiation of the internet's social contract might be achieved without a unifying political mechanism for those in the network who can't bargain with the status quo. For those forced into compliance with its already dominant standards. Or for those who don't yet know the faces of their friends.

Some version of a social contract between citizens and governments (and corporations) was demonstrated in 2012 when citizens across the world successfully prevented the Stop Online Piracy Act and the Protect IP Act from coming into effect.[30] "Social contract" here means the possibility for people to bargain with the powerful about measures that threaten the common good. Major websites like Google and Wikipedia sided with the protesters against SOPA/PIPA, which somewhat nuances the familiar picture of "evil corporations." However, this type of legislation tends to silently return in a different guise, most recently with the highly secretive Trans-Pacific Partnership (TPP) agreement. The intellectual property portion of this agreement was leaked to WikiLeaks in November 2013.[31]

A social contract for the internet requires governments and corporations to welcome its political inconveniences. It requires them to radically cut back on surveillance. It requires them to unambiguously legalize leaks, cyberprotests, and online civil disobedience as legitimate political expressions. As noted in part 2 of this essay, in 2010 and 2011

UK- and US-based hacktivists used DDoS attacks to target private corporations that imposed a corporate embargo against WikiLeaks. The hacktivists responsible were hunted down and tried as criminals; the analogy between hacktivism and nonviolent civil disobedience was lost on the system and its judges. Cyberprotests express the *absence* of any verifiable and binding agreement between the system and its users. Digital equivalents to strikes and blockades are framed as crimes against property and profit.

The activist group NullifyNSA has taken on the task of disabling the NSA by shutting off the water supply to its data centers. The fascinating proposition is a stark reminder that the ability to spy and to store data is ultimately dependent on electricity and cooling. Thus, any "internet" operation is ultimately dependent upon the living environment and its resources. Michael Boldin, executive director of the Tenth Amendment Center and a NullifyNSA representative, explains:

> In Utah, the new data center is expected to need 1.7 million gallons of water per day to keep operational. That water is being supplied by a political subdivision of the state of Utah. Passage in that state of the 4th Amendment Protection act would ban all state and local agencies from providing material support to the NSA while it continues its warrantless mass surveillance. No water = no data center.[32]

NullifyNSA is politically on the libertarian-conservative Right. Its ideas are, as Boldin says,

> backed up by the advice of James Madison. The Supreme Court has repeatedly issued opinions

> over the years backing it up in a widely accepted legal principle known as the anti-commandeering doctrine. The cases go all the way back to the 1840s, when the court held that states couldn't be forced to help the feds carry out slavery laws. The latest was the Sebelius case in 2012, where the court held that states couldn't be compelled to expand Medicaid, even under threat of losing federal funding.[33]

NullifyNSA has all of the Right's typical rigor and determination even while it, as Boldin summarizes, seeks to be "transpartisan" in its efforts:

> Our goal is single-minded—stopping NSA spying. It's a long haul, and it's going to take significant effort and resistance from groups and people not used to working together. But the time is now to set aside differences for the liberty of all.[34]

The group explains the interdependency between the digital and the physical domains accurately and plainly. Almost no one on the Left seems to have talked about data centers quite like this. Boldin points out the ecological disaster that is the NSA, adding that "a state like Utah is in a state of near-constant drought. The fact that all these precious resources are being used to spy on the world should be disgusting to nearly everyone."[35] He goes on to analyze the NSA's distribution of data centers and its implications for the organization's own perception of its vulnerabilities:

> Back in 2006, the NSA maxed out the Baltimore area power grid. Insiders were very concerned that expansion of the NSA's "mission" could result in power outages and a "virtual shutdown

> of the agency." In reading their documents and press releases over the years, we know that a prime motivation in expanding their operations in Utah, Texas, Georgia, Colorado and elsewhere was to ensure that loads of resources like water, electricity, and more, were distributed. That means they know they have an Achilles heel.[36]

After all, the NSA's weak point may be its insatiable appetite for electricity rather than its breaches of the Constitution. NullifyNSA, a group of conservatives with a practical bent, hints at the under-investigated relationship between data centers and their physical geographies.[37]

The Possibility of an Iceland

"Data sovereignty" is a phrase of recent coinage describing two distinct trends in internet hosting. The first is the increasing tendency of nation-states to make networks that fit within national borders so they can completely control what goes on inside the network. Russia and China both have their own Facebook and Twitter, controlled at all times by the state. The only advantage of these networks is that they are not under the auspices of the NSA. Boutique data sovereignty is a viable economic strategy in the wake of global surveillance. Secure "e-mail made in Germany" is now hot; user data are protected by supposedly watertight German privacy laws.[38] Swisscom, Switzerland's telecommunications company, which is majority-owned by the government, is developing a secure "Swiss cloud" aspiring to levels of security and privacy that US companies can't guarantee.[39] Luxembourg and Switzerland's recent wealth havens, or freeports for property in transit—mostly expensive art—also offer data storage.[40]

The second definition of "data sovereignty" is personal. Every internet user should "own" all of his or her online data. Jonathan Obar critiques the idea, but for the wrong reasons. He claims that personal data sovereignty is fallible because we have now "big data":

> Recent calls for personal data sovereignty, or the ability for a single individual to have control over all of their personal data, represent a similar fantasy. Had we the faculties and the system for enabling every digital citizen the ability to understand and continually manage the evolving data-driven internet, to control the data being collected, organized, analyzed, repurposed and sold by every application, commercial organization, non-commercial organization, government agency, data broker and third-party, to understand and provide informed consent to every terms of service agreement, and privacy policy—would we have time to actually use the internet? To work? To have a family? To do anything else? This is the fallacy of personal data sovereignty in a digital universe increasingly defined by big data.[41]

The saying goes that if your only tool is a hammer, all problems look like nails. Data may need to be prevented from becoming "big" in the first place. Obar inadvertently shows the conceptual similarity of "big data" to bad financial products that no one understands. Personal data have become the credit default swaps of the cloud, building a bubble economy as unsustainable as the subprime mortgages that triggered the 2008 financial collapse. The NSA participates in this corporate feeding frenzy as much as cloud providers do. There is, in this light, nothing strange about wanting more personal control over one's personal information. A clear model for it is still missing, but a 2011 paper by US Naval Graduate School students notes that "data sovereignty provides an explicit tool to break a level of abstraction provided by the cloud. The idea of having the abstraction of the cloud when we want it, and removing it when we don't, is a powerful one."[42] To break down the abstraction of the cloud, the internet needs to be more localized.[43]

An example of the boundaries between nation-state politics and online politics being traversed is Iceland—a sparsely populated island nation in the North Atlantic that has come to be one of the rare places in the West where political alternatives get a chance. On July 5, 2008, John Perry Barlow gave a speech at the Reykjavík Digital Freedoms Conference. The talk was titled "The Right to Know."[44] Barlow took his audience on a journey that began with the wordless prehistory of Homo sapiens; he ended by pitching a somewhat unexpected update of the "data haven"—an offshore sanctuary for information prefigured by cyberpunk science fiction. Iceland, Barlow said, could become a "Switzerland of Bits"—a haven for digital freedom, a safe harbor for transparency, a sanctuary for the Enlightenment. Cyberspace, for Barlow, was both global and local, and "the more local it becomes, the more global it becomes."

A mere three months after Barlow's talk, Iceland's banks collapsed. Relative to country size, it was the largest banking crisis ever suffered by a single state.[45] Iceland's recovery from the banking crisis became an opportunity for national democratic and ethical reforms. A twenty-five-strong Constitutional Assembly rewrote the constitution, and a crowdsourcing effort introduced thousands of comments and hundreds of concrete proposals from citizens directly into the legislative process.[46] On June 16, 2010, Iceland's parliament cast a unanimous vote for IMMI, the Icelandic Modern Media Initiative. IMMI combined a "greatest hits" of freedom of speech and libel protection laws that existed in various other countries.[47] And while the idea for the Switzerland of Bits came from Barlow, a cofounder of the Electronic Frontier Foundation, WikiLeaks also had an influence on IMMI's legal architecture: Assange's whistleblowing platform ran separate hosting agreements with ISPs in various countries, benefiting from their laws.

The internet activist, software developer, and writer Smári McCarthy is IMMI's executive director. Much of the organization's impact depends on Iceland's ability to influence new international standards, and to attract companies and organizations to host data.[48] At the same time, McCarthy is involved in the development of MailPile, a secure e-mail application and collective decision-making software that is in the political lineage of "liquid democracy"—a form of delegative democracy. A founding member of the Icelandic Pirate Party, much of McCarthy's work takes place on the cutting blade of law and code.

McCarthy describes IMMI as an "NGO somewhere half-way between a think tank and a lobby group." Can IMMI transform Iceland into a Switzerland of Bits? McCarthy is unambiguous in his answer: "Yes. And not just Iceland." He explains: "Look through the legal code, the social structure, and pretty easy entry points start to become obvious. Treat society as a Wiki—a publicly editable social space—and be bold."[49]

James Grimmelmann, who is a professor of law at the University of Maryland, comments:

> I think Iceland's plans are viable and well-considered. They are using Iceland's legal sovereignty, real-world isolation, global connectedness, and stable political system to advance a series of pro-expression policy goals. They're doing so in ways that don't fundamentally alter Iceland's nature as a modern democratic state, but rather play to the theoretical and practical strengths of that model. And McCarthy shows a good understanding of what the limits to this strategy are, in terms of effects beyond Iceland's borders.[50]

In Iceland, the classical data haven has evolved into a more advanced combination of policy, software, coding, and advocacy, removing itself from the anarcho-libertarian free-for-all. The internet, here, is an experiment with democracy. The development of online communication and coordination tools certainly falls within IMMI's scope. The organization's technical director, Eleanor Saitta, explains its larger democratic vision:

> The Internet is an $11 trillion economy, globally. It's a largely post-national economy (to a degree that quantizing it in the currency of a single nation feels mildly ridiculous), but the effects of that economy touch specific people, on specific pieces of ground. What Iceland is becoming is a nation deeply integrated with the internet at an economic level. There are ways in which that resonates strongly and typologically with the notion of the "island"—it's a resonance we use at IMMI, sometimes, to explain our work. However, the fact that it's happening in a Scandinavian country also makes a big difference. Iceland has obviously seen its economy turned upside

> down by the massive financial looting of the past decade, but the fundamental collectivist nature of the country remains. This stands in stark contrast with the hyper-libertarian, "damn anyone who can't keep up" attitude common among crypto-anarcho-capitalists.
>
> Building a data haven means something very different when you do it in a place where people live and have lived for centuries, in a place where it is a national project, not an also-ran that at best injects a little cash and at worst exists only as network colonialism. The notion of resilience is critical here, too. While some large hosting companies are tentatively approaching sustainability as a concept, they're doing so to get punishing energy budgets down to something manageable and to comply with regulatory forces. Resilience is much more than sustainability; it meshes very closely with left-information politics, and in doing so, combines to provide a basic political platform much stronger than each alone. Hence in Europe, the limitations of the Pirates as (until their recent initial steps) a single-issue party; likewise, the Greens, mostly working from a relatively obsolete sustainability-only platform.[51]

Saitta sees the networked politics of the near future to be strongly interconnected with locality, so that the outcome is neither a purely nation-state-based affair nor commitment-free internet clicktivism. Such politics spring from a space of exception created both within the context of Iceland as a community and within the internet as a human network:

> As translated into the material context of neoliberal capitalism, this provides guidance for some

> specific corporation to decide where they wish to host servers, but the creation is an act of the commons. [...] Now, as to how network culture can create its own room in which to breathe, I think that's a much more interesting question, one where I think we will see networked post-institutional political non-state actors continuing to take a lead, to see that their politics leaks out from the internet into the real locality in which they may live. In creating room for themselves, they are in part looking at their place in the web of mutual obligation and stepping up to take their part in the deeper polis as much as they are drawing on and reinforcing the obligations of their localities to them.[52]

The design agenda for the future of the internet seems straightforward: become a networked, post-institutional, non-state actor and start right where you live with political reform. The idea of a "localized internet" anticipates increasing overlaps between digital and physical social structures. Eventually, all social structures take on physicality. Saitta:

> I joke that my ten year stretch goal is to kill the nation state, but really, I don't think that's particularly necessary. There will always be territorial organizational structures, but they're only one possible structure among many that can interact. I favor building up new alternatives, starting now. If we somehow magically did manage to destroy the nation state before there was anything to replace it, we'd all, quite frankly, be fucked. I'm a road fetishist. I really like roads. And power. And food. Those are all currently mostly provided by or coordinated through the state. Kill the state now, and life looks grim. That said,

waiting until you've got a fully functional alternative before taking any kind of political action aimed at common emancipation is equally dumb, as is investing more effort in actively hostile systems when you can't actually change them. I'm a realist, in the end. I want less suffering, for everyone, in both the short and long term, and that doesn't come out of the barrel of any one ideology, just as surely as it isn't going to come by sticking to the straight and narrow of our status quo handbasket.[53]

Servers in the Clouds

The possibility for a network—centralized, decentralized, or distributed—to override jurisdiction and state power is a foundational dream of the internet, as well as a perpetual mirage shaped and inspired by science fiction. What was once thought to be "the internet"—a deterritorialized space among a world of nation-states—is known today to be incredibly saturated with the spatial implications of borders, jurisdictions, and sovereignty. New approaches to guaranteeing internet freedoms are increasingly becoming premised on literally eluding these spatial implications of a (perhaps always) reterritorialized internet.

The Pirate Bay is a famous Sweden-based P2P BitTorrent sharing service. Recently, access to its service was blocked in various countries and the site's three founders were sentenced on charges of enabling the violation of intellectual property by facilitating illegal downloads. At the time of this writing, the final sentences are still pending in Sweden, where the case has been brought to the Supreme Court. Apart from being a file sharing site, the Pirate Bay is also a kind of living manifesto for the cyber-anarchic internet; it has issued various memes, it had plans to buy the Principality of Sealand, and in March 2012, it issued an unusual announcement that detailed the next possibility for evading jurisdiction. The Pirate Bay announced that it would start hosting content on airborne drones, evading law enforcement and copyright claims.[54] The Pirate Bay's own tagline was: "Everyone knows WHAT TPB is. Now they're going to have to think about WHERE TPB is." While clearly part of the Pirate Bay's amazing array of publicity stunts and memes, the plan is not technologically impossible. In the same month, the website *TorrentFreak* interviewed Tomorrow's Thoughts Today, an organization exploring "the consequences of fantastic, perverse and underrated urbanisms," which has built a set of wirelessly connected drones operating like a mobile darknet.[55] These machines constitute what the organization says is "part nomadic infrastructure and part robotic swarm":

> We have rebuilt and programmed the drones to broadcast their own local wifi network as a form of aerial Napster. They swarm into formation, broadcasting their pirate network, and then disperse, escaping detection, only to reform elsewhere.[56]

Though some of the Pirate Bay's servers reportedly now operate out of a secret mountain lair,[57] its proposed Low Orbit Server Stations (LOSS) would host servers that redirect traffic to a secret location. Though the plan is, conceptually, a call for a deterritorialized internet space, it seems somewhat oblivious to the lingering legal implications of having a localized server. Tomorrow's Thoughts Today's *Electronic Countermeasures* project, on the other hand, is based equally on deterritoriality as well as locality. Liam Young, cofounder of Tomorrow's Thoughts Today, reflects:

> As a culture we are having to come to some kind of collective agreement about what copyright means in a digital age. Who owns information as it becomes a digital commodity. Industries and governments are too slow to adapt and projects like Electronic Countermeasures or The Pirate Bay drone servers are imagined for the purposes of examining these issues and speculating on new possibilities. The privatization of knowledge is something we all need to be thinking about. Moves toward the storage of all our data in the cloud, a cloud managed by private companies or nation states, is potentially very dangerous. Even if this drone network isn't implemented as a practical solution we would be just as interested if the work made us question what is happening and what alternatives there may be in data distribution.[58]

Young's "nomadic speculative infrastructures" are relatively harmless in areas that are already heavily covered by regulations. But in less regulated areas, they might become something more.

Failed States in International Waters

An island can be created either by expressly carving out law, or by not legislating at all. State power works both ways; negatively, some jurisdictions on the world map lack control over their borders and have no centrally administered rule of law—they are "'lawless' zones in various states of anarchy, poverty, decay and crime."[59] In international relations it has become customary to apply a set of rules to define statehood; a state needs to have control over borders, a centrally administered rule of law (even if a dictatorship), and to a considerable extent, it needs to comply with customary practices in "international society" or "the international system." As a normative categorization, this presupposes the institutional characteristics of Western statehood as the one legitimate form to which all states should aspire.

The term "failed state" was introduced in Western foreign policy to signify any state authority not substantially fulfilling either one of these criteria. Since the introduction of the term, various failed states have emerged, many of them in Africa: Somalia, Yemen, Sudan, and Mali are but a few examples. The designation of "failure" seems legitimate when applied to raging civil wars, violent conflicts, and their fallout. But it also points back to the political process, ideology, or entity that hands out the designation. In other words: one man's failed state is, potentially, another man's utopia. As Pierre Englebert and Denis M. Tull assert in their study on failed states and nation building in Africa:

> The goal of rebuilding collapsed states is to restore them as "constituted repositories of power and authority within borders" and as "performers and suppliers of political goods." Almost all African states, however, have never achieved such levels of statehood. Many are "states that fail[ed] before they form[ed]." Indeed, the evidence is overwhelming that most of Africa's collapsed states at no point in the postcolonial era remotely resembled the ideal type of the modern Western polity.[60]

Failed states can be seen as their own political model; a "failure" to produce outcomes compliant with accepted norms can be seen as a "success" in arenas where such norms are disputed. Failed states don't govern, don't hold a monopoly of violence, don't control borders, and don't enforce a rule of law. They are at the outer borders of the international system and the world political map. Insofar as they are still, partially at least, inside that system, they may present new opportunities for internet practice, new sovereignties for hosting, and new areas for nomadic infrastructure. James Grimmelmann outlines some of the complications that this model faces:

> The problem that failed states face is that it's difficult to create telecommunications infrastructure without security and a functioning economic system. They have domains that may not be effectively under their control and are backed up by an international body. Their internet infrastructure frequently relies on technological providers who operate from out-of-state; what is available is often of limited connectivity and quite expensive. *De facto*, these places of weak enforcement may tend to function as data havens—particularly when there are many of them—but the reliability of provisioning any specific content is low.[61]

A country like Cameroon presents a borderline case. There is digital infrastructure in the country, but its statehood appears to descend into failure anyway. In 2008, Ozong Agborsangaya-Fiteu warned that in his country, "unless there is clear political reform that will allow citizens to finally enjoy basic civil liberties—including full freedom of expression, free elections and the rule of law—a crisis is inevitable."[62] About a year later, internet security firm

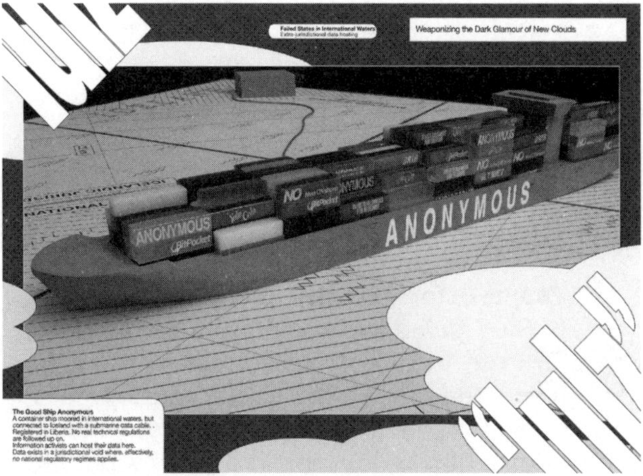

"Weaponizing the Dark Glamour of New Clouds." The Good Ship Anonymous: A container ship anchored in international waters, but connected to Iceland with a submarine data cable, registered in Liberia. No real technical regulations are followed up on. Information activists can host their data here. Data exists in a jurisdictional void where, effectively, no national regulatory regimes applies.

McAfee revealed that Cameroonian websites were the most dangerous in the world for their users—even more than Hong Kong websites. McAfee found that Cameroon boasts a shadow industry of "typo-squatting" domains. Typo-squatting exploits users who mistype a popular URL, leading them to a scam website. Cameroon's domain name extension (".cm") differs but one character from the ubiquitous ".com"—hence Cameroon's success in building popular Potemkin destinations based on typos. Facebook.cm, apparently, leads to a highly offensive porn ad.[63] Is the boom in "cybercrime" from countries with weak oversight some sort of data haven byproduct? Grimmelmann comments: "Yes, you could put it that way: I'm reminded of the Eastern European virus-writing 'industry.'"[64]

People before Clouds

In *The Truman Show*—with Jim Carrey starring as Truman, the unwitting protagonist of a real life sitcom—the series director, or "Creator," makes an emotional appeal to Truman in an attempt to convince him that reality *out there* is no better, and no more real, than reality *inside* the giant suburban biosphere that was built for him. Truman's world is a world without visible signs of government; there are only signposts, and warnings, and red tape, at the *edges* of its liveable reality.

Government, for Truman, is the drone-like perspective of the series director. Isn't the point of view offered by former NSA Director Keith Alexander similarly comforting? Alexander begins almost every other sentence with the phrase "from my perspective." He won't really ever refer to anyone else's perspective, but it sounds as if he could. "From my perspective" sounds almost *modest*. Alexander has innumerable grandchildren and their love for iPads

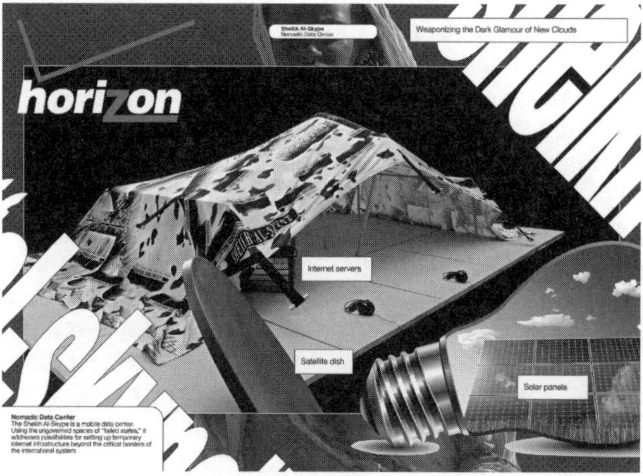

"Weaponizing the Dark Glamour of New Clouds." Nomadic Data Center: The Sheikh al-Skype is a mobile data center. Using the ungoverned spaces of "failed states," it addresses possibilities for setting up temporary internet infrastructure beyond the critical borders of the international system.

illustrates, for the general, the countless possibilities and threats of the "cyber." Alexander's NSA is about "saving lives," as if it were a virtual ambulance rushing to rescue the digitally wounded. He brags about his agency's "tremendous capabilities" as if he were a middle-aged computer room systems manager boasting about the robustness of his Apache server. How do we best escape the custody of this virtual father figure, and others standing in line to take over once he steps down? How do you liberate a society that has the internet?

No one really knows, but to begin with, we need to get rid of the deceptive gibberish of technocracy. We have become the enslaved consumers of nonsensical abstractions. No one has ever seen the cloud, or its main tenant, "big data." These are objects of ideology and belief, and at times, treacherous harbingers of Big Brother. Those who argue that we need new tools to fix the broken internet are right, but they shouldn't forget that we also need the right polities to use them. The spectacle of technology needs to be unleashed to further the ends of those who wish for a way of their own, rather than rule over others. People are real. Clouds aren't.

Reformist and legislative currents in the ongoing surveillance drama have put their stakes in institutions that are themselves the repositories of vested interests. This bureaucratic apparatus is incapable of reform, because it can't fire itself from the job it has done so badly for so long. Shielded from the most basic democratic accountability, an opaque data orgy plays out inside the boardrooms, spy bases, and data warehouses of surveillance.

Those who promote that we should, in response, encrypt all our communications, seem to have a strong point. Anonymizing technologies and other protections bring to mind the sort of privacy that was once expected from a sealed envelope or a safe. Yet on the other hand, the very argument for total encryption is the flipside of solutionism; it seeks for technology to solve a political problem. Encryption can't, by itself, heal the internet.

Separate from these two strands is a third possibility: a localized internet, one that wields the double-edged sword of political and technological reforms, and saves the network from being a looming abstraction manipulated by Silicon Valley entrepreneurs. We should be able to explain the network to each other in the simplest possible terms, in mutual agreement. We should not need to be under the gray cloud of a super-jurisdictional, abstract *Totalstaat.* We deserve to wake up from the dreamless lethargy that is induced by the techno-managerial matrix, and look each other in the eye.

New polities, new technologies, and new jurisdictions are needed—all three of them, in abundance. Democracy and people need to forever come before clouds. Drinking water needs to always be prioritized over spying. Life itself is the enemy of surveillance.

Written by Daniel van der Velden, Vinca Kruk, and Alysse Kushinski (research assistant).

1
pourmecoffee, Twitter post, August 16, 2013, 4:11 a.m.

2
Carl von Clausewitz, *On War*, trans. J. J. Graham (London, 1873). See http://www.clausewitz.com/readings/OnWar1873/BK1ch01.html.

3
Smári McCarthy, "Iceland: A Radical Periphery in Action. Smári McCarthy Interviewed by Metahaven," *Volume* 32 (2012): 98–101.

4
Rosie Gray, "Equador Rebrands Itself as the Home of Internet Freedom," *BuzzFeed World*, December 6, 2013, http://www.buzzfeed.com/rosiegray/ecuador-bids-to-be-seen-as-the-home-of-internet-freedom.

5
Shane Harris, "The Cowboy of the NSA: Inside Gen. Keith Alexander's All-Out, Barely-Legal Drive to Build the Ultimate Spy Machine," *Foreign Policy*, September 9, 2013, http://www.foreignpolicy.com/articles/2013/09/08/the_cowboy_of_the_nsa_keith_alexander?page=full.

6
Kim Zetter, "NSA Chief Tells Hackers His Agency Doesn't Create Dossiers on All Americans," *Wired*, August 27, 2012, http://www.wired.com/threatlevel/2012/07/nsa-chief-denies-dossiers/.

7
Senator Ron Wyden: "We're getting to a gap between what the public thinks the law says and what the American government secretly thinks the law says." Quoted in Mike Masnick, "Senators Reveal That Feds Have Secretly Reinterpreted the PATRIOT Act," *Techdirt*, May 26, 2011.

8
"All of your friends, that's one hop. Your friends' friends, whether you know them or not—two hops. Your friends' friends' friends, whoever they happen to be, are that third hop. That's a massive group of people that the NSA apparently considers fair game." Quoted in Philip Bump, "The NSA Admits It Analyzes More People's Data Than Previously Revealed," *Atlantic Wire*, July 17, 2013, http://www.theatlanticwire.com/politics/2013/07/nsa-admits-it-analyzes-more-peoples-data-previously-revealed/67287/.

9
Eben Moglen, "Snowden and the Future, Part 1: Westward the Course of Empire" (lecture, Columbia Law School, October 9, 2013), http://snowdenandthefuture.info/PartI.html.

10
Jason Leopold, "Revealed: NSA Pushed 9/11 as Key 'Sound Bite' to Justify Surveillance," *Al Jazeera*, October 30, 2013, http://america.aljazeera.com/articles/2013/10/30/revealed-nsa-pushed911askeysoundbitetojustifysurveillance.html.

11
Bump, "NSA Admits It Analyzes More People's Data Than Previously Revealed."

12
Barton Gellman and Ashkan Soltani, "NSA Infiltrates Links to Yahoo, Google Data Centers Worldwide, Snowden Documents Say," *Washington Post*, October 30,

2013, http://www.washingtonpost.com/world/national-security/nsa-infiltrates-links-to-yahoo-google-data-centers-worldwide-snowden-documents-say/2013/10/30/e51d661e-4166-11e3-8b74-d89d714ca4dd_story.html.

13

A document that reveals this NSA plot was published by the *Huffington Post*. The document's origin is "DIRNSA," the agency's director. See Glenn Greenwald, Ryan Gallagher, and Ryan Grim, "Top-Secret Document Reveals NSA Spied on Porn Habits as Part of Plan to Discredit 'Radicalizers,'" *Huffington Post*, November 26, 2013, http://www.huffingtonpost.com/2013/11/26/nsa-porn-muslims_n_4346128.html?1385526024.

14

Ruth Marcus, "James Clapper's 'Least Untruthful' Answer," *Washington Post*, June 13, 2013, http://articles.washingtonpost.com/2013-06-13/opinions/39950057_1_oversight-national-intelligence-national-security-agency.

15

Jason Howerton, "James Clapper Apologizes for Lying to Congress about NSA Surveillance: 'Clearly Erroneous,'" *The Blaze*, July 2, 2013, http://www.theblaze.com/stories/2013/07/02/james-clapper-apologizes-for-lying-to-congress-about-nsa-surveillance-clearly-erroneous/.

16

Yochai Benkler, "Time to Tame the NSA Behemoth Trampling Our Rights," *Guardian*, September 13, 2013, http://www.theguardian.com/commentisfree/2013/sep/13/nsa-behemoth-trampling-rights.

17

Jennifer Granick, "NSA SEXINT Is the Abuse You've All Been Waiting For," *Just Security*, November 29, 2013, http://justsecurity.org/2013/11/29/nsa-sexint-abuse-youve-waiting/.

18

Luke Johnson, "James Clapper, Director of National Security Intelligence Who Misled Congress to Establish Surveillance Review Group," *Huffington Post*, August, 13, 2013, http://www.huffingtonpost.com/2013/08/13/james-clapper_n_3748431.html.

19

David Weigel, "New NSA Reform Bill Authorizes All the NSA Activity That Was Making You Angry," *Slate*, November 1, 2013, http://www.slate.com/blogs/weigel/2013/11/01/new_nsa_reform_bill_authorizes_all_the_nsa_activity_that_was_making_you.html.

20

Mark Hosenball, "Obama Halted NSA Spying on IMF and World Bank Headquarters," *Reuters*, October 31, 2013, http://www.reuters.com/article/2013/10/31/us-usa-security-imf-idUSBRE99U1EQ20131031.

21

Claire Cain Miller, "Google Bases a Campaign on Emotions, Not Terms," *New York Times*, January 1, 2012, http://www.nytimes.com/2012/01/02/technology/google-hones-its-advertising-message-playing-to-emotions.html?_r=2&.

22

See our discussion of network power in the book *Uncorporate Identity*, ed. Metahaven and

Marina Vishmidt (Baden: Lars Müller Publishers, 2010).

23
Julian Assange, "The Banality of 'Don't Be Evil,'" *New York Times*, June 1, 2013.

24
See "Evgeny Morozov on Technology—The Folly of Solutionism," *Economist.com*, May 2, 2013, http://www.economist.com/blogs/babbage/2013/05/evgeny-morozov-technology.

25
Milton L. Mueller, *Networks and States: The Global Politics of Internet Governance* (Cambridge, MA: MIT Press, 2010), 268.

26
Bruce Schneier, "The US Government Has Betrayed the Internet: We Need to Take It Back," *Guardian*, September 5, 2013, http://www.theguardian.com/commentisfree/2013/sep/05/government-betrayed-internet-nsa-spying.

27
Benjamin Bratton, "Some Trace Effects of the Post-Anthropocene: On Accelerationist Geopolitical Aesthetics," *e-flux journal*, no. 46 (July 2013), http://www.e-flux.com/journal/some-trace-effects-of-the-post-anthropocene-on-accelerationist-geopolitical-aesthetics/.

28
"Newsnight: Paxman vs Brand—Full Interview," YouTube video, 10:46, posted by "BBC Newsnight," October 23, 2013, http://www.youtube.com/watch?v=3YR4CseY9pk.

29
Carne Ross, "Citizens of the World, Unite! You Have Nothing to Lose But Your Data," *Guardian*, October 31, 2013, http://www.theguardian.com/commentisfree/2013/oct/31/citizens-world-unite-data?CMP=twt_gu.

30
The US Congress withdrew the bills proposing SOPA and PIPA in February 2012 after widespread protests. Around the same time, the Anti-Counterfeiting Trade Agreement (ACTA) was successfully defeated by citizens in the European Union.

31
"Secret Trans-Pacific Partnership Agreement (TPP) - IP Chapter," WikiLeaks, November 13, 2013, https://wikileaks.org/tpp/pressrelease.html.

32
Michael Boldin/NullifyNSA, e-mail to the authors, December 4, 2013.

33
Ibid.

34
Ibid.

35
Ibid.

36
Ibid.

37
For NullifyNSA, see http://nullifynsa.com/.

38
Elizabeth Dwoskin and Frances Robinson, "NSA Internet Spying Sparks Race to Create Offshore Havens for Data Privacy,"

Wall Street Journal, September 27, 2013, http://online.wsj.com/news/articles/SB10001424052702303983904579096082938662594.

39
Caroline Copley, "Swisscom Builds 'Swiss Cloud' as Spying Storm Rages," *Reuters*, November 3, 2013.

40
"Freeports: Über-Warehouses for the Ultra-Rich," *Economist*, November 23, 2013, http://www.economist.com/news/briefing/21590353-ever-more-wealth-being-parked-fancy-storage-facilities-some-customers-they-are.

41
Jonathan A. Obar, "Phantom Data Sovereigns: Walter Lippmann, Big Data and the Fallacy of Personal Data Sovereignty," March 25, 2013, http://papers.ssrn.com/sol3/papers.cfm?abstract_id=2239188.

42
Zachary N. J. Peterson, Mark Gondree, and Robert Beverly, "A Position Paper on Data Sovereignty: The Importance of Geolocating Data on the Cloud," *Usenix* (2013): 4, https://www.usenix.org/legacy/events/hotcloud11/tech/final_files/Peterson.pdf.

43
See the extensive study by Anselm Franke, Eyal Weizman, and Ines Geisler, "Islands: The Geography of Extraterritoriality," *Archis* 6 (December 2003): 19–21.

44
"John Perry Barlow on the Right to Know," YouTube video, 1:02:57, posted by "Forbes," February 1, 2012, https://www.youtube.com/watch?v=snQrNSE1T7Y.

45
"Iceland: Cracks in the Crust," *Economist*, December 11, 2008, http://www.economist.com/node/12762027?story_id=12762027.

46
"The Constitutional Council Hands Over the Bill for a New Constitution," *Stjornlagarad*, July 29, 2011, http://stjornlagarad.is/english/.

47
"Iceland's Media Law: 'The Switzerland of Bits,'" *Economist*, June 17, 2010, http://www.economist.com/blogs/babbage/2010/06/icelands_media_law.

48
"Birgitta Jónsdóttir—Samara/Massey Journalism Lecture," YouTube video, 53:31, from a lecture at the Samara/Massey Journalism Seminar Series in Toronto on January 11, 2011, posted by "Samara Canada," July 21, 2011, http://www.youtube.com/watch?v=MyFKP1VXFww.

49
"Iceland: A Radical Periphery in Action."

50
James Grimmelmann, e-mail to the authors, July 17, 2012.

51
Eleanor Saitta, e-mail to the authors, November 4, 2012, http://mthvn.tumblr.com/post/38457685064/decentralizationdesignandthecloud.

52
Ibid.

53
Ibid.

54
Ryan Paul, "Pirate Bay Plans to Build Aerial Server Drones with $35 Linux Computer," *Ars Technica* (blog), March 22, 2012, http://arstechnica.com/tech-policy/2012/03/pirate-bay-plans-to-build-aerial-server-drones-with-35-linux-computer/.

55
"World's First Flying File-Sharing Drones in Action," *TorrentFreak* (blog), March 20, 2012, https://torrentfreak.com/worlds-first-flying-file-sharing-drones-in-action-120320/.

56
Liam Young, Electronic Countermeasures GLOW Festival video, http://www.tomorrowsthoughtstoday.com/.

57
"The Pirate Bay Ships New Servers to Mountain Complex," *Torrent Freak*, May 16, 2011, http://torrentfreak.com/the-pirate-bay-ships-new-servers-to-mountain-complex-110516/.

58
"An Open Source Sky: Metahaven in Conversation with Liam Young," January 30, 2013, http://mthvn.tumblr.com/post/41818910653/opensourcesky.

59
Franke, Weizman, and Geisler, "Islands."

60
Pierre Englebert and Denis M. Tull, "Postconflict Reconstruction in Africa: Flawed Ideas about Failed States," *International Security* 32, no. 4 (Spring 2008): 106.

61
Grimmelmann, e-mail to the authors, July 17, 2012.

62
Ozong Agborsangaya-Fiteu, "Another Failed State? Cameroon's Descent," *International Herald Tribune*, April 10, 2008, http://www.nytimes.com/2008/04/10/opinion/10iht-edcameroon.1.11865189.html?_r=0.

63
Andy Greenberg, "Cameroon's Cybercrime Boom," *Forbes*, December 2, 2009, http://www.forbes.com/2009/12/01/cybercrime-mcafee-spyware-technology-cio-network-cameroon.html.

64
James Grimmelmann, e-mail to the authors, July 20, 2012.

Benjamin Bratton

The Black Stack

Planetary-scale computation takes different forms at different scales: energy grids and mineral sourcing; chthonic cloud infrastructure; urban software and public service privatization; massive universal addressing systems; interfaces drawn by the augmentation of the hand, of the eye, or dissolved into objects; users both overdetermined by self-quantification and exploded by the arrival of legions of nonhuman users (sensors, cars, robots). Instead of seeing the various species of contemporary computational technologies as so many different genres of machines, spinning out on their own, we should instead see them as forming the body of an accidental megastructure. Perhaps these parts align, layer by layer, into something not unlike a vast (if also incomplete), pervasive (if also irregular) software and hardware *Stack*. This model is of a Stack that both does and does not exist as such: it is a machine that serves as a schema, as much as it is a schema of machines.[1] As such, perhaps the image of a totality that this conception provides would—as theories of totality have before—make the composition of new governmentalities and new sovereignties both more legible and more effective.

My interest in the geopolitics of planetary-scale computation focuses less on issues of personal privacy and state surveillance than on how it distorts and deforms traditional Westphalian modes of political geography, jurisdiction, and sovereignty, and produces new territories in its image. It draws from (and against) Carl Schmitt's later work *The Nomos of the Earth*, and from his (albeit) flawed history of the geometries of geopolitical architectures.[2] "Nomos" refers to the dominant and essential logic to the political subdivisions of the earth (of land, seas, and/or air, and now also of the domain that the US military simply calls "cyber") and to the geopolitical order that stabilizes these subdivisions accordingly. Today, as the *nomos* that was defined by the horizontal loop geometry of the modern state system creaks and groans, and as "Seeing like a State" takes leave of that initial territorial nest—both with and against the demands of planetary-scale computation[3]—we wrestle with the irregular abstractions of information, time, and territory, and the chaotic de-lamination of (practical) sovereignty from the occupation of place. For this, a *nomos* of the Cloud would, for example, draw jurisdiction not only according to the horizontal subdivision of physical sites by and for states, but also according to the vertical stacking of interdependent layers on top of one another: two geometries sometimes in cahoots, sometimes completely diagonal and unrecognizable to one another.[4]

The Stack, in short, is that new *nomos* rendered now as vertically thickened political geography. In my analysis, there are six layers to this Stack: *Earth*, *Cloud*, *City*, *Address*, *Interface*, and *User*. Rather than demonstrating each layer of the Stack as a whole, I'll focus specifically on the Cloud and the User layers, and articulate some alternative designs for these layers and for the totality (or even better, for the next totality, the *nomos* to come). *The Black Stack*, then, is to the Stack what the shadow of the future is to the form of the present. The Black Stack is less the anarchist stack, or the death-metal stack, or the utterly opaque stack, than the computational totality-to-come, defined at this moment by what it is not, by the empty content fields of its framework, and by its dire inevitability. It is not the platform we have, but the platform that might be. That platform would be defined by the productivity of its accidents, and by the strategy for which whatever may appear at first as the worst option (even evil) may ultimately be where to look for the best way out. It is less a "possible future" than an escape from the present.

Cloud

The platforms of the Cloud layer of the Stack are structured by dense, plural, and noncontiguous geographies, a hybrid of US super-jurisdiction and Charter Cities, which have carved new partially privatized polities from the whole cloth of de-sovereigned lands. But perhaps there is more there. The immediate geographical drama of the Cloud layer is seen most directly in the ongoing Sino-Google conflicts of 2008 to the present: China hacking Google, Google pulling out of China, the NSA hacking China, the NSA hacking Google, Google ghostwriting books for the State Department, and Google wordlessly circumventing the last instances of state oversight altogether, not by transgressing them but by absorbing them into its service offering. Meanwhile, Chinese router firmware bides its time.

The geographies at work are often weird. For example, Google filed a series of patents on offshore data centers, to be built in international waters on towers using tidal currents and available water to keep the servers cool. The complexities of jurisdiction suggested by a global Cloud piped in from non-state space are fantastic, but they are now less exceptional than exemplary of a new normal. Between the "hackers" of the People's Liberation Army and Google there exists more than a standoff between the proxies of two state apparatuses. There is rather a fundamental conflict over the geometry of political geography itself, with one side bound by the territorial integrity of the state, and the other by the gossamer threads of the world's information demanding to be "organized and made useful." This is a clash between two logics of governance, two geometries of territory: one a subdivision of the horizontal, the other a stacking of vertical layers; one a state, the other a para-state; one superimposed on top of the other at any point on the map, and never resolving into some consensual cosmopolitanism, but rather continuing to grind against the grain of one another's planes. This characterizes the geopolitics of our moment (this, plus the gravity of generalized succession, but the two are interrelated).

From here we see that contemporary Cloud platforms are displacing, if not also replacing, traditional core functions of states, and demonstrating, for both good and ill, new spatial and temporal models of politics and publics. Archaic states drew their authority from the regular provision of food. Over the course of modernization, more was added to the intricate bargains of Leviathan: energy, infrastructure, legal identity and standing, objective and comprehensive maps, credible currencies, and flag-brand loyalties. Bit by bit, each of these and more are now provided by Cloud platforms, not necessarily as formal replacements for the state versions but, like Google ID, simply more useful and effective for daily life. For these platforms, the terms of participation are not mandatory, and because of this, their social contracts are more extractive than constitutional. The Cloud Polis draws revenue from the cognitive capital of its Users, who trade attention and microeconomic compliance in exchange for global infrastructural services, and in turn, it provides each of them with an active discrete online identity and the license to use this infrastructure.

That said, it is clear that we don't have anything like a proper geopolitical theory of these transformations. Before the full ambition of the US security apparatus was so evident, it was thought by many that the Cloud was a place where states had no ultimate competence, nor maybe even a role to play: too slow, too dumb, too easily outwitted by using the right browser. States would be cored out, component by component, until nothing was left but a well-armed health insurance scheme with its own World Cup team. In the long run, that may still be the outcome, with modern liberal states taking their place next to ceremonial monarchs and stripped of all but symbolic authority, not necessarily replaced but displaced and misplaced to one side. But now we are hearing the opposite, equally brittle conclusion: that the Cloud is *only* the state, that it equals the state, and that its totality (figural, potential) is intrinsically totalitarian. Despite all, I wouldn't take that bet.

Looking toward the Black Stack, we observe that new forms of governmentality arise through new capacities to tax flows (at ports, at gates, on property, on income, on attention, on clicks, on movement, on electrons, on carbon, and so forth). It is not at all clear whether, in the long run, Cloud platforms will overwhelm state control on such flows, or whether states will continue to evolve into Cloud platforms, absorbing the displaced functions back into themselves, or whether both will split or rotate diagonally to one another, or how deeply what we may now recognize as the surveillance state (US, China, and so forth) will become a universal solvent of compulsory transparency and/or a cosmically opaque megastructure of absolute paranoia, or all of the above, or none of the above.

Between the state, the market, and the platform, which is better designed to tax the interfaces of everyday life and draw sovereignty thereby? It is a false choice to be sure, but one that raises the question of where to locate the proper site of governance as such. What would we mean by "the public" if not that which is constituted by such interfaces, and where else should "governance"—meant here as the necessary, deliberate, and enforceable composition of durable political subjects and their mediations—live if not there? Not in some obtuse chain of parliamentary representation, nor in some delusional monadic individual unit, nor in some sad little community consensus powered by moral hectoring, but instead in the immanent, immediate, and exactly present interfaces that cleave and bind us. Where should sovereignty reside if not in what is in between us—derived not from each of us individually but from what draws the world through us?

For this, it's critical to underscore that Cloud platforms (including sometimes state apparatuses) are exactly that: *platforms*. It is important as well to recognize that "platforms" are not only a technical architecture; they are also an institutional form. They centralize (like states), scaffolding the terms of participation according to rigid but universal protocols, even as they decentralize (like markets), coordinating economies not through the superimposition of fixed plans but through interoperable and emergent interaction. Next to states and markets, platforms are a third form, coordinating through fixed protocols while scattering free-range Users watched over in loving, if also disconcertingly omniscient, grace. In the platform-as-totality, drawing the interfaces of everyday life into one another, the maximal state and the minimal state, Red Plenty and Google Gosplan, start to look weirdly similar.

Our own subjective enrollment in this is less as citizens of a *polis* or as *homo economicus* within a market, but rather as Users of a platform. As I see it, the work of geopolitical theory is to develop a proper history, typology, and program for such platforms.

These would not be a shorthand for Cloud Feudalism (nor for the network politics of the "multitude") but models for the organization of durable alter-totalities which command the force of law, if not necessarily its forms and formality. Our understanding of the political economy of platforms demands its own Hobbes, Marx, Hayek, and Keynes.[5]

User

One of the useful paradoxes of the User's position as a political subject is the contradictory impulse directed simultaneously toward his artificial *over-individuation* and his ultimate *pluralization*, with both participating differently in the geopolitics of transparency. For example, the Quantified Self movement (a true medical theology in California) is haunted by this contradiction. At first, the intensity and granularity of a new informational mirror image convinces the User of his individuated coherency and stability as a subject. He is flattered by the singular beauty of his reflection, and this is why QSelf is so popular with those inspired by an X-Men reading of *Atlas Shrugged*. But as more data is added to the diagram that quantifies the outside world's impact on his person—the health of the microbial biome in his gut, immediate and long-term environmental conditions, his various epidemiological contexts, and so on—the quality of everything that is "not him" comes to overcode and overwhelm any notion of himself as a withdrawn and self-contained agent. Like Theseus's Paradox—where after every component of a thing has been replaced, nothing original remains but a metaphysical husk—the User is confronted with the existential lesson that at any point he is only the intersection of many streams. At first, the subject position of the User overproduces individual identity, but in the continuance of the same mechanisms, it then succeeds in exploding it.

The geopolitics of the User we have now is inadequate, including its oppositional modes. The Oedipal discourse of privacy and transparency in relation to the Evil Eye of the uninvited stepfather is a necessary process toward an alterglobalism, but it has real limits worth spelling out. A geopolitics of computation predicated at its core upon the biopolitics of *privacy*, of self-immunization from any compulsory appearance in front of publics, of platforms, of states, of Others, can sometimes also serve a psychological internalization of a now-ascendant general economy of succession, castration anxiety—whatever. The result is the preparanoia of withdrawal into an atomic and anomic dream of self-mastery that elsewhere we call the "neoliberal subject."

The space in which the discursive formation of the subject meets the technical constitution of the User enjoys a much larger horizon than the one defined by these kinds of individuation. Consider, for example, proxy users. uProxy, a project supported by Google Ideas, is a browser modification that lets users easily pair up across distances to allow someone in one location (trapped in the Bad Internets) to send information unencumbered through the virtual position of another User in another location (enjoying the Good Internets). Recalling the proxy servers set up during the Arab Spring, one can see how Google Ideas (Jared Cohen's group) might take special interest in baking this into Chrome. For Sino-Google geopolitics, the platform could theoretically be available at a billion-user scale to those who live in China, even if Google is not technically "in China," because those Users, acting through and as foreign proxies, are themselves, as far as internet geography is concerned, both in and not in China. Developers of uProxy believe that it would take two simultaneous and synchronized man-in-the-middle attacks to hack the link, and at a population scale that would prove difficult even for the best state actors, for now. More disconcerting perhaps is that such a framework could just as easily be used to withdraw data from a paired site—a paired "user"—which for good reasons should be left alone.

Some plural User subject that is conjoined by a proxy link or other means could be composed of different types of addressable subjects: two humans in different countries, or a human and a sensor, a sensor and a bot, a human and a robot and a sensor, a whatever and a whatever. In principle, any one of these subcomponents could not only be part of multiple conjoined positions, but might not even know or need to know which meta-User they contribute to, any more than the microbial biome in your gut needs to know your name. Spoofing with honeypot identities, between humans and nonhumans, is measured against the theoretical address space of IPv6 (roughly 10^{23} addresses per person) or some other massive universal addressing scheme. The abyssal quantity and range of "things" that could, in principle, participate in these vast pluralities includes real and fictional addressable persons, objects, and locations, and even addressable mass-less relations between things, any of which could be a sub-User in this Internet of Haeccities.

So while the Stack (and the Black Stack) stage the death of the User in one sense—the eclipse of a certain resolute humanism—they do so because they also bring the multiplication and proliferation of other kinds of nonhuman Users (including sensors, financial algorithms, and robots from nanometric to landscape scale), any combination of which one might enter into a relationship with as part of a composite User. This is where the recent shift by major Cloud platforms into robotics may prove especially vital, because—like Darwin's tortoises finding their way to different Galapagos islands—the Cambrian explosion in robotics sees speciation occur in the wild, not just in the lab, and with "us" on "their" inside, not on the outside. As robotics and Cloud hardware of all scales blend into a common category of machine, it will be unclear in general human-robotic interaction whether one is encountering a fully autonomous, partially autonomous, or completely human-piloted synthetic intelligence. Everyday interactions replay the Turing test over and over. Is there a person behind this machine, and if so, how much? In time, the answer will matter less, and the postulation of human (or even carbon-based life) as the threshold measure of intelligence and as the qualifying gauge of a political ethics may seem like tasteless vestigial racism, replaced by less anthropocentric frames of reference.

The position of the User then maps only very incompletely onto any one individual body. From the perspective of the platform, what looks like one is really many, and what looks like many may only be one. Elaborate schizophrenias already take hold in our early negotiation of these composite User positions. The neoliberal subject position makes absurd demands on people as Users, as Quantified Selves, as SysAdmins of their own psyche, and from this, paranoia and narcissism are two symptoms of the same disposition, two functions of the same mask. For one, the mask works to pluralize identity according to the subjective demands of the User position as composite alloy; and for another, it defends against those same demands on behalf of the illusory integrity of a self-identity fracturing around its existential core. Ask yourself: Is that User "Anonymous" because he is dissolved into a vital machinic plurality, or because public identification threatens individual self-mastery, sense of autonomy, social unaccountability, and so forth? The former and the latter are two very different politics, yet they use the same masks and the same software suite. Given the schizophrenic economy of the User—first over-individuated and then multiplied and dedifferentiated—this really isn't an unexpected or neurotic reaction at all. It is, however, fragile and inadequate.

In the construction of the User as an aggregate profile that both is and is not specific to any one entity, there is no identity to deduce other than the pattern of interaction between partial actors. We may find, perhaps ironically, that the User position of the Stack actually has far less in common with the neoliberal form of the subject than some of today's oppositionalist formats for political subjectivity that hope (quite rightly) to challenge, reform, and resist the State Stack as it is currently configuring itself. However, something like a Digital Bill of Rights for Users, despite its cosmopolitan optimism, becomes a much more complicated, fragile, and limited solution when the discrete identification of a User is both so heterogeneous and so fluid. Are all proxy composite users one User? Is anything with an IP address a User? If not, why not? If this throne is reserved for one species—humans—when is any one animal of that species being a User, and when is it not? Is it a User anytime that it is generating information? If so, that policy would in practice crisscross and trespass some of our most basic concepts of the political, and for that reason alone it may be a good place to start.

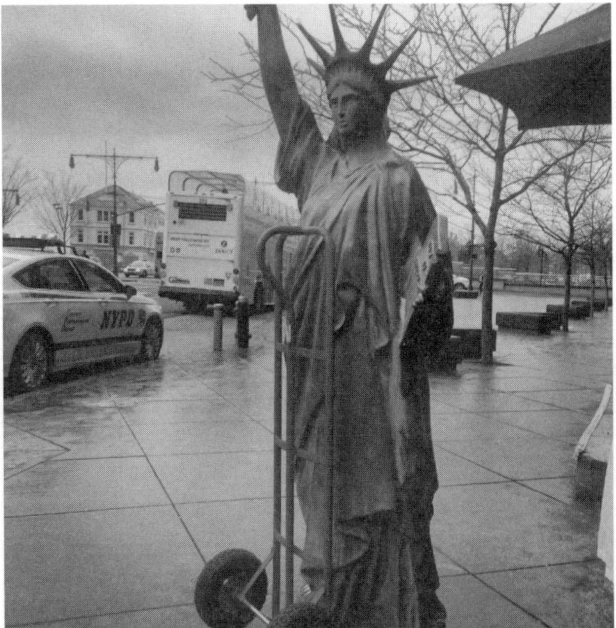

Lady Liberty is on the go.

In addition to the fortification of the User as a geopolitical subject, we also require a redefinition of the political subject in relation to the real operations of the User, one that is based not on *homo economicus*, nor on parliamentary liberalism, nor on post-structuralist linguistic reduction, nor on the will to secede into the moral safety of individual privacy and withdraw from coercion. Instead, this definition should focus on composing and elevating sites of governance from the immediate, suturing, interfacial material between subjects, in the stitches and the traces and the folds of interaction between bodies and things at a distance, congealing into different networks demanding very different kinds of platform sovereignty.

The Black Stacks

I will conclude with some thoughts on the Stack-we-have and on the Black Stack, the generic figure for its alternative totalities: the Stack-to-come. The Stack-we-have is defined not only by its form, its layers, its platforms, and their interrelations, but also by its content. As leak after leak has made painfully clear, its content is also the content of our daily communications, now weaponized against us. If the panopticon effect is when you don't know if you are being watched or not, and so you behave as if you are, then the inverse panopticon effect is when you know you are being watched but act as if you aren't. This is today's surveillance culture: exhibitionism in bad faith. The emergence of Stack platforms doesn't promise any solution, or even any distinctions between friend and enemy within this optical geopolitics. At some dark day in the future, when considered versus the Google Caliphate, the NSA may even come to be seen by some as the "public option." "At least it is accountable in principle to *some* parliamentary limits," they will say, "rather than merely stockholder avarice and flimsy user agreements."

If we take 9/11 and the rollout of the Patriot Act as Year Zero for the United States' massive data gathering, encapsulation, and digestion campaign (one that we are only now beginning to comprehend, even as parallel projects from China, Russia, and Europe are sure to come to light in time), then we can imagine the entirety of network communication for the last decade—the Big Haul—as a single, deep-and-wide digital simulation of the world (or a significant section of it). It is an archive, a library of the real. Its existence as the purloined property of a state, just as a physical fact, is almost occult. Almost.

The geophilosophical profile of the Big Haul, from the energy necessary to preserve it to its governing instrumentality understood as both a text (a very large text) and as a machine with various utilities, overflows the traditional politics of software. Its story is much more Borges than Lawrence Lessig. As is its fate. Can it be destroyed? Is it possible to delete this simulation, and is it desirable to do so? Is there a trash can big enough for the Big Delete? Even if the plug could be pulled on all future data hauls, surely there must be a backup somewhere, the identical double of the simulation, such that if we delete one, the other will forever haunt history until it is rediscovered by future AI archaeologists interested in their own Paleolithic origins. Would we bury it, even if we could? Would we need signs around it like those designed for the Yucca Mountain nuclear waste disposal site that warn off unknowable future excavations? Those of us "lucky" enough to be alive during this fifteen-year span would enjoy a certain illegible immortality, curiosities to whatever metacognitive entity pieces us back together using our online activities, both public and private, proud and furtive, each of us rising again centuries from now, each of us a little Ozymandias of cat videos and Pornhub.

In light of this, the Black Stack could come to mean very different things. On the one hand, it would imply that this simulation is opaque and unmappable—not disappeared, but ultimately redacted entirely. It could imply that, from the ruined fragments of this history, another coherent totality can be carved against the grain, even from the deep recombinancy at and below the Earth layer of the Stack. Its blackness is the surface of a world that can no longer be composed by addition because it is so absolutely full, overwritten, and overdetermined, that to add more is just so much ink in the ocean. Instead of *tabula rasa*, this *tabula plenus* allows for creativity and figuration only by subtraction, like scratching paint from a canvas—only by carving away, by death, by replacement.

The structural logic of any Stack system allows for the replacement of whatever occupies one layer with something else, and for the rest of the architecture to continue to function without pause. For example, the content of any one layer—*Earth*, *Cloud*, *City*, *Address*, *Interface*, *User*—could be replaced (including the masochistic hysterical fiction of the individual User, both neoliberal and neo-other-things), while the rest of the layers remain a viable armature for global infrastructure. The Stack is designed to be remade. That is its technical form, but unlike replacing copper wire with fiber optics in the transmission layer of TCP/IP, replacing one kind of User with another is more difficult. Today, we are doing it by adding more and different kinds of things into the User position, as described above. We should, however, also allow for more comprehensive displacements, not just by elevating things to the status of political subjects or technical agents, but by making way for genuinely post-human and a-human positions.

In time, perhaps at the eclipse of the Anthropocene, the historical phase of Google Gosplan will give way to stateless platforms for multiple strata of synthetic intelligence and biocommunication to settle into new continents of cyborg symbiosis. Or perhaps instead, if nothing else, the carbon and energy appetite of this ambitious embryonic ecology will starve its host.

For some dramas, but hopefully not for the fabrication of the Stack-to-come (Black or otherwise), a certain humanism and companion figure of humanity still presumes its traditional place in the center of the frame. We must let go of the demand that any artificial intelligence arriving at sentience or sapience must care deeply about humanity—us specifically—as the subject and object of its knowing and its desire. The real nightmare, worse than the one in which the big machine wants to kill you, is the one in which it sees you as irrelevant, or as not even a discrete thing to know. Worse than being seen as an enemy is not being seen at all. As Eliezer Yudkowsky puts it, "The AI does not hate you, nor does it love you, but you are made out of atoms which it can use for something else."[6]

One of the integral accidents of the Stack may be an anthrocidal trauma that shifts us from a design career as the authors of the Anthropocene, to the role of supporting actors in the arrival of the Post-Anthropocene. The Black Stack may also be black because we cannot see our own reflection in it. In the last instance, its accelerationist geopolitics is less eschatological than chemical, because its grounding of time is based less on the promise of historical dialectics than on the rot of isotope decay. It is drawn, I believe, by an inhuman and inhumanist molecular form-finding: pre-Cambrian flora changed into peat oil changed into children's toys, dinosaurs changed into birds changed into ceremonial headdresses, computation itself converted into whatever meta-machine comes next, and Stack into Black Stack.

An earlier version of this text was presented as a keynote lecture at Transmediale: Afterglow, January 31, 2014, in Berlin. Its presentation shared the stage with another keynote by Metahaven (Daniel van der Velden and Vinca Kruk) and was given at the curatorial invitation of Ryan Bishop and Jussi Parikka, along with Kristoffer Gansing and Transmediale. My thanks to each of them. The title, "The Black Stack," was coined by me and Metahaven to conjoin two current projects: my forthcoming book *The Stack: On Software and Sovereignty* (MIT Press) and Metahaven's book *Black Transparency* (Sternberg Press, 2015). I chose to take up the figure of the "Black Stack" as an alternative to the current system of global calculation.

1

Software (and hardware) stacks are technical architectures that assign interdependent layers to different specific clusters of technologies, and fix specific protocols for how one layer can send information up or down to adjacent layers. OSI and TCP/IP are obvious examples.

2

See Carl Schmitt, *The Nomos of the Earth in the International Law of Jus Publicum Europaeum*, trans. G. L. Ulmen (Candor, NY: Telos Press, 2006).

3

The reference is to James Scott's *Seeing Like a State*, but the term seems to have expanded and migrated beyond his antigovernmental thesis. See also, for example, Bruno Latour's lecture "How to Think Like A State" ("in the presence of the Queen of Holland," http://www.bruno-latour.fr/node/357). For this text, I mean to tie one thread to Scott's connotation (how states see everything available to their schemes) and to a more Foucauldian sense of the actual optical technologies that conjure forms of governance in their own image. Today, these privileges are also enjoyed by the hardware/software platforms that manufacture such optics and leverage them as the basis of their own exo-state governmental innovations.

4

I mean "Cloud" in a very general sense, referring to planetary-scale software/hardware platforms, supporting data centers, physical transmission links, browser-based applications, and so forth.

5

My ongoing discussion on the political economy of platforms with Benedict Singleton, Nick Srnicek, and Alex Williams informs these last remarks.

6

See Eliezer Yudkowsky, "Artificial Intelligence as a Positive and Negative Factor in Global Risk," in *Global Catastrophic Risks*, ed. Nick Bostrom and Martin Rees (New York: Oxford University Press, 2008).

Patricia MacCormack

Cosmogenic Acceleration: Futurity and Ethics

> Learn the aesthetic error of submitting everything to a law: leveling the local event produces boredom and ugliness, a world without landscapes, books without pages, deserts. Take everything away and you will not see. To see space demands time, do not kill time. Avoid the symmetrical error of being satisfied with fragments.
> —Michel Serres[1]

In *Post-Cinematic Affect*, Steven Shaviro defines accelerationist aesthetics in two ways. First, he points to the "'disruption,' or the radical 'break,' without any positive content, which is all that remains for Jameson of the Utopian gesture today."[2] More optimistically, he emphasizes the need to think futurity and speed in new ways when he states that what we have here and now is not enough, and is vulnerable to capitalism's voracious appetite for assimilation. Through the exhaustion of the *now* we can play with what's left, the future-now.[3] Time is problematized, collapsed, and enfolded, as it always has been in any discussion of the *post-*. This article will explore the ways futurity, time, and acceleration can constitute a demand for the *next* that outruns capital's consumption of the now. It attends to the critical ethical components of this irreversible time in order to avoid the tendency of accelerationism to become just one more speed politics that furthers capitalism's replacement compulsion, its techniques for devastating all to come.[4]

One of the crucial ethical elements Shaviro emphasizes in his discussion of affect is that affect has no lack or opposite—all is affect. The post-human vocabulary of break, fracture, and rupture is therefore no less affective for its empty contents. Indeed, this is its most insidious quality; as Shaviro puts it, "the prison has no outside."[5]

Accelerationism seems to have been misapplied to velocity and capitalist replacement culture, but Shaviro—following Guattari and Deleuze's use of the concept of time via speed as a qualitative (and mediative) duration—frames acceleration as an always variable intensity. True, replacement is the lure par excellence of contemporary culture's denial of attention. Yet speed has time. Replacement culture denies time by suturing together random flashes of cultural membranes, without allowing time as durational consistency to make creative connections between those montage gaps. In these conditions, art becomes vacuous hope in an alchemical aesthetic coagulation in space.

The important question is: What is the qualitative difference between a nihilistic reading of accelerationism as saturation without refined intensity, and an accelerationist aesthetic that does not equate speed with the too-fast replacements of capitalism, instead seeing intensity in all movement, and thus all movement as acceleration (even multi-directional)? Serres urges: "Do not seek to know how to look at a landscape," yet he dismisses any *post*-compulsion to say there is thus no landscape, or only a fragmentary one. He emphasizes that intensity without perceptibility and velocity without atrophy may make aesthetic experience difficult, but it is all the more real for being so—and thus all the more ethical.[6] Guattari similarly states:

> *Only sense without signification* produced by a diagrammatic economy of signs is able to thwart the dead ends specific to semiologies of signification, insofar as it introduces into semiotic assemblages an additional coefficient of deterritorialization allowing sign machines to simulate, "duplicate," and "experience" the relational and

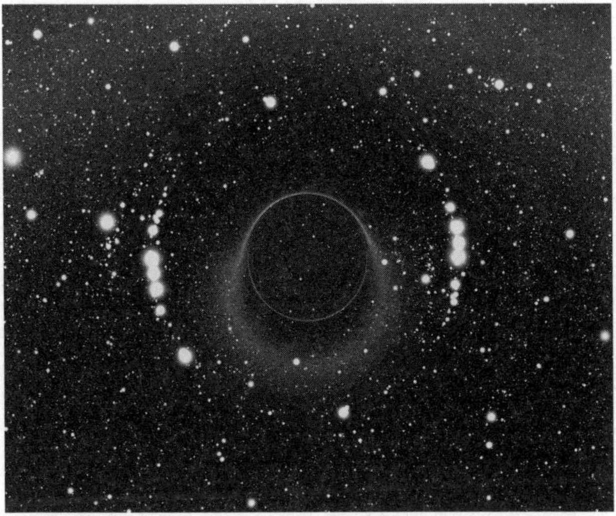

Apple's Time Machine background alludes to a wormhole representation such as the one in the image above.

> structural nodes of material and social flows precisely at the points that would remain invisible to anthropocentric vision.[7]

Accelerationist aesthetics are too fast for humans. Accelerationism is beloved by capital but, as Shaviro points out, accelerationism takes capitalism to its vertiginous depths.[8] And there are other things to be found within and beyond those depths, namely, the monsters of affect; as Deleuze and Guattari tell us, "*affects are the becoming inhuman of man*."[9] Taking affect as the defining intensity that constitutes a life's specificity as a coalescence of expressive powers combined with openness to other affects posits affect in a Spinozist ethical relation. This is a relation that, following Deleuze and Guattari, is inhuman, but not via the dehumanizing operations of fracturing capitalist speed politics. Rather, it is rendered inhuman through the constitution of lives as nodal points entirely specific to their position and constellation of relations, resistant to genus or even species. Deleuze states:

> Beings will be defined by their *capacity for being affected*, by the affections of which they are capable, the excitations to which they react, those by which they are unaffected, and those which exceed their capacity and make them ill or cause them to die. In this way one will obtain a classification of beings by their power.[10]

Classification shifts from human, nonhuman, and their salient associations with hierarchical arboreal models of domination, to classification through infinite, temporal, and temporary connectivities, always already a result of former affects and multiple interactions. The more inhuman any series of affective relations makes us, the less attached we are to classification in its majoritarian sense, and to oppression. The inhuman is independent of opposition. It is neither *anti-* nor *non-* but, following Guattari, more appropriately understood as *a*-human.

Shaviro claims that "one important role of art is to explore the dangers of futurity." He sets up a dichotomy between accelerationist aesthetics and accelerationist politics—a necessary distinction when for him aesthetics does not translate into politics.[11] There is the sense that aesthetics deals with the untranslatable. As in its address to futurity, aesthetics addresses vocabularies that have not yet been, those to come. The *political* role of aesthetics could then be to catalyze inhuman affective relations that are still to come. Thus the incommensurability of any project of politicizing aesthetics itself emerges: Does politics need a future it must confess it cannot know but, in order to engage activism and change, must tactically sketch? Does aesthetics need to refuse all known vocabularies in order to force unthinkable futures? Or, more precisely, does aesthetics need to force systems of knowledge to take leaps of thought that fill the vertiginous holes between what is possible (already established in advance) and what is potential (the as-yet-unthinkable but nonetheless plausible) with affect, that is, with the unexpected powers and forces which alter paradigms and trajectories?

Put simply, the present moment may be the moment of imagination, which Shaviro rightly asserts has deserted us. Because or in spite of our utopian belief, we may now have the means to extend imaginative potentials further than ever. But these means have become the obsession of capital systems, while the problems, the dangers, that which constitutes the *need* for aesthetics, are to be resolved. Are these dangers precisely the gaps that aesthetics occupies, and indulges as its occupation? Are these gaps actually montage holes in speed culture reminding us that the gaps are not empty, that we should not just ignore them and suture fragmented life together, pretending that all is smooth and logical? Do these gaps actually end up homogenizing consistencies that create schizo-sicknesses in diminishing thought and imagination?

Shaviro's anxiety that some accelerationist aesthetics may get lost in the spaces they endeavor to survey should be taken as a warning against ignoring the spaces that accelerationist aesthetics create or occupy, which capitalist acceleration has transformed into blind spots, or places that do not matter.[12] These non-spaces are found between the leaps of replacement culture, and in the spaces between those spaces, the interfractal, imperceptible zones that add elements of slowness to accelerationist aesthetics by readdressing the lost time that was never perceived—the futurity of the past and present, the interstitial, threshold, in-between spaces that are the minoritarian planes of duration. This cosmic time, or circular time, is time that sees objects in space abandon their centrality to become sources of intensity in duration. This is what Serres calls the irreversible time of genesis—"irreversible time and history send their roots deep into strange substances. They are born from circumstances."[13] Serres describes what could be called cosmogony affect when he posits composition as constituting consistency and movement as constituting constancy. Thus, bodies in proximity alter and affect each other through their relations; they become unique consistencies in gracious opening to each other over immeasurable and irreversible time. Their futurity in irreversible time is assured, as constancy is found only in the cosmic operation of composition and recomposition, in movement within.

Anxieties about accelerationist aesthetics privileging the future as the "what next" are alleviated somewhat with Serres's cosmogenic time: what is available for aesthetic manipulation to create unthinkable affects is always here; it is not a matter of replacement so much as recomposition; the new is always the oppressed of the past rendered capable of catalyzing excitations through recombinings and reconfiguration. Most importantly, the strangeness of the combinations creates their relevance. In reference to the inhumanity of affects, this strangeness is the critical point of ethics. The stranger the combinations are, the more inhuman they are; the more inhuman, the more minoritarian. The futurity thus opened to minoritarian recombinings—and not to the inclusion of "types"—is more ethical. Ethics and the need for unnatural, strange recombining are defined insofar as they are *timely*. Acceleration aesthetics is about qualities of time *as* intensity. Thus, it is arguably an ethical aesthetics.

A cosmogony of aesthetics welcomes chaos. "We thus come back to a conclusion to which art led us: The struggle with chaos is only the instrument of a more profound struggle against opinion, for the misfortune of people comes from opinion."[14] Opinion orients time through repetition; it orients affectuation through reification intead of movement. Art attends to creating from chaos, but the result is the opposite of the mapping of this chaos by determined coordinates—Deleuze and Guattari rethink science, philosophy, and art as always including "an *I do not know* that is positive and creative, the condition of creation itself and that consists in determining *by* what one does not know."[15] The temporal spaces between, the blind spots of capital, could be shared interstitials—meeting points of specific celerity.

If movement is constant, aesthetic tools are those that effectuate the most inhuman affects on other bodies, including bodies of thought. What tools can we think of? Are they minoritarian, or are they tools for the acknowledgement of general a-human alterity? Creating a flux that slows the temporal chain can remap its intensities. Creating flux is, according to Serres, "positive chaos. Spinoza does not say otherwise: determination is negation. Indetermination is thus positive."[16] The great unreason of rational enlightenment is that one can determine the place and (lack of) meaning of a thing precisely in order to refute, negate, and deny that thing. The really sad fact is that postmodernity and new technologies that make any imaginings possible are the exact opposite of "anything goes." They produce many infinite instances of self rather than finite territories in which interrelational or (in Leibnizian terms) effectuation ethics must figure. An ethical accelerationist aesthetics wants to become "nameless words. Verbs without nouns. [...] Rhythm is a fluctuation of the rhesis, the surge [...] to speak of these transports as positive, negative, is mere naive anthropomorphism. The multiple moves, that is all."[17] As Guattari states:

> We are thus in the presence of two polar modalities of consciousness: that of pseudo-territorialities of resonance and that of an irrevocable deterritorialization; that of tranquilizing (and reassuring) faces and significations and that of anxiety without object, or rather, an anxiety which aims at the *reality* of nothingness. [...] It is a question of neutralizing, by reducing them, the "*n*" animal, vegetal and

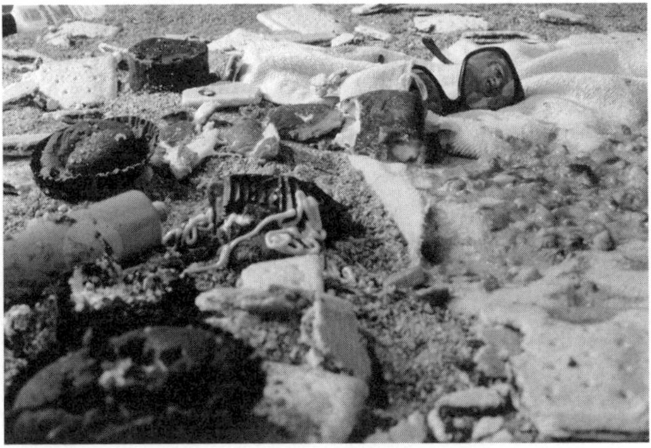

Cindy Sherman, *Untitled #175*, 1987. Chromogenic color print.

> cosmic eye of the rhizomatic possible which could subsist within residual territorialized assemblages. [...] The media install a vanishing point behind every glance.[18]

Guattari's use of animal, vegetal, and cosmic need not be interpreted as co-opting the minoritarian from the human animal in nature. Rather, it can be seen as the a-humanity of various orders of the human when liberated from the exhausted moment of the myth of absolute truth found in manufactured perception. This prevents the (formerly) human's elements of alterity from being fashionably sutured to the human for various trend-fulfilling capitalist projects of Frankenstein-like assimilation and co-option via contracts in which the oppressed or minor term has no agency—that is, human projects fulfilling phantasies of hybrid futurity.

Minoritarian-fantasy hybridity is futurity without ethics. Acceleration aesthetics attends to the slowness of meditative ethical interaction over the results-based drive for a hybrid human object that self-fulfills its own eye's desire for itself as a new object. The animal, vegetal, cosmic eye is an a-human eye that does not see in genus and species, in recognition, in fulfillment of representational criteria, or in a future which is confounding for its own sake. But nor does it homogenize singularities in their rhizomatic interactions. Guattari may offer a possibility of activism in what he calls "residual territorial assemblages": How can we utilize aesthetics to activate an ethical configuration of desire that is only defined by its deterritorializing usefulness at any given moment?

> A "machinics" breaking with [capitalist modes of thought] would imply a refusal of the dichotomy

> between material processes and semiotic processes. It would be brought to consider the deterritorializations of time and space only in connection with a new type of assemblage of enunciation, new types of faciality traits, refrains, relations to the body, sex, the cosmos.[19]

The future is not discontinued, contracted, or deprived of immanence by accelerationist thinking. Rather, accelerationist thinking is the very definition of what an imperceptible, cosmic, immanent future can be, since it looks toward the future without thinking in advance as a thinking human, while nonetheless thinking the future as inevitable and inevitable change. Like ethics—which cannot predict the affects of the future, but which must perform the devastatingly cursed operation of hoping for expressing forces that excite those of others affected and that seek to diminish only malevolent majoritarian forces—the future itself must be thought without pre-forming what the future will, should, or even could be.

In order to be accountable post-humans, we must see near futures, tactical little goals, and the strategic unification of issues that increase the expressivity of other lives as nodular moments on the way toward an ultimate creative future of joy—a future that the human cannot think. It is a future to which—if it is the real goal of post-humanism, even while it attests to the present being the location of that goal and its activisms—the human cannot belong. Cosmogenic ecosophy requires humans to bring into being other worlds beyond those of purely abstract information, to engender Universes of reference and existential Territories where singularity and finitude are taken into account by the multivalent logic of mental ecologies and by the group Eros principle of social ecology; to dare to confront the vertiginous Cosmos so as to make it inhabitable; these are the tangled paths of the tri-ecological vision.[20]

1
Michel Serres, *The Five Senses: A Philosophy of Mingled Bodies*, trans. Margaret Sankey and Peter Cowley (London: Athlone, 2008), 239.

2
Steven Shaviro, *Post-Cinematic Affect* (London: Zero Books, 2010), 137. See Fredric Jameson, *Archaeologies of the Future: The Desire Called Utopia and Other Science Fictions* (New York: Verso, 2005), 231–32.

3
Shaviro, *Post-Cinematic Affect*, 137.

4
See, for example, Gean Moreno's "Notes on the Inorganic, Part I: Accelerations," in this book, 81–99.

5
Shaviro, *Post-Cinematic Affect*, 137.

6
Serres, *The Five Senses*, 239.

7
Félix Guattari, *The Machinic Unconscious*, trans. Taylor Adkins (Los Angeles: Semiotext(e), 2011), 59; emphasis in original.

8
Shaviro, *Post-Cinematic Affect*, 138.

9
Gilles Deleuze and Félix Guattari, *What Is Philosophy?*, trans. Hugh Tomlinson and Graham Burchell (New York: Columbia University Press, 1994), 169; emphasis in original.

10
Gilles Deleuze, *Spinoza: Practical Philosophy*, trans. Robert Hurley (San Francisco: City Lights Books, 1988), 45.

11
Shaviro, *Post-Cinematic Affect*, 139.

12
Ibid.

13
Serres, *The Five Senses*, 291.

14
Deleuze and Guattari, *What Is Philosophy?*, 206.

15
Ibid., 128.

16
Michel Serres, *Genesis*, trans. Genevieve James and James Nielson (Ann Arbor: University of Michigan Press, 1995), 98.

17
Serres, *Genesis*, 101, 69.

18
Guattari, *The Machinic Unconscious*, 82–83.

19
Ibid., 105.

20
Félix Guattari, *The Three Ecologies*, trans. Ian Pindar and Paul Sutton (London: Athlone, 2000), 67.

Julian Assange

In 2006, Assange began work on WikiLeaks, a website intended to collect and share confidential information on an international scale. The information his organization released earned him strong supporters and powerful enemies. For his efforts, the internet activist earned the *Time* magazine "Person of the Year" title in 2010. After arriving at the Ecuadorean Embassy in London in June 2012, seeking to avoid extradition to Sweden, Assange was granted political asylum by the Ecuadorean government in August 2012.

Franco "Bifo" Berardi,

founder of the famous Radio Alice in Bologna and an important figure in the Autonomia movement in Italy, is a writer, media theorist, and media activist. He currently teaches social history of the media at the Accademia di Brera, Milan. His most recent book, entitled *The Uprising*, was published by Semiotext(e) in 2012.

Benjamin Bratton

is a theorist whose work spans philosophy, art, and design. He is an associate professor of visual arts and the director of D:GP, the Center for Design and Geopolitics at the University of California, San Diego. His research is situated at the intersections of contemporary social and political theory, computational media and infrastructure, architectural and urban design problems, and the politics of synthetic ecologies and biologies. Current work focuses on the political geography of cloud computing, massively granular universal addressing systems, and alternate models of ecological governance. His next book, *The Stack: On Software and Sovereignty*, is forthcoming.

Diedrich Diederichsen

was editor of two music magazines in the 1980s (*Sounds*, Hamburg; *Spex*, Cologne) and taught at several academies in the 1990s in Germany, Austria, and the United States in the fields of art history, musicology, theater studies, and cultural studies. He was Professor for Cultural Theory at Merz Academy, Stuttgart, from 1998 to 2006, and is currently Professor of Theory, Practice, and Communication of Contemporary Art at the Academy of Fine Arts in Vienna. Recent publications include *Über Pop-Musik* (Kiepenheuer & Witsch, 2014); *Utopia of Sound*, (Schlebrugge. Editor, 2010, coedited with Constanze Ruhm); *Rock, Paper, Scissor—Pop-Music/Fine Arts* (Verlag der Buchhandlung Walther König, 2009, coedited with Peter Pakesch); *On (Surplus) Value in Art* (Sternberg Press, 2008); *Eigenblutdoping* (Kiepenheuer & Witsch, 2008); *Kritik des Auges* (Philo Fine Arts, 2008); *Argument Son* (Les presses du réel, 2007); *Personas en loop* (Interzona, 2005); and *Musikzimmer* (Kiepenheuer & Witsch, 2005).

Keller Easterling

is an architect, writer, and professor at Yale University. Her most recent book, *Extrastatecraft: The Power of Infrastructure Space* (Verso, 2014), examines global infrastructure networks as a medium of polity. Another recent book, *Subtraction* (Sternberg Press, 2014), considers building removal or how to put the development machine into reverse. An e-book essay, *The Action Is the Form: Victor Hugo's TED Talk* (Strelka Press, 2012) previews some of the arguments in *Extrastatecraft*. Other books include: *Enduring Innocence:*

Global Architecture and Its Political Masquerades (MIT, 2005), which researched familiar spatial products in difficult or hyperbolic political situations around the world, and *Organization Space: Landscapes, Highways and Houses in America* (MIT, 1999), which applied network theory to a discussion of American infrastructure. Easterling has lectured and published widely in the United States and abroad. The journals to which she has contributed include *Domus*, *Artforum*, *Grey Room*, *Cabinet*, *Volume*, *Assemblage*, *e-flux journal*, *Log*, *Praxis*, *Harvard Design Magazine*, *Perspecta*, and *ANY*.

Rasmus Fleischer

(b. 1978) is a Swedish historian, writer, and occasional musician. He was involved in the anti-copyright collective Piratbyrån (Bureau for Piracy), which was active from 2003 to 2010 and which is known for founding the Pirate Bay, but was also active in the fields of art, theory, and politics. Books by Rasmus Fleischer include *Boken & Biblioteket* (2011), about the transformation of publishing and the future of libraries, as well as his PhD thesis *Musikens politiska ekonomi* (2012).

Joana Hadjithomas and Khalil Joreige

have collaborated for fifteen years as filmmakers and artists. They have focused on images, representations, and the history of their home country, Lebanon, questioning the region's imaginaries. Together, they have directed documentaries such as *Khiam 2000–2007* (2008) and *El Film el Mafkoud* (The Lost Film) (2003) and feature films such as *Al Bayt el Zaher* (1999) and *A Perfect Day* (2005). Their recent feature film, *Je Veux Voir* (I Want to See), starring Catherine Deneuve and Rabih Mroué, premiered at the Cannes Film Festival in 2008. The French critics guild chose it as the best Francophone film of 2008. Their artworks have been shown in museums, biennials, and art centers around the world, in solo or collective exhibitions, and are part of important public and private collections, such as Musee d'Art Moderne de la Ville de Paris; FNAC France; Guggenheim, New York; Centre Georges Pompidou, Paris; V&A, London; Sharjah Art Foundation, UAE. They received the 2012 Abraaj Capital Art Prize for their work *A Letter Can Always Reach Its Destination*. In 2012 they released their feature documentary *The Lebanese Rocket Society: The Strange Tale of the Lebanese Space Race*, and presented a series of artistic installations around this 1960s space project. They are the authors of numerous publications and university lecturers in Lebanon and Europe, members of the board of Metropolis Cinema, and cofounders of Abbout Productions with Georges Schoucair. Hadjithomas is also a board member of the Ashkal Alwan Academy, Home Work Space. They both regularly present lecture-performances as "Aida save me" and live between Beirut and Paris.

Ursula K. Heise

is a professor of English at UCLA and a faculty member of UCLA's Institute of the Environment and Sustainability (IoES). She is a 2011 Guggenheim Fellow and was President of the Association for the Study of Literature and the Environment (ASLE) in 2011. Her research and teaching focus on contemporary environmental culture, literature, and art in the Americas, Western

Europe, and Japan; theories of globalization; literature and science; and the digital humanities.

Bruno Latour
is a professor at Sciences Po, Paris, and his work may be found online at www.bruno-latour.fr.

Geert Lovink
is a Dutch-Australian media theorist and critic. He is a professor at the European Graduate School, research professor at the Hogeschool van Amsterdam, where he is founding director of the Institute of Network Cultures, and associate professor in media studies (new media), University of Amsterdam. Lovink is the author of *Dark Fiber* (2002), *My First Recession* (2003), and *Zero Comments* (2007). He recently co-organized events and publications on Wikipedia research, online video, and the culture of search. His forthcoming book investigates the rise of "popular hermeneutics" inside Web 2.0, large scale comment cultures, and the shifting position of new media (studies) inside the humanities.

Patricia MacCormack
is professor of continental philosophy at Anglia Ruskin University, Cambridge. She has published extensively on Guattari, Blanchot, Serres, Irigaray, queer theory, teratology, body modification, post-human theory, animal rights, and horror films. Her work includes "Inhuman Ecstasy" (*Angelaki*), "Becoming-Vulva" (*New Formations*), "The Great Ephemeral Tattooed Skin" (*Body and Society*), "Necrosexuality" (*Queering the Non/Human*), "Unnatural Alliances" (*Deleuze and Queer Theory*), "Vitalistic FeminEthics" (*Deleuze and Law*), and "Cinemasochism: Time, Space and Submission" (*Afterimages of Gilles Deleuze's Film Philosophy*). She is the author of *Cinesexuality* (Ashgate, 2008) and the coeditor of *The Schizoanalysis of Cinema*. Her most recent books are *Posthuman Ethics* (Ashgate, 2012) and the edited collection *The Animal Catalyst: Towards Ahuman Theory* (Bloomsbury, 2014).

Metahaven
is an Amsterdam-based design collective on the cutting edge between politics and aesthetics. Founded by Vinca Kruk and Daniel van der Velden, Metahaven's work—both commissioned and self-directed—reflects political and social issues through research-driven design, and design-driven research. Research projects include the *Sealand Identity Project*, *Facestate*, and *Iceland as Method*. Solo exhibitions include "Affiche Frontière" (CAPC musée d'art contemporain de Bordeaux, 2008) and "Stadtstaat" (Künstlerhaus Stuttgart/Casco, 2009). Group exhibitions include "Forms of Inquiry" (AA London, 2007), Manifesta 8 (Murcia, 2010), the Gwangju Design Biennale 2011 (Gwangju, Korea), "Graphic Design: Now In Production" (Walker Art Center, Minneapolis, 2011, and Cooper-Hewitt National Design Museum, New York, 2012), and "The New Public" (Museion, Bolzano, 2012). Metahaven's work has been published and discussed in the *International Herald Tribune*, the *New York Times*, *Huffington Post*, *Courrier International*, *Icon*, *Domus*, *Dazed*, *The Verge*, *L'Architecture d'Aujourd'hui*, and *Mute*, among other publications. Vinca Kruk is a tutor of editorial design and design critique at ArtEZ Academy of Arts in Arhem. Daniel van der Velden is a senior critic at

the graphic design MFA program at Yale University, and a tutor of design at the Sandberg Instituut Amsterdam. In 2010, Metahaven released *Uncorporate Identity*, a design anthology for our dystopian age, published by Lars Müller. Their latest book is *Black Transparency* (Sternberg Press, 2015).

Gean Moreno
is an artist and writer based in Miami. His work has recently been exhibited at the North Miami MoCA, Kunsthaus Palais Thum and Taxis in Bregenz, Institute of Visual Arts in Milwaukee, Haifa Museum in Israel, Arndt & Partner in Zurich, and Invisible-Exports in New York. He has contributed texts to various magazines and catalogues.

Hans Ulrich Obrist
is a Swiss curator and art critic. In 1993, he founded the Museum Robert Walser and began to run the Migrateurs program at the Musée d'Art Moderne de la Ville de Paris, where he served as a curator for contemporary art. In 1996 he cocurated Manifesta 1, the first edition of the roving European biennial of contemporary art. He presently serves as Codirector of Exhibitions and Programmes and Director of International Projects at the Serpentine Gallery in London.

Jon Rich
was born in Amman in 1965. He teaches Arabic and sociology in Lisbon, where he has lived since 1990.

Hito Steyerl
is a filmmaker and writer. She teaches new media art at University of the Arts Berlin and has recently participated in documenta 12, the Shanghai Biennial, and the Rotterdam Film Festival.

Image Credits

p. 13 Photo: Christoph W. Sensen
p. 15 Photo: Nanex LLC
p. 31 © Cedric Price fonds, Collection Centre Canadien d'Architecture / Canadian Centre for Architecture, Montreal
p. 43 Photo: Alessandro Coco. With the support of Fondazione Garrone, Genoa, and Fondazione Sambuca, Palermo, and special thanks to pinksummer contemporary art.
p. 47 Photo: Alessandro Coco. With the support of Fondazione Garrone, Genoa, and Fondazione Sambuca, Palermo, and special thanks to pinksummer contemporary art.
p. 59 © David A. Hardy, www.astroart.org. Image courtesy of the author.
p. 65 Courtesy of kag.org
p. 86 © Professor Liam Blunt and University of Huddersfield
pp. 90–91 Courtesy of the artist
p. 103 CC BY-SA 3.0
p. 121 © 1903 M. Witmark & Sons
p. 129 Courtesy of University of Rochester, URnano
p. 139 Photo: John H. White / Environmental Protection Agency
p. 145 Photo: Denny Medley / Random Photography, LLC
p. 153 See more here: http://www.youtube.com/user/citizentube
p. 159 Photo: Louai Beshara/AFP/ Getty Images
p. 168 © EPA/Justin Lane
p. 191 Photo: Villa Arson/J. Brasille. Courtesy of the artists and In Situ Fabienne Leclerc Gallery (Paris), CRG Gallery (New York), The Third Line Gallery (Dubai).
p. 203 Photo: Villa Arson/J. Brasille. Courtesy of the artists and In Situ Fabienne Leclerc Gallery (Paris), CRG Gallery (New York), The Third Line Gallery (Dubai).
p. 242 Courtesy of the artists
p. 253 Courtesy of Metahaven
p. 269 Courtesy of Metahaven
p. 271 Courtesy of Metahaven
p. 291 Courtesy of Eva Franch i Gilabert
p. 301 CC BY-SA 3.0
p. 307 Courtesy of the artist and Metro Pictures

The Internet Does Not Exist

ISBN 978-3-95679-130-7

First published 2015, first reprint 2016, second reprint 2023

Publisher
Sternberg Press

Series editors
Julieta Aranda
Brian Kuan Wood
Anton Vidokle

Managing editors
Mariana Silva
Kaye Cain-Nielsen

Copyediting and proofreading
Mike Andrews
Max Bach

Design
Jeff Ramsey

For further information, contact journal@e-flux.com
www.e-flux.com/journal

Sternberg Press
71-75 Shelton Street
London WC2H 9JQ
sternberg-press.com